Feeling at Home

Also by Alexandra Stoddard

Open Your Eyes

The Decoration of Houses

Living in Love

Gracious Living in a New World

Mothers: A Celebration

The Art of the Possible

Alexandra Stoddard's Tea Celebrations

Alexandra Stoddard's Book of Days

Making Choices

Grace Notes

Creating a Beautiful Home

Daring to Be Yourself

Gift of a Letter

Alexandra Stoddard's Book of Color

Alexandra Stoddard's Living Beautifully Together

Living a Beautiful Life

The Postcard as Art

Reflections on Beauty

A Child's Place

Style for Living

Feeling

Also by Alexandra Stoddard

Open Your Eyes

The Decoration of Houses

Living in Love

Gracious Living in a New World

Mothers: A Celebration

The Art of the Possible

Alexandra Stoddard's Tea Celebrations

Alexandra Stoddard's Book of Days

Making Choices

Grace Notes

Creating a Beautiful Home

Daring to Be Yourself

Gift of a Letter

Alexandra Stoddard's Book of Color

Alexandra Stoddard's Living Beautifully Together

Living a Beautiful Life

The Postcard as Art

Reflections on Beauty

A Child's Place

Style for Living

Feeling

at Home

Defining Who You Are
and How You Want to Live

Alexandra Stoddard

Quill

A HarperResource Book
An Imprint of HarperCollins*Publishers*

HarperCollins books may be purchased for educational, business, or sales promotional use. For information please write: Special Markets Department, HarperCollins Publishers Inc., 10 East 53rd Street, New York, NY 10022.

First HarperResource Quill paperback edition published 2001

A hardcover edition of this book was published by William Morrow and Company in 1999.

Designed by Marysarah Quinn

The Library of Congress has cataloged the hardcover edition as follows:

Stoddard, Alexandra.
Feeling at home : defining who you are and how you
want to live / Alexandra Stoddard.
p.   cm.
Includes index.
ISBN: 0-688-15905-2
1. Conduct of life.   2. Identity (Psychology)   3. Home—
Psychological aspects.   I. Title.
BF637.C5S714   1999
158.1—dc21   99–24156
CIP

ISBN 0-38-073145-2 (pbk.)

01 02 03 04 05 ❖/QW 10 9 8 7 6 5 4 3 2 1

With love to
Alexandra, Brooke, and Peter,
who always
make me feel at home

Contents

Acknowledgments

With admiration
and affection to
my literary agent,
Carl Brandt,
and my editor,
Toni Sciarra

Note to the Reader

*A home is not dead but living, and like all living things, must obey
the laws of nature by constantly changing.*
—CARL LARSSON

Most books about the home understandably dwell simply on the
exterior and interior architecture, the furnishings, and the decoration
in order to help the reader make the house or apartment look attractive and function efficiently.

Although these things are necessary and desirable, what is missing is the most important element of all.

Home can and should be the place where we get in touch with
our individuality, our true nature. Home can and should be a place
where we regularly experience our most sublime emotions. If we
know the truth about how we feel, we'll be far better able to
enhance the atmosphere of our house or apartment and
express our innate genius in our home. In this way, we rise
to a new level of consciousness, transforming ourselves and
our homes as well.

Feeling at Home is devoted, on this higher level of self-
awareness, to the essential qualities of living with happiness
and love every day.

*We create an ideal atmos-
phere, where we feel at
home, by transcending ordinary thinking into enlightened vision.*

This book defines the concept of feeling at home. Here, at home, we give birth to a whole new way of seeing the world and our relationship to it. Our hunger for meaningful experiences and a sense of belonging is satisfied when we seek depth in our daily living experiences. Whatever we do at home, we are doing for ourselves. Our surroundings can teach us to live with more reverence, more focus, and more flexibility.

Home is there for us as our inner self.

There is more to life than learning how to exist efficiently in environments that often do not reflect ourselves. We have seen what damage is caused by living in a dehumanized world. We shop by catalogue and television, can't always reach a human being on the telephone, and check out at the supermarket with a cashier who uses a scanner without making eye contact. No matter how efficient these technological "advances" may be, we all seem to be marching to a less loving, less caring, less gracious, less spiritually illuminating drumbeat.

All the more reason to ask ourselves: Are we living with harmony, fulfillment, and joy at home? Are we receptive to the feelings of our loved ones? Do we spend enough time in quiet contemplation, where we retreat from the marketplace into our private haven to affirm and confirm what our life is all about? Do we even spend enough time at home? Are we living as well as we would like, or are we too often anxious, emotionally exhausted, and stressed?

Life is a cornucopia centered in the home. Here is our personal castle. We should think of it that way and make this come true.

PETER MEGARGEE BROWN

Feeling at home with ourselves and being able to create a spirit of place that nourishes us physically, emotionally, and spiritually is a goal worthy of our highest priority. We can raise our sights high when we're willing to break free from being conformists who live a conventional life simply because we are too afraid to express our uniqueness.

Being at home can and should be a sacred experience. Feeling content, at peace, serene and, at the same time, enthusiastic, is a gift of grace we receive when we learn to trust ourselves, take risks, and connect to our deeper selves. It is in this vast, broader perspective, where we have moments of awesome clarity, that our attitude toward life at home can be uplifted.

Being at home is a coming home to yourself, your spirit and your vital energy. We find our true home in the atmosphere, mood, and soul of our intimate, personal surroundings. Here we're free to get into the spirit and swing of the joys of our daily domestic rhythms. If something isn't working out for us, we can change it—immediately. Even the most minor improvements can make us feel more at ease, more relaxed, more at home.

Have we forgotten that meaningful living takes time? The simple, quiet graces of a well-lived life have been abandoned. The nonmaterial things you and I can't buy and sell are at the very core of our sense of freedom and joy. Shooting the waves at the beach after a storm, walking through the woods at sunrise, sitting quietly alone in a garden, having a siesta with your spouse, are not wastes of time. If we don't take time to wonder, to stargaze, to be in awe of nature's sheer majesty, we're focusing on all the problems mankind brings to us that are less important in the long run. We should feel free to spend more time in contemplation, prayer, and meditation, when we fill our own hearts with light and faith and hope. We don't have to go to a chapel or a synagogue or a mosque to do this. We can meditate standing over the dishes in the kitchen sink, or fall to our knees in appreciation of our blessings as we wipe up the bathroom floor after a bath.

Living a civilized, cultivated, and joyful life at home is not only a possibility but should be our goal. We should open ourselves wide to the precious, magical possibilities of accepting the richness within us as well as in all of life. We can experience this inner awareness each moment wherever we are, whatever we are doing. All our endeavors can be spiritual acts, once we open our hearts to some fundamental truths about our nature and human nature, our living and our dying.

Our personal objects can become spiritual when viewed in this light because they are full of wonder and beauty, and collectively they inspire love and express our taste and our style for living. We see them, touch them, speak to them, and they teach us that while we can experience them concretely while we are alive, they also contain a mystery, a spirit, and an energy, a life force we cannot fully know.

This is meeting time again. Home is the magnet . . . All that is dear, that is lasting, renews its hold on us: we are home again . . .

ELIZABETH BOWEN

To be moral is to discover fundamentally one's own being.

SIMONE DE BEAUVOIR

You may have a beautiful table that you love. You can sit at it and feel whole. Why does this table hold such powerful feelings for you? You wonder about the tree that made this table possible. Where was the tree planted? It is fruitwood; what kind of fruit? Pear? Apple? What did the tree look like that later became a table? Was it tall? When was it cut down? Why was it cut down? Did it fall down in a storm? Who made your favorite table? Who, before you, sat at this table? You know there is something more to this table than its being just another table. It has an energy, a spirit, an invisible force.

We often have these feelings about a house, an apartment, or another person. We know when something speaks to us on a deep inner level, connecting us to who we are, who we were, and who we will become. And it is at this profound place when we have tinges of this sense of oneness, of wholeness and connection, that we trust our own truth. Who we are becomes a way of life at home.

We have to give ourselves permission to seek this higher self. The practical necessities of everyday living at home are important, but they are only a partial reality. I have a need for privacy at home so that I can take time to examine my feelings. It is at home when we're private that we're able to tap into our deepest passions, take time to heal, live with a sense of fulfillment, satisfaction, and meaning. There must be times at home when there are no interruptions, when we pay close attention to how we feel as we go about the business of doing what has to be done. It is in these precious moments of solitude that we learn to be open to our intuition and trust what we experience inwardly.

Feeling at Home shows us how to set ourselves free in order to live with greater joy, love, and spontaneity every day. How each of us feels about ourselves and life as we read the newspaper, set the table, wash the dishes, write a thank-you note, recycle the trash, read to a child, wash our clothes, make the bed, dress and undress, bathe, prepare for sleep, awaken to a new day, is essential to our overall happiness and well-being.

Each of us is eccentric because each of us is unique and no one else is like us. We can best express our individuality in unusual, uncommon ways at home. Our home is an autobiography, a journal, a scrapbook of our past, our present, and future dreams. Living at home is a dynamic, creative process.

Our home is our essence, the ultimate earthly place where we live and love and have our being. The personal objects around us create a welcoming feeling, one of warmth and comfort we all yearn for. Each of us can create a unique atmosphere that represents us, nourishes us, in all our moods and changing situations.

I hope through reading this book you receive the assurance an[d] energy to live as close as possible to your ideal at home. We can a[ll] be happy with what we have, no matter how simple, when we loo[k] beyond the material, and value what makes life worth living well an[d] loving. We all have particular, individual feelings about life. We a[re] need to establish our own philosophy and style, reflecting our fai[th] and spiritual enlightenment. To know our truth, to be true to wh[o] we are at our core, is to feel at home.

Feeling at Home is a guide to help you live an inner-directe[d,] dynamic life every day in your private haven. Here is where yo[u] know what's best for you, and you can live just the way you choo[se] to. Your surroundings will have a profound effect on your moo[d,] outlook, health, and psychic energy.

Feeling at home is a positive energy, a vital process, and a [ ] way to improve the quality of our daily lives, wherever our [ ] journey takes us, because, ultimately, home is inside each of [ ] us. By seeing our true nature and expressing this truth, home welcomes us, renews us, liberates us, and most of all, enlarges us to embrace the mystery and value of the unknown. Feeling at home helps us to be less controlling, more humble, more aware of our higher nature and our divine gifts.

else is like us. We can best express our individuality in unusual, uncommon ways at home. Our home is an autobiography, a journal, a scrapbook of our past, our present, and future dreams. Living at home is a dynamic, creative process.

Our home is our essence, the ultimate earthly place where we live and love and have our being. The personal objects around us create a welcoming feeling, one of warmth and comfort we all yearn for. Each of us can create a unique atmosphere that represents us, nourishes us, in all our moods and changing situations.

A lifestyle is an art form. It brings life and wonder, joy and hope to persons otherwise condemned to superficial living.

MATTHEW FOX

I hope through reading this book you receive the assurance and energy to live as close as possible to your ideal at home. We can all be happy with what we have, no matter how simple, when we look beyond the material, and value what makes life worth living well and loving. We all have particular, individual feelings about life. We all need to establish our own philosophy and style, reflecting our faith and spiritual enlightenment. To know our truth, to be true to who we are at our core, is to feel at home.

Feeling at Home is a guide to help you live an inner-directed, dynamic life every day in your private haven. Here is where you know what's best for you, and you can live just the way you choose to. Your surroundings will have a profound effect on your mood, outlook, health, and psychic energy.

Feeling at home is a positive energy, a vital process, and a way to improve the quality of our daily lives, wherever our journey takes us, because, ultimately, home is inside each of us. By seeing our true nature and expressing this truth, home welcomes us, renews us, liberates us, and most of all, enlarges us to embrace the mystery and value of the unknown. Feeling at home helps us to be less controlling, more humble, more aware of our higher nature and our divine gifts.

The greatest thing in the world is to know how to be one's own self.

MONTAIGNE

You may have a beautiful table that you love. You can sit at it and feel whole. Why does this table hold such powerful feelings for you? You wonder about the tree that made this table possible. Where was the tree planted? It is fruitwood; what kind of fruit? Pear? Apple? What did the tree look like that later became a table? Was it tall? When was it cut down? Why was it cut down? Did it fall down in a storm? Who made your favorite table? Who, before you, sat at this table? You know there is something more to this table than its being just another table. It has an energy, a spirit, an invisible force.

We often have these feelings about a house, an apartment, or another person. We know when something speaks to us on a deep inner level, connecting us to who we are, who we were, and who we will become. And it is at this profound place when we have tinges of this sense of oneness, of wholeness and connection, that we trust our own truth. Who we are becomes a way of life at home.

We have to give ourselves permission to seek this higher self. The practical necessities of everyday living at home are important, but they are only a partial reality. I have a need for privacy at home so that I can take time to examine my feelings. It is at home when we're private that we're able to tap into our deepest passions, take time to heal, live with a sense of fulfillment, satisfaction, and meaning. There must be times at home when there are no interruptions, when we pay close attention to how we feel as we go about the business of doing what has to be done. It is in these precious moments of solitude that we learn to be open to our intuition and trust what we experience inwardly.

Feeling at Home shows us how to set ourselves free in order to live with greater joy, love, and spontaneity every day. How each of us feels about ourselves and life as we read the newspaper, set the table, wash the dishes, write a thank-you note, recycle the trash, read to a child, wash our clothes, make the bed, dress and undress, bathe, prepare for sleep, awaken to a new day, is essential to our overall happiness and well-being.

Each of us is eccentric because each of us is unique and no one

The sole purpose of human existence is to kindle a light in the darkness of mere being.

CARL JUNG

To change one's life: start immediately. Do it flamboyantly. No exceptions.

WILLIAM JAMES

vital energy. We find our true home in the atmosphere, mood, and soul of our intimate, personal surroundings. Here we're free to get into the spirit and swing of the joys of our daily domestic rhythms. If something isn't working out for us, we can change it—immediately. Even the most minor improvements can make us feel more at ease, more relaxed, more at home.

Have we forgotten that meaningful living takes time? The simple, quiet graces of a well-lived life have been abandoned. The nonmaterial things you and I can't buy and sell are at the very core of our sense of freedom and joy. Shooting the waves at the beach after a storm, walking through the woods at sunrise, sitting quietly alone in a garden, having a siesta with your spouse, are not wastes of time. If we don't take time to wonder, to stargaze, to be in awe of nature's sheer majesty, we're focusing on all the problems mankind brings to us that are less important in the long run. We should feel free to spend more time in contemplation, prayer, and meditation, when we fill our own hearts with light and faith and hope. We don't have to go to a chapel or a synagogue or a mosque to do this. We can meditate standing over the dishes in the kitchen sink, or fall to our knees in appreciation of our blessings as we wipe up the bathroom floor after a bath.

Living a civilized, cultivated, and joyful life at home is not only a possibility but should be our goal. We should open ourselves wide to the precious, magical possibilities of accepting the richness within us as well as in all of life. We can experience this inner awareness each moment wherever we are, whatever we are doing. All our endeavors can be spiritual acts, once we open our hearts to some fundamental truths about our nature and human nature, our living and our dying.

Our personal objects can become spiritual when viewed in this light because they are full of wonder and beauty, and collectively they inspire love and express our taste and our style for living. We see them, touch them, speak to them, and they teach us that while we can experience them concretely while we are alive, they also contain a mystery, a spirit, and an energy, a life force we cannot fully know.

This is meeting time again. Home is the magnet ... All that is dear, that is lasting, renews its hold on us: we are home again ...

ELIZABETH BOWEN

To be moral is to discover fundamentally one's own being.

SIMONE DE BEAUVOIR

PART ONE

Self-Attune-ment

Connect our inner light
to the external light of our
environment.

—GOETHE

Self-Attune-ment

Connect our inner light
to the external light of our
environment.

—GOETHE

CHAPTER 1

Defining Who You Are Now

The immense value and beauty of the human being lies precisely in the fact that he belongs to the two kingdoms of nature and the spirit.
— THOMAS MANN

Feeling at Home

Several years ago, my daughter Brooke was sitting at a favorite café in Paris, reflecting on how central France is to her life. Not only did she find her true self in France but her love of this country led her to a career in design and style. Something extraordinary happens to Brooke's face whenever she sets foot on French soil. She gets dimples. Ever since she was five, France has been a living reality in her philosophy and her way of experiencing the world. At that café that particular afternoon, reflecting on her good fortune to be able to make her home in Paris after graduating from college, she did something I would do—she got out her pen and a sheet of paper from her Filofax and wrote down the ten things that define who she is. She kept that list in her notebook all these years and came across it recently. What's powerful about this exercise is how true to her center these words continue to be. These words tumbled

> *All thought is a feat of association; having what's in front of you bring up something in your mind that you almost didn't know you knew.*
>
> ROBERT FROST

from pen to paper without conscious thought. They symbolize all the true meaning of her being.

Inspiration	Blue
Paris	Elephants
Flowers	Light
Beauty	Artists
Design	Creativity

When we feel at home we move through our daily lives in tune with our superior spirit. At home we get in touch with our truth.

Whenever we feel at home, our soul is nourished with loving energy.

Over lunch in a French bistro on Madison Avenue, she shared with me these ten symbols that define who she is. I reached for pen and paper and wrote mine down. My husband, Peter, joined in and wrote down his. We laughed and laughed. Tears of joy rolled down our cheeks because of the ineffable liberation of our spirits. Here we are, three people who love each other dearly, who have shared a home together happily ever since Peter and I married in May 1974, yet each of us expresses our true self so differently. That lunch was memorable because of the intimacy we felt toward each other and the feeling of freedom each of us experienced in defining who we are.

Because this experience was so powerful for all of us, I suggest you get out a pencil or pen and a piece of paper and write down the ten word symbols that tell who you truly are. Don't think. Your subconscious does all the work. Be there to record what emerges from the deepest recesses of your heart. This may be one of the sweetest moments of your entire life. Try it, and see for yourself how you feel.

I returned to the house, took the penholder (this is my flute) and with a gentle shudder, leaned over the paper.

NIKOS KAZANTZAKIS

Your Personal Book

The brilliant result of the exercise you just completed is that you see your individuality in front of you. You have a unique mind and spirit. No matter what social conventions or habits you've learned, you are different from anyone else on earth. Once you tap into that awareness of your self, then the joy is in expressing that unique soul.

Buy a notebook to use as an exercise book as you read *Feeling at Home*. Think of this book as a place to discover your own personal truth. By getting in tune and in touch with your truths, you can create a home that echoes your true spirit. When I ask you a question, write the answer in your notebook. The notebook will be our creative interaction.

I am going to share some deeply felt truths about our feelings at home. I want you to be challenged by them. Make notes, write your questions, answer those you wish to, and remember, there are no right answers. You will see that the questions lead you to your own reality, your own truth, your own answers. Your answers can't be answered by me (or anyone else), nor will I ask you all the right questions. Some will cause painful self-analysis and others will help you to see how well your needs are met at home. I want to stimulate your thinking about your daily life, your needs, and your desires.

The notebook you use to accompany *Feeling at Home* might be the best book ever written because it will be you at your core, free of social expectations and the anxieties of day-to-day living. Once you can touch that essential nature, you are free to live not only a beautiful life but a joyful existence in your earthly home.

I can think only when the pencil is in my hand.

NIKOS KAZANTZAKIS

By taking personal inventory, you learn more about your needs.

Ten Personality Traits

The ten symbols that define who I am are:

Love   Food
Sunlight   Family
Gardens   Color
Beaches   Ribbons
Children   Home

Words are a form of action, capable of influencing change. Their articulation represents a complete lived experience.

INGRID BENGIS

Later, I will share examples of how and why I've been untrue to my self at different periods of my life and how I got back on my path.

Peter told me he'd be happy to share his ten defining symbols:

Love	Dancing
Beaches	Music
Old friends	Wine
Children	Lunch
Reading	Memories

I smile every time I think of this because anyone who knows Peter understands this is pure Peter Megargee Brown. One of the most important lessons I've learned from Peter is how true he always is to who he really is. No matter who he's with, whether he's alone with me, with family, with a mentor, a client, a friend, or a waiter, with rare exceptions he is quintessentially himself. He is a playful fourth child of four, always the baby, and as the youngest he had invaluable time to learn from his mother, who was happy and resourceful, beautiful and graceful in spirit. Simply, he got away with being himself. To the extent he could separate himself from others' demands, he managed to do so. Often he just played dumb, politely listening to others' advice, while following his own.

On Becoming Who We Are

It took me longer to break free for many simple and complex reasons. My mother was easy to get along with as long as you agreed with her. Perhaps she felt somewhat trapped in her own life, unable to liberate herself to the degree she felt she needed to in order to feel harmony in her core. The words from *Hamlet* were her motto:

This above all: To thine own self be true,
And it must follow, as the night the day,
Thou canst not then be false to any man.

While she wanted desperately to be true to herself, it was hard for her to let her children go off in their own different directions. Although I was often forced to toe the line, my instinct was to stir up the pot. In many ways, I think my mother believed deeply in her soul that each of her four children must be on a quest to find out who they were at their center. In contrast, Peter's mother was not a controlling personality, and he gained the confidence at an early age to do what felt right to him. Peter manages to be a free spirit no matter what obstacles face him. He continues to enjoy music, dancing, wine, and lunch because he has learned how to celebrate life through all its losses, and he regularly sees new opportunities, new fresh ways to express his love of life.

Words are only painted fire; a look is the fire itself.

MARK TWAIN

What have you learned about yourself from writing the ten symbols that define who you are now? What do you see about yourself that you feel needs more nourishing? If you wrote down dancing, as Peter did, how often do you actually dance? Look at each of the ten symbols and analyze what it represents to you. Thirty years ago, I would have had tennis as one of my ten words. I was a passionate tennis player. Because I will never play tennis again due to a tricky back and a bad knee, I have moved on. After I herniated and slipped a disc, my literary agent, who knew what my doctor's orders were, told me "Sandie, if you ever play tennis again, get another agent." He meant what he said. I've fantasized about tennis, dreaming I've played, but I am no longer a tennis player. One key lesson you learn is to evaluate who you are now. If you see something on your list of ten symbols that is no longer possible, you'll be living in the past, frustrated in your current life. We should not spend our psychic energy, valuable time, and money longing for something that is no longer possible. We must learn to let go and open new doors, letting in fresh light. My spiritual mentor, John Bowen Coburn, who married Peter

Your motto: Be Bold, Be Free, Be Truthful.

BRENDA UELAND

and me, told me one day, "Alexandra, we live our life in chapters. You can't live chapter three until you've lived chapters one and two." When one part of our life dies, we feel a loss, but without loss there is no gaining of new challenges, new opportunities, new understanding.

The Reality Versus the Myth

Look at your list. Where are you now? Are there symbols that represent important things that you want to do more of that you're not currently doing? Perhaps you want to read or garden more. Or, maybe, you need more color in your home. If there is any one thing you're not doing that you really want to do, look at your list to see if it's there.

For reasons I don't know, my friend Mysty stopped playing the piano when she was eight years old. One day she read that people should follow their dreams. She was in her early thirties at the time. A light went on in her soul: "I want to play the piano." She saved up for five years and with great satisfaction bought a piano. Now she's taking lessons, practices every morning before going to work, and is working toward performing in a recital. The living room of her sweet house is dominated by the presence of the piano. It is not stuck in the corner. It commands center stage, a far more appealing focal point than a fireplace that doesn't work or a television. Mysty wrote down her ten symbols, and the piano was one of them.

Designing Your Life

If there's any one thing you're not doing that you really want to do, write it in your notebook. Some people feel strong urges to pursue things neglected over the years. Whether the cause is lack of time, money, other distractions, poor health, or whatever reason, identify what you want to do to add to the fullness of your life. Perhaps you want to write a novel. If you get up one hour earlier than you do now and write one page a day, you will have a rough first draft in a year. If you want to write poetry, you can set a goal to write one poem a week. In time, you can increase that to two or three or seven. Start small and build.

Needs and Wants

Just as important as knowing what you want to add to your life is knowing what to eliminate. Examine carefully how you actually spend your time. Look for fudging when you are being unconsciously self-deceptive. Evaluate how you feel when you are engaged in certain activities. Look at what you are doing, compared to what you want to be doing. Spell out what you have to do compared to what you want to do. Identify these activities in your notebook. Draw a vertical line down the center of the page. On the top left, write *Needs*, and on the top right, write *Wants*. Spend a few minutes to freely express what are clearly necessary chores and what are grace notes, *needs* versus *wants*. Next to each item, write down how much time it takes you to accomplish it each week. For example, how long does it take you to clean out the cat litter, do the laundry, dust, or iron? In Chapter 4 we will work on time management, how we balance what we do at home.

If I have a creed, it is this: I don't want to be labeled or have any person or group limit my vision.

At home you have the freedom to be quiet and alone and feel connected to everyone and everything.

Getting to Your Core

On another page in your notebook, in a stream of consciousness, write down what you most like about your life right now. What's good about you? What are your strengths? What are your weaknesses? Are there areas that you need to work on to improve the quality of your life? If you are a Type-A personality, for example, what are you

We achieve immortality by becoming so insistently and inimitably ourselves.

ERNEST BECKER

doing to become more relaxed? Do you garden? If you are
disorganized, what are you doing to put your life back in
order? If you are artistic and feel frustrated that you haven't
managed to find time to express yourself, what are you
doing to turn that situation around? See if there is an art
class you can go to one night a week. If you work over
eighty hours a week at the office but really want to begin a family,
what are you doing to resolve this conflict of interests? Be as honest as possible. Do you have any habits that are life threatening?
Are some of your habits interfering with the harmony at home?

How well are you getting along with your spouse? What is your
relationship with your children? How close are you to your
extended family? Who, if anyone, do you not get along with?
Can you identify why? Who is paid to come help you
around the house? Write their names down, if any. How do
you get along with these helpers? Do you work alongside
them, or do they work independently? If you don't have any
help, do you wish you did? What kind of work would you
want someone else to do? Would you want someone to help
clean the house? Do the laundry? Garden? Run errands? Pay
the bills?

How much privacy do you require? Do you have a room of your
own, a thinking room or a space where you can retreat that is sacrosanct, a place where only you are allowed? How well do you handle
interruptions? Do you wish you had your own study?

How healthy are you right now? Do you have a doctor you trust?
How do you rate your energy? On a scale of one to ten, rate your
vital energy. Are you getting enough sleep? How much sleep
would be ideal? How do you feel about the future? Are you
hopeful? Are there specific goals you have in place and are
you working toward them?

Do you feel you've found your passion? What is your
passion? If you were to leave this earth today, how would
you want the world to think of you? What are your gifts? Do
you consider yourself to be kind? Compassionate? Generous?
Caring?

What do you want to do that you are not doing? How

do you want to spend your psychic energy? Do you consider yourself an optimist or a pessimist? Do you tend to brood? What mood are you in now? Rate your mood from one to ten. Describe your temperament. Do you tend to be cheerful or grumpy? What causes you to become upset? How well do you handle stress? How anxious do you tend to become? Do you consider yourself objective or subjective? While many intelligent people consider themselves objective, all human happiness is subjective.

Each of us should take personal responsibility to meet our own emotional, spiritual, and physical needs at home.

How Do You Want Your Home to Feel?

A talented interior designer, Charles Gandy, asks his clients to think of three symbols that would best describe the way they want their home to feel. One client, living on a ranch in Montana, said, "Chocolate chip cookies." When the house was complete, Charles baked chocolate chip cookies so it smelled of warm chocolate, sugar, and the perfume of baking. When they walked in the front door, the sweet scent wafted on the crisp mountain air, expressing a warm homecoming. What are the three symbols that evoke the spirit of your home? Peter's and mine are welcoming, comforting, and loving.

Questions I Ask Clients

How long have you lived in this home?
When was it built?
Do you know who the architect was?
How long do you intend to live here?
What do you like most about your house?
What do you want to change?
Over what time period?
What is your budget for the next six months?

When you get converted, you still have the same personality. You merely exercise it in terms of a different set of values.

ROBERT PENN WARREN

What dreams do you have for your house?

Show me your favorite piece of furniture. Why are you so attached to this particular piece of furniture?

Show me your favorite window. Why are you drawn to this particular window?

Do you feel your house gets enough natural light?

Have you thought about ways to lighten up the spaces?

What room do you like the most?

Why do you like this room best of all in your entire house?

What room reveals your personality the most?

What are the objects that speak to you and for you?

Show me your most meaningful photographs. Tell me who these people are and how you feel about them.

Where do you like to sit?

Show me five favorite places where you enjoy sitting.

Tell me what you like to do when you're at home.

You like to read. How much time do you actually spend reading per day?

Where do you sit to read?

Do you read a daily newspaper?

What time do you read the newspaper?

Where do you like to read the newspaper?

Where do you actually read the paper?

(Try reading the newspaper in seven different places for the next seven days. By changing your pattern, you may find a more ideal spot. If you don't like to be disturbed while reading the paper, select a more secluded place. Try placing your chair facing a window with the back of the chair toward the door. The placement of the chair will make it obvious that you need to be alone to concentrate. Also, by changing the place where you choose to read the paper, you will feel stimulated by the variety of locations in your house where you can enjoy reading.)

Become intimately involved with all the various dimensions of your day-to-day living.

Believe, that you may understand.

SAINT AUGUSTINE

How important is television to you?

How often do you watch television per week?

What kind of programs do you watch?

How much time do you spend watching television per week?

How do you feel after you've watched television?

What books are you currently reading?

If you feel you don't have enough time to read, can you limit your television viewing to the evening news, after you've spent several hours reading?

How much time do you spend eating?

Where do you sit for breakfast? Lunch? Tea? Dinner?

How many times do you entertain per month?

In a year, how many parties do you have?

How do you entertain?

How many people do you tend to have for a reception?

How often do you have cocktail parties? dinner parties? teas?

How many dinner parties have you had in the last twelve months?

What seasons do you like best for celebrations?

How many people did you actually entertain in the past year besides your extended family?

Do you use your dining room table for family dinners and perhaps breakfast and lunches during the weekends?

Things seen and unseen affect the harmony of our sense of reverence for life at home.

Not a single other creature in all the history of the world has been just as ourselves. Not another will be like us.

WILLIAM SOUTAR

A client bought a house that had a room on the floor plan called a dining room. She paid a fortune for the room's furnishings, including a traditional sideboard, a mirror, and expensive silk brocade for the Chippendale chair seats. This family has a wonderful large kitchen where they eat all their family meals. The dining room is used for a child's birthday party or Thanksgiving dinner, but rarely for entertaining because the husband and wife both work and the children are still young. This lovely space is a still life most of the time. What a shame to have a room not used every day.

A Library at Home

Let the light that shines brightly inside you become the light that guides the energy of your home.

When I married Peter, the dining room in his apartment had been a dormitory for several daughters before they left for college. When they left home, rather than turning the room back into a dining room, we decided to build bookcases. I was appalled that a man who loves books had no books in his apartment. He kept his library at his law office on Wall Street. (Peter's law firm had built him bookcases when he went to work there.) With a large family and so many tuitions to pay, he couldn't rationalize the expense of bookcases at home. Looking back, this was certainly a mistake because he could have bought a series of ready-made bookcases at a reasonable price, and they could have housed his children's books as well. In contrast, my apartment had a library–dining room with books everywhere.

One Saturday, over lunch at Le Veau D'Or, a popular Manhattan brasserie where Peter had proposed to me only a few months beforehand, we had a slight fight. I couldn't believe he didn't live with his books at home. "What if you want to reread a book late one night or look up a reference? If your library is four miles away, isn't it frustrating? I need my books with me. I love my books. They are all my friends. I need them around me for comfort and security. They speak to me even when they're not being read. They are a major part of my life."

Peter listened, held my hand, and said, "I will build bookcases in the apartment and bring up my favorites from the law firm, and we'll make the old dining room into the library for the enjoyment of everyone."

That was a defining moment because I knew I couldn't live without lots of books and a place to house them. We all make mistakes, but we can correct them. We should remember that all mistakes are in the past. By identifying our needs, we can incorporate them in tangible ways at home. We should never say we cannot afford to do something until we've investigated the cost and practicality. Have confidence in your self-awareness. As long as you believe in change, you are free.

Every soul has to learn the whole lesson for itself. It must go over the whole ground. What it does not see, what it does not live, it will not know.

EMERSON

I knew I also needed bookcases in our bedroom. I bought an inexpensive wall unit at the Door Store and filled it with books floor to ceiling. There was a drop-front desk where I could sit and work. For several years, I thought this was what I needed and wanted. But I grew to know this was the wrong use of space. I love light and shouldn't face into a wall unit. This entire wall was devoted to the storage of books and we longed for a comfortable sitting area where we could both sit and read together. Also, I grew not to like lying in bed looking up at masses of books, feeling I should get up and read. I ended up putting the units in a child's room, and we created a much-desired sitting area in the space. I had a carpenter build bookcases underneath a wide window ledge. I still live with books in our intimate bedroom, but they aren't threatening anymore.

If you don't like something one way, you can change it. My rule is that if it feels right, don't change it. If it doesn't feel right, fix it. Also keep in mind that something can be right for us at one time; later we may come to understand it is wrong. Don't be afraid to admit you made a mistake. The only error is not to learn from what we do and make practical improvements.

By building the bookcases in the library, Peter not only gave us a place to join our books but also opened up an opportunity for us to collect books together. The bookcases went from floor to ceiling along the entire length of our room as well as on either side of the windows on the adjacent wall. At first we didn't have enough books to fill the shelves. We mixed in paintings and decorative objects. Now, more than twenty-five years later, we have books on the shelves, on the floor, and stacked on tables. Everywhere there is a surface, there are books.

My client who had the dining room she never used became inspired to build bookcases in the room to make a place where she and her family could go to read and study at the dining room table, surrounded by books. After the bookcases were built and more time was spent in this room reading at the table, everyone felt comfortable having meals there as a change of atmosphere from the kitchen, where the cooking and cleaning up take place.

A bird does not sing because it has an answer. It sings because it has a song.

CHINESE PROVERB

We should always be pointing toward the ideal.

I am what I am and that's what I am.

POPEYE

One of the luxuries of having a dining room is using the table to spread out your papers and books and having room to work. Peter and I bring our books, newspapers, and magazines to the dining room at our cottage in Stonington, where we often have breakfast and end up sitting for hours afterward relishing the luxury of time and a place to read and write. There is no right answer for how we should put our spaces to use. Our lives are a dynamic process unfolding. As we open up to new ways, we can live more richly in our spaces, and find ways to make our rooms more comfortable for us and our family.

Who Are You?

When you are alone in your house, what do you most like to do? Where do you go? What is your mood when you're alone? What is your attitude about the circumstances of your life at home? Do you ever turn inward and feel sorry for yourself? Do you tend to complain to family members or friends or do you keep your feelings to yourself? Do you ever feel envious or jealous about other people's good fortune? Do you sometimes feel overwhelmed by details and demands on your time and wish you could push the world aside and escape? Do you ever feel trapped at home?

What do you want that you don't have? List things as well as feelings. You may want a new dishwasher and you might want peace of mind. Maybe you want the screen door repaired or you'd like a bird-bath outside your breakfast room window or a wind chime on your willow tree.

What are the last three books you've read? Why did you read them? What did you get out of them? How important is reading to you? Do you read to learn or to escape? How many books do you read a year? Do you tend to read fiction or nonfiction?

Do you consider yourself a grateful person? How many times do you say "thank you" per day? What are some of the ways you give thanks? Do you say grace before a meal? Have you ever been burned out? What caused it? How did you feel? What did you do to change your patterns to regain your equilibrium? Do you have a tendency to blame others when something goes wrong? Do you make excuses? If you want to write a book, you can't blame your husband or your boss or your children, logically, but do you? Do you ever deceive yourself into believing there is no time when all you have in your lifetime is time, twenty-four hours every day? If we don't have time, it means we're not taking charge of our time, claiming certain times for ourselves alone.

Do you feel something is wrong in your life and you can't put your finger on it? Clients often tell me they're stuck. All questions cut to the truth. Have some of these questions made you feel uncomfortable? Why? Did one or two hit a nerve?

How intuitive are you? How often do you have immediate insights or understanding? How have your learned to trust your intuition? Are you usually right when you pay attention to this way of knowing? Did you ever have a sharp insight where you knew something to be true without conscious reasoning, and you didn't follow through? Why? What blocked you from trusting yourself?

How introspective are you? How often do you contemplate your own thoughts, feelings, and motives? How often do you tend to examine your self, to look within? Do you meditate each day? Do you pray? Do you believe in a force beyond your self? How highly evolved do you believe you are spiritually? Are you religious? Are you a practicing member of a religious order? Do you have any prejudices against other people who feel differently than you do about faith? Why?

How sophisticated are you? Are you naive? Have you ever felt superior to someone else? Why? Have you ever felt yourself to be a snob? How did it make you feel?

Have you developed a personal philosophy for your life? Are you able to identify your gifts and talents? On a scale of one to ten, how creative do you feel you are? Are you using your gifts to capacity or are you burying many of them while you're on another path? How can you cultivate your creativity? Are you contributing only things you personally create as your ideal?

Who are some of your role models who help you to be true to your core?

Borrow the best from the past.

You want to come home only if there's peace when you arrive. The fine part of our lives is the calm in our house. When you get there, you love it.

SHERRY SIUB COHEN

In your notebook, write down each of your gifts. Identify them specifically. Your greatest gift could be to "listen with a loving heart," words of the presiding bishop of the Episcopal Church, Frank T. Griswold III. Your gifts might include letter writing or baking bread or your enthusiasm for life that rubs off on all those whose lives cross yours. Your gift could be your intuition or your caring heart. You could sing like an angel or dance like the wind. By writing down the gifts you were given, you can clearly see you are happiest when you use them. Creative energy gives us our enthusiasm and passion for life. The more you exercise your gifts, the more you're in tune with yourself. You become attuned to bringing your life into harmony, making adjustments in order to perform to your greatest power.

All the answers to your questions are in your heart.

Do you consider yourself inner directed or outer (other) directed? Do you care more about how you feel than about anyone else's opinions? Do you care more what other people think of you than what you believe to be the truth about yourself? How daring are you to be and express your true self? Are there people you are afraid of? Who are they? Are there authority figures who try to control your behavior? When other people dictate what you do and tell you what to think, how does this make you feel?

How much of an effort do you make to encourage other people to be happy? Do you generally try to impress other people? Do you find your behavior changes when you are with "important" people?

Are there some people who get under your skin, who find fault no matter what you do? Identify these people. It is far easier to see what's wrong with someone else than ourselves, but usually if someone is highly critical of another, it is out of self-loathing, not self-love.

Think globally, but act locally.

RENÉ DUBOS

On a scale of one to ten, do you feel free, independent, and in control? Do you feel confined? Do you ever feel claustrophobic at home? In what spaces? Try to identify why. Is the space dark and crowded?

What are the biggest burdens in your life right now? Are they beyond your control? If wisdom tells us that it is not always what happens to us in life but how we react to what happens that is of key importance, how are you reacting to these burdens? Do you ever think, "Why me?" Do some painful situations prove to be pathways to deeper spiritual insights? How do you handle the times when things are completely beyond your control? Are you able to say to yourself, "What can I do?"

How disciplined do you think you are? Are you willing to take the necessary time to improve your skills, practice regularly in order to learn your craft and accomplish your goals? Have you ever quit something you should have worked on until it was completed? How did it make you feel? Have you ever stuck with something long after you knew it was wrong for you? When you let someone else down, how bad do you feel? How do you feel when you let yourself down? On a scale of one to ten, are you extremely hardworking or quite lazy?

How do you feel about yourself when you completely focus your attention on the task at hand and complete it as best you can? When something needs to be done, do you tend to procrastinate? When you rush and just get by, doing something half-heartedly, how does it make you feel? When you rush around the house, does the hurrying up make you nervous? Why do you think that you do some things so rapidly that you aren't fully aware of what you're doing?

How good are you at motivating yourself, setting goals, making plans, and sticking with them? Do you value time as your most precious resource? Do you have too little or too much time on your hands? When was the last time you were bored? Who were you with? Why did you feel weary and dull? Were the people you were with uninspired? Or were they tedious or obnoxious? Why were you in this situation? Were you at home? Do you like having uninteresting business people to your house, or would you prefer to see them in a restaurant?

How do you rate your self-esteem, your self-love? Are you extremely confident or do you feel you lack the self-worth to follow your own dreams and desires? Were your childhood experiences generally positive or negative? Have you had successful long-term relationships with others? Do you feel you know where you stand, what your boundaries are, what your limits are, so that you behave in a

The task of education is to make the individual so firm and sure that, as a whole being, he can no longer be diverted from his path.

FRIEDRICH NIETZSCHE

Take stock of where you are now on your path to yourself.

If I had lost confidence in myself, I have the Universe against me.

EMERSON

manner that makes others feel comfortable, and you never have to compromise your integrity? How strong are you?

How we regard ourself resonates in all our relationships to people, to things, and to the spirit of place. The very atmosphere sends out vibrations either intensifying life's psychic energy or diminishing it. Coming to terms with who we are and how we identify ourselves is not vain or selfish, but self-centering, helping us know on our deepest level who we are. By exploring the complexities of our personality, we increase our understanding of just who we are. If you are an individualist, willing to express originality, being idiosyncratic, even eccentric, these characteristics are a virtue because you are being true to the quirky aspects of your personality. As famously suggested by Dr. Karl Menninger, if we are dead-center normal, we have no personality at all. The qualities, the totality of distinctive traits, compose who we are, our persona. Do we wear a mask? Are we willing to take it off and expose our honest, true, authentic self in order to live our life in sincerity?

My experience is that many people are unduly hard on themselves. They want to please others, many different people, and in the process they lose their identity as individuals. In other cases, people will take on too much work, stretching themselves in all different directions, agreeing to requests that are clearly not only inconvenient but impossible, not being able to say no because they want other people's approval. We all have a longing to be part of a community. We want fellowship. But we don't have to try so hard. You could have a beautiful garden, and if a few dead leaves fall from the tree, you may feel you should run and pick them up so they don't destroy the beauty of the lawn; yet most people see the miraculously beautiful garden, not the minute natural flaws. The falling leaves can teach us to be more real and more realistic.

Do you think of yourself as a nurturer of others? Write in your notebook before reading on, yes or no. Now, do you think you treat yourself as well as you do others? Many of my readers confide that they find it difficult to nurture themselves. Often people neglect themselves as they become caregivers to others. But how can you give fully to others from a hollow, dry well? How can we give some-

I see the folly of attempting to hitch one's wagon to a star with a harness that does not belong to it.

HELEN KELLER

thing we don't have? How can we give happiness to someone else if we don't feel this fine inner attunement ourselves?

Healthy Versus Neurotic Guilt

Having fresh flowers in a pitcher on the kitchen table, even if the room's paint is peeling and you need to get out the sandpaper, is a way of having the kitchen greet you with a smile. I would wither up and be spiritually diminished if I couldn't live with flowers. They are as important to me as food, and food is one of life's greatest blessings. Flowers nurture my soul. They give us hope. If you have some purple iris on the kitchen table, you will be surprised by joy every time you see them. Their delicate beauty is speaking to you of a divine mystery because they are God-made, not man-made. Their majesty rubs off on you, and you think more lofty thoughts about yourself and your family. You have a grace-filled moment and feel grateful. The irises are there for no other reason than to bring happiness to your moment. You need no justification for their existence. You don't need to feel guilty for buying them or growing them.

The best way to know the Truth or Beauty is to try to express it.

BRENDA UELAND

I have come to believe that a substantial portion of decent, conscientious people feel guilty when they're doing something pleasant for themselves and having a good time at home. They feel guilty about their own happiness because of the suffering of the rest of the world. Yet, wise men throughout recorded history have urged us to live a life of perfect freedom and joy. How can we give ourself permission to do whatever it takes for us to find freedom and joy if deep down we feel guilty? There are possibly two kinds of guilt—healthy guilt and neurotic guilt. Taking time for yourself is essential. If you feel guilty when you're doing things to nurture and nourish yourself, this is neurotic guilt. If you haven't done anything nice for your spouse or children for a month, this is healthy guilt and you might be prompted to be more available to your family. If you constantly feel that you should be doing something more for other people, that you should be accomplishing something useful

At home you feel yourself breaking free, opening up to new levels of awareness of who you are.

rather than being content to appreciate what is unfolding in front of you, you will never feel serenity at home or anywhere. Self-love means treating ourselves well, living well, and finding more and more ways to love and embrace life. Once you are in this illuminated consciousness, it is possible you are then able to inspire numbers of people to mobilize themselves into right action and right being. So often in the rush of immediate daily demands we forget that our higher self is yearning to be recognized and nourished. When we take time to care for our whole selves, it is never a waste of time because whatever needs to be done will be accomplished with greater ease and appreciation.

Those who have spent the time, done the thinking, and put themselves in the center of their own lives, their own home, are our teachers. They are our role models. Who are your role models, the people who know themselves and live a life at home that uplifts their spirit? When families sensitively accommodate all the people who live there, where everyone feels the loving psychic energy whenever they approach the front door, this is truly feeling at home.

If you are fortunate to have had a mentor—a mother, a father, or a grandparent—who lived with grace and dignity at home, who loved every day, living in the intimacy of family and a few well-selected friends, who loved beauty, books, music, good food, and conversation, who understood home as their private center, you are richly blessed. Our home can empower those who live there to greater faith and hope because of the positive feelings it radiates. Only by investing in yourself, recognizing your personal needs, and understanding that what you like matters, will your home take on this magical quality.

Believe in something larger than yourself.

BARBARA BUSH

Your home is more than simply an echo of yourself. Your home is your higher self. It is a place you love up by loving yourself. Your home is your true center, your true self, integrated, accommodating your interests, hobbies, and practical needs as well as those of each family member. Whenever I need to heal myself, I always return to our home in Stonington. By taking an ugly, old, taupe wreck of a house that I intuitively felt had an innate sweetness to it, we continuously love it up, tend to its ever-present needs, and in this process we make fresh discoveries about ourselves. We connect to nostalgic memories of our childhood and we feel blessed. We see our small treasured possessions everywhere; they delight us with their presence.

Everyone talks about the effect that world crises will have on our future, but deep down each of us feels home is central to us and our family. To be happy at home is the highest accomplishment on earth. Finding your true self and having a sacred place where you can express yourself is the most significant achievement, because we can improve our self and our home each day, combining the practical needs of eating, sleeping, and bathing with satisfaction of our spiritual yearnings.

My loving challenge to you is to see yourself and your home in a whole new way. When you work to achieve this paradigm shift, you will know elements of paradise on earth and be able to live in this atmosphere and beauty all the days of your life because you will be happy at home.

What you think and feel matters.

We all find magic in different parts of our homes.

DOMINIQUE BROWNING

CHAPTER 2

Shaping Your Home

The art of living is always to make a good thing out of a bad thing.
—E. F. SCHUMACHER

A Client's Taking Stock

I interviewed a family who lives in a house in Massachusetts. Diane is forty-five years old, a freelance journalist who works from home and who loves to garden, read, and cook. She is married to John, a surgeon. They have two children, Bonnie, age ten, who is artistic, and Michael, age fifteen, an athlete.

By reading this family's dialogue with me about their needs, wishes, and dreams, you can better understand how to glean this information and use it for your own needs at home. As you evaluate your spaces, you'll see how to express yourself in the shaping of your home. All the questions I asked in Chapter 1 you can now see in operation with clear, specific solutions. The core of this chapter is to help you to make the connections between the abstract and conceptual, and the practical, useful, and concrete.

Do what you can, with what you have, where you are.

THEODORE ROOSEVELT

25

For the interview: A = Alexandra
                      D = Diane
                      J = John
                      B = Bonnie
                      M = Michael

A: How would you describe how you want your house to feel?

D: Comfortable, light, colorful, and cheerful.

A: How formal do you want it to be?

D: Not formal. Relaxed and informal. I want the house to be inviting, welcoming, and flexible.

A: What do you like the most about the house?

D: The openness of the spaces. The ample windows that go to the floor. The light.

A: What do you least like about the house?

D: It is ordinary. The builder wasn't an architect. The house has no character. It's a modern house. I've always lived in old houses. While I love the openness of the spaces, I miss having architectural details. I miss traditional molding, raised-panel doors, and chair rails. I miss the good workmanship of an older house.

A: How long do you intend to live in this house?

D: As long as it works for us. We're open. When the children go off to college, we'll use their rooms in some useful way.

A: Do you have parents or in-laws who will be visiting you?

D: Yes. John's mother and father live in California and will visit once or twice a year. My mother lives twenty minutes away. She comes to stay with the children when John and I are away on a vacation or at a conference.

A: I see you have a guest room with twin beds. Do you regularly have house guests?

D: No. John works long hours at the hospital. I'm always under deadline. We're really not free to entertain house guests. Because I love to cook, we have friends over for dinner but not to spend the night.

A: What do you do when friends invite themselves to come stay with you for a few days?

D: (Laughing) Awkwardly, I make excuses for why it isn't convenient. Because I work from home, it just doesn't work out. John leaves for the hospital at six o'clock and I go to my desk to work after breakfast. I can't have people underfoot. I need your help putting this guest room off the kitchen area to daily use, Alexandra. We don't have house guests.

A: I understand. It does seem a shame to have this great room used so infrequently. Have you ever thought about turning it into your work room? This would work except for the few times John's parents come because when your mother spends the night you and John are away. You could use the twin beds as banquettes, one on the north wall and the other on the east wall, adjacent to each other. With bolster cushions and lots of pillows, the thirty-nine-inch-wide beds become daybeds. In the evenings, you and John can use this room for reading and watching videos. Just a thought.

D: That makes sense. My desk is now in a closet and I have no natural light. This will make a huge difference to me.

A: Tell me about the pattern of your day. What are your habits? What time do you get up? Walk me through a typical day.

D: John gets up at five o'clock and jogs for half an hour. He makes coffee for me and brings it to me in bed, and then I get up and awaken Michael and Bonnie. We say good-bye to John and the children have breakfast with me.

A: Where?

D: It depends. The kitchen table most of the time, but we like to eat on the terrace when the weather is nice.

A: How many months of the year, weather permitting, do you have breakfast on the terrace?

D: From April through September, when it's not raining.

A: Where do you usually eat dinner?

D: The myth is we use the dining room regularly, but the reality is we end up here in the kitchen.

A: Where would you ideally like to eat dinner?

D: The dining room. Growing up, we always sat at the

All good things are cheap: all bad are very dear.

HENRY DAVID THOREAU

Rooms have to have a lilt, an element of fun.

PATRICIA CORBIN

What we learn to do, we learn by doing.

ARISTOTLE

dining room table and I have fond memories of the conversations and laughter.

A: Who served your dinner?

D: A maid.

A: Do you have anyone helping you serve your dinners?

D: Only when we have a dinner party, usually for over eight
people. I can manage cooking and serving for six to eight.

A: Why do you think you don't dine regularly in the dining
room?

D: It's too much work. I'd give almost anything to knock this
wall down or open it up partially so I could easily serve a
gracious meal in that attractive space.

A: Why don't you?

D: Are you serious?

A: Yes, I'm serious.

D: This wall separating the kitchen from the dining room has always
been a huge emotional barrier. I always feel cut off from the conversation. I only hear bits and pieces.

A: How often do you have friends over? How many dinner parties
do you have a year?

D: About once a month. The children have friends over all the time
but they become family. I would say we have friends for dinner
twelve to fifteen times a year.

A: Is that enough, too much, or too little?

D: Alexandra, if I could have dinner parties with more ease, I'd like
to have friends over once a week.

A: Really?

D: Really.

A: How elaborate are your dinner parties?

D: I love to cook, but one of my favorite parts of the meal is setting
a pretty table. I always have fresh flowers on the table, and we
always light candles. We have a variety of sets of china. I love our
collection of cotton napkins and often I like using a favorite tablecloth.

A: What do you really think of knocking down part of this entire
wall?

D: I would feel forever liberated, grateful, and happy.

A: How do you feel about the dining room furniture?

D: I like it. Why do you ask? What are you thinking?

A: If we put the dessert table on the far wall, you'd have a free wall you could remove completely, if it's structurally sound, opening up the entire room to join the kitchen. This way, when you're in the kitchen, you'll have the view and light from the dining room windows. Even if there are support issues, we can at least join the two rooms. Lighting will be key. You'll be able to use undercounter lights in the kitchen that will be practical yet soft and unobtrusive when you're seated at the dining table.

D: I can see it. I wish we could do it today. This dining room is an anachronism, out of date with the reality of our lives. We can still retain the grace without all the inconveniences and wasted time and energy. When we have more than eight people for a meal we can use the kitchen table as well.

A: How do you think John will feel about this idea?

D: He won't be in favor of it.

A: Why do you say that?

D: John worked hard to have a beautiful home. Having a dining room, not a dining space, means a great deal to him. He wants more formality than I do.

A: Obviously, you'll have to take into careful consideration how he feels, and in all homes there are necessary compromises, but there is no need to precompromise. A designer once lectured to some students urging them not to design scared. Don't be afraid. The truth will come out. Let me speak with John.

D: I'm afraid of what he'll say.

A: Don't be afraid. Wait and see.

D: What do we have to do architecturally to join the two rooms, creating one space?

A: First, we have to hire an engineer to see if we can open up the whole elevation or just a portion. Then you have to decide on integrating the floor. You could run the old

If a house has character, the fact is obvious immediately.

CLAIRE JOYES

I've never been in a room that couldn't be improved. Spaces should be contoured to meet your needs. Consider turning your living room into a garden sunroom.

Every room should be used every day. The most successful rooms are the ones where you spend the most time.

sugar pine into the kitchen, but I wouldn't suggest having the terra-cotta run into the dining area. It will be too informal for the furniture.

D: I'd love the idea of the wood floor in the kitchen, but will it be practical?

A: Yes, if we put six or eight coats of polyurethane on it.

D: The walls are fine the way they are. The windows are fine. We're fortunate we don't have to give up any cabinets. There's really very little involved because there's no plumbing on the drywall. I'd be surprised if we can't open up the whole expanse.

A: Without any unforeseen problems, the demolition of the eight-foot wall and the plastering will be relatively inexpensive. The floor will cost something, but has great value in integrating the spaces. So far, because you love to cook and really want to use your dining room regularly, it looks as though this idea should be a priority if John agrees. Let's not worry unnecessarily. Let's look at the rest of the house. Before we leave, envision your new space opening up to the terrace. The French doors in both spaces are the same proportions. All we're doing is taking down a useless wall that was blocking you from living more freely and having a more integrated space and view.

D: Alexandra, I trust you will listen well to John and be able to make this dream come true.

A: I have no doubt. When something is right, it's right for all concerned.

D: Alexandra, one of the reasons John fell in love with this odd house is the dining room.

A: Ah, yes, Diane, but won't John be happier to be able to use the dining room table for meals every day?

D: He'll be so happy.

A: Let's move on. Let's review sleeping and bathing now that you have thought through where you wish to eat. Show me your bedroom.

D: This room needs work.

A: What do you like most about your bedroom?

D: The privacy. The view.

A: How much time do you spend here other than when you are sleeping?

D: We don't spend much time here now because there's no sitting area. I'd like to turn this room into a private sanctuary, a place John and I can retreat to when I'm not working. I need help.

A: What isn't working out for you in this room?

D: John and I have no comfortable place to sit together. The furniture is odds and ends, a hodgepodge. All the space is taken up with chests of drawers storing clothes.

A: Do you like where the bed is located?

D: No.

A: Why?

D: If I had my way, I'd put the bed off center, move it way over to the left, creating space in front of the fireplace for comfortable upholstered chairs and an ottoman. This way, John and I could see the lake from our bed.

A: What's holding you back?

D: I thought I had to have the bed centered opposite the mantel.

A: Who told you that?

D: I read it in a book, I think.

A: But whoever wrote that rule didn't know your specific space. How could you center the bed if it means giving up the view of the swans on your lake? Let's move the bed over now.

D: Now?

A: Right now.

D: Okay.

A: Sit on your side of the bed. Now sit on John's side. How does it feel?

D: Heavenly.

A: Do you read in bed?

D: I love to read in bed. John does, too.

A: Do you ever like to have breakfast in bed? I know where you have your first cup of coffee, but do you and John ever have breakfast in bed on a weekend?

Home is a sacred place where we find contentment and daily blessings as gifts of grace. What are your daily activities at home?

Everything is relevant to everything else.

RENÉ DUBOS

To develop in taste, quality, and personality, one is obliged to respect the past, accept the present, and look with enthusiasm toward the future.

ELEANOR MCMILLEN
BROWN

D: No, not unless one of us is sick, and then we bring in a bed tray. If I had another of those bed trays, however, I'd sure love to have breakfast in bed with John if the children were off spending the night with friends and John and I were alone in the house. Now, John prefers sitting at a table because he hates juggling the tray on his knees.

A: Do you feel the light is adequate?

D: No. We need better reading light.

A: Are your end tables big enough?

D: No. Other than the bed, nothing in this room appeals to me.

A: May I look in your closets? You and John are so neat. I admire your organization. May I look to see what you have stored in the chests of drawers?

D: None of the things in these chests are used regularly. The drawers stick and are too shallow so I put odd things in them—out-of-season things, wrapping paper, and gifts to give in the future.

A: Would you like a small desk in front of a window to write letters, away from the computer screen?

D: I'd love it.

A: Let's look at the adjoining bathroom.

D: I love the bathroom.

A: Who wouldn't? It's great.

D: It's light, cheerful, easy to maintain. Because everything is white it seems a lot larger than it really is. All the surfaces are tiled so it is practical. John likes taking long steamy showers. That's why we decided to tile the ceiling also. I like to take baths and look out at the lake.

A: May I see your linen closet?

D: It is not neat at the moment. Could you help me with a better way to arrange these shelves?

A: I can see they are too deep. If they were cut back into a U-shape, you could see and reach everything more easily.

D: Perfect.

A: Show me some towels you like and also show me some that you're tired of or that are faded, worn out, and dreary.

D: (Laughing) I need new towels. The all-white bathroom is crying out for new towels. What color should I buy?

A: Buy several different colors you like that coordinate well together and mix and match them depending on the season and your mood. How old are these towels?

D: Most of them are twenty years old, purchased when we got married or given to us as shower or wedding gifts.

A: What about the sheets? Show me ones you like the most.

D: I love these blue-and-white striped ones. I also like the blue-and-white patterned ones. I guess I really like blue and white, especially in our bedroom.

A: Are there some sheets you no longer enjoy, ones you rarely use?

D: Yes. All of these in this stack.

A: Would you miss them if they weren't there?

D: Never. I don't find it hard to give things away. What I need to do is to edit the things out I don't really like because ideally I like having everything in the house be current, where I enjoy using one thing as much as another.

A: We all need editors, people who see repetitions, redundancies, where our true style is choked because of all the things that no longer represent who we are now.

D: Sometimes, Bonnie helps me to weed out the clutter and make room for what I really like.

A: I see your color palette has evolved. Tell me about the colors you now enjoy. Also tell me the colors you've outgrown your attraction to—what colors are no longer you?

D: As I said, I love blue. The cooler the better. I'm a water person. Blue makes me think of water and sky. I love the freedom I feel at a beach. I'm grateful we have this lake because I adore seeing the reflection of the blue sky and the clouds in the water.

A: What are some other colors you like?

D: I like greens, yellows, and pinks. I'm not crazy about orange, and

I knew very well what I was undertaking, and very well how to do it, and have done it very well.

SAMUEL JOHNSON

I should love to satisfy all, if I possibly can; but in trying to satisfy all, I may be able to satisfy none.

MOHANDAS K. GANDHI

A man must consider what a rich realm he abdicates when he becomes a conformist.

EMERSON

I know of no more encouraging fact than the unquestionable ability of man to elevate his life by a conscious endeavor.

HENRY DAVID THOREAU

dusty rose makes me crazy; I associate dusty rose with old people who are ill. The color makes me sad.

A: I feel the same way you do about dusty rose—dusty anything. For me the killer color is taupe, although many people disagree with my loathing for taupe. Another color that turns my stomach is olive-drab green. I love intense acid greens and I'm wild about chartreuse (the grandchildren it call chartreusie) but the war zone green worn by soldiers as camouflage is profoundly depressing to my spirit.

D: Are there any colors you don't like in my house?

A: Diane, are there any colors *you* don't like in your house?

D: Yes. The colors of the living room. The whole room feels brown to me.

A: May we go have a look?

D: Let's.

A: Speak to me. Tell me what you envision.

D: First of all, we rarely use this room.

A: Why?

D: Because it isn't us. I inherited some of this formal reproduction furniture when my father died and my mother bought a smaller house. It's my grandparents' furniture and I find it heavy and dark.

A: What does John think?

D: He feels it's heavy and dark, too, but it's furniture and it fills a room that would otherwise have to go unfurnished for a while as furniture is so expensive.

A: Have you ever considered bleaching the mahogany to make it more of a fruitwood tone, lightening it up and making it look less heavy?

D: It never occurred to me that was an option.

A: It could make a huge difference. Something to think about.

D: John and I have talked about the possibility of starting from scratch with this room. The rigidity of the furniture isn't me, and now that we're thinking of opening up the dining room to the kitchen, I know we'll spend more and more time there. Unless we change the whole spirit of the living room, it will never be used. Bonnie and Michael would never go in there to read or listen to music, for example. Yet, look at the views. We have the same French doors leading out to the terrace. We have a large well-proportioned space with a high ceiling. We have a fireplace that draws well. We can see the lake and my precious garden. It's such a waste not to have a cheerful, relaxed, informal room that we could all enjoy every day. I haven't spoken with John about a less formal room, but I feel now is the time.

A: Few people live well in their living rooms. Most living rooms are too stiff and sterile because they aren't used regularly. They're fussier than the rest of the house. If you were to make a major transformation in this space, what would you visualize? What would you want to call this new room?

D: I'd love to create a garden-reading room.

A: You could have bookcases on either side of the fireplace.

D: I'd love that. As you can see, we have books everywhere except in this room. That's another problem. I'm uncomfortable without books around me. The baker's rack in the kitchen is filled with our reading books. The cookbooks are all on the two shelves above the desk area. I have newspapers, magazines, and catalogues in big rectangular baskets that stack. I'd love to create a garden atmosphere with books everywhere.

A: If the room were empty, it would be easier for you to envision an entirely new atmosphere. Try to experience this room as empty, with nothing in it but the mantel. Remove the curtains from the windows and French doors. Take out every stick of furniture. Remove the rug, the lamps, the objects—do this visualization now. Mentally, strip the room bare. Take a few minutes to clear it out in your head and let me know when you have. I will go outside to walk around the terrace and walk in your garden. Come find me when you're ready. We'll sit out on the terrace in the wicker rocking chairs, look at the swans on the lake, and dream up a whole new atmosphere.

D: Okay, I've mentally emptied the room and it feels so right. That

When it becomes necessary to do a thing, the whole heart and soul should go into the measure, or not attempt it.

THOMAS PAINE

A home is not for other people. It is for every day—and for you.

Very often it happens that a discovery is made whilst working upon quite another problem.

THOMAS ALVA EDISON

furniture was bought during the Depression; it depresses me. While I love my grandparents, I can no longer be the custodian of their ugly furniture. They couldn't take it with them when they died, and I shouldn't feel guilty about no longer needing it. Mother can have it back to give to another family member.

A: Is there anything at all you like in the old living room?

D: Not really. I guess I wasn't myself when we put that space together. It makes me feel old, tired, and sad.

A: Nothing? Not even a lamp? A chair?

D: For now I'd like to have a fresh start. I often envy young people starting out with little money. They're still in touch with their feelings. They have so little and think honestly about each purchase. They like knotty pine, for example. I wouldn't select it today. I'd prefer fruitwood here.

A: I agree. I remember working with a young couple who had just married, helping them decorate their first house. Mrs. Brown, my boss and mentor, came to see it when we fixed it up. She was so excited. At age eighty-five, she told me in the car coming back to the office in New York, "Sandie, I want to sell my house and buy something small and decorate it more casually. My life has changed. I no longer entertain formally." I was so impressed that someone in her mid-eighties would be so open to change. But then again, Mrs. Brown was a visionary, way ahead of her time. She and her husband, Archie Brown, lived in a converted amateur theater with a forty-foot-square room in the 1930s, long before open plan architecture.

D: I'm ready for a big change. So is John. We truly love this house and this room doesn't belong to us. It's dreary. I don't know how we got off track but we've turned our back long enough. While our friends have always congregated in the kitchen, I embrace the idea of having an equally relaxed, comfortable space for John and me, for Bonnie and Michael, and for their friends and our friends.

A: How do you envision your garden-reading room? Describe it to me in detail. I'll take notes.

D: Where do I start? Where does one begin in a space?

A: Are there any architectural changes you want to make? We can go back in there in a minute, but I want you to speak from your heart about the actual space. I have an idea but I'd rather hear from you.

D: We're better off not looking at it now because I'm afraid I'll chicken out and not dare to make really radical changes.

A: I agree. There's always the fear of the cognitive imperative—you later feel you might have made a mistake and want to go back to the other choice. Be bold. You know the truth, so don't be frightened. Speak your truth. Dream.

D: I always dreamed I could have a French door leading to the garden. Those two windows could be larger and bring in more light.

A: Exactly. When I was in your garden, I visualized a curving brick path leading to a pair of French doors to literally bring your garden inside. The trees are so beautiful. You can light them at night.

D: I see trellis. Greens, yellows, and white. I see bookcases. The floor is too dark. We stained the floor dark to go with the dark furniture. I see bleached floors. I see natural rattan furniture covered in a flowered chintz with a dark-green background. Even the paintings in the room are dark. Those landscape pictures are well painted and I inherited them from my grandparents, but I've grown to realize I don't like a dark background in a painting. What happens is I stop looking at the trees because the background is so murky. I'll find a place for them but not in the new room. I'd like some botanical prints. I see potted geraniums and pansies and some trees, so that when it's snowing outside I can sit by the fire in my indoor garden and sift through my seed catalogues and plan the next season's garden. I even visualize some garden furniture thrown into the mix. For example, we could have a card table with French garden chairs. What do you think, Alexandra?

Fearlessness is the first requisite of spirituality.

MOHANDAS K. GANDHI

The greater the difficulty, the greater the glory.

CICERO

A: I can see it. You painted such a vivid picture. It sounds warm, soft, cozy, and utterly charming. Isn't it amazing how powerful the atmosphere of a place is and how one mood is so right for one person and so wrong for another? Whenever we are afraid to face our true feelings we die a little inside.

D: Did this ever happen to you, Alexandra, or did you always know what you wanted?

A: Diane, I always knew, ever since I was three, but when I married Peter I made some serious mistakes. He married a lively, enthusiastic person with an ebullient personality. And he loved me just the way I was. I was thirty-two and he was fifty-two. I looked up to him and respected him and didn't have the confidence to be myself. I wanted to please him and felt that I needed to become more mature in order for him to be happy with me.

D: Tell me what mistakes you made.

A: Well, I wore bright pastels on our honeymoon to Paris. I remember wearing a sexy, long, clinging, peach Halston dress and I felt glamorous, simply beautiful. I remember wearing it to dinner one evening and everything was magical as we dined together in a candlelit restaurant, feeling the preciousness of being married to the true love of my life. We went from Paris to Bermuda, where I wore silk slacks at night in hot, chromatically intense colors, and Thai silk tunic tops in wild prints bought on a buying trip in Bangkok, Thailand, when I worked for the Singapore government.

I was in heaven. Soon after we returned from our dreamy honeymoon, we took a train from our apartment in New York to New Haven to attend Peter's thirtieth Yale reunion. Alexandra and Brooke, ages six and four, wore their matching yellow smocked dresses with pale blue French knots and precious white ballet slippers. They looked like angels scampering around in the grass on the Branford College common. I wore a spring-green, ultrasuede shirt dress and pale green stockings. I felt terrific until I looked around. All the women were mature and appropriately dressed. I was perhaps the youngest woman there. I was also just married. I stood out. I was a stranger. And while Peter's class-

People have a right to live their own lives.

KATE MILLET

Hope is the essential ingredient of moving forward.

PETER MEGARGEE BROWN

mates and their wives embraced me, I felt somewhat uncomfortable and out of place.

Whenever we're insecure, we want to hide. I went out and bought matronly clothes—dark, lots of pleats, and too long. The sexy peach dress was put in the back of the closet. I bought an evening dress in a color that made me look like a nun; it had long baggy sleeves and a full skirt completely hiding my figure. I was seriously off my path.

D: What pulled you back in?

A: Fortunately, my two daughters, Alexandra and Brooke, took charge and became my stylists. They laughed at me. They would go into my closet and take everything out, editing all the "mature" things. Peter was delighted. He never wanted to insult me by telling me he didn't like the way I dressed, but he was grateful to the girls for enlightening me and encouraging me to be myself.

D: Did you make any decorating mistakes after you married Peter?

A: Of course. One thing leads to another. I was afraid to make radical changes at first. Fortunately, we bought new upholstered furniture in a cheerful peach twill. The walls were a fresh lemon yellow with white trim and the ceiling was soft blue. We had white shutters at the windows and a pretty dhurrie patterned rug in greens, yellows, and peach tones. The paintings Peter adored. Most of them were by Roger Mühl, who remains our favorite contemporary artist. They are all windows into Provence, sun-drenched scenes of simple natural beauty. Yes, the living room, thank the stars, never got off track. However, the library and kitchen are another story. Big mistakes. But let's go back to *your* house.

D: What's next? Do you want to see Bonnie and Michael's rooms?

A: I'd like to let Bonnie and Michael show me their rooms when they come home. My daughter Brooke told me when she was quite young that her room was not a room, it was her world. I'm always happy when children invite me into their world and tell me their story.

These are no precedents: you are the first you that ever was.

CHRISTOPHER MORLEY

There's a divinity that shapes our ends, Rough-hew them how we will.

SHAKESPEARE

Those things are dearest to us that cost us most.

MONTAIGNE

D: Perfect. Let's look at the children's bathroom, then. They share the hall bath.

A: Does that work for them?

D: I think so, but you might want to ask them.

A: Good.

D: Come see the laundry room. I spend a lot of time in this space. I want to make it even brighter, more attractive. I really enjoy doing the laundry. It gives me a chance to be by myself; I can think of lots of things without interruption.

A: Do you have someone help you with the housework?

D: We have a cleaning service come when I call them. I used to have someone come regularly, but because I work at home, I don't like to have anyone underfoot. Frankly, it's a lot cheaper, too.

A: I understand. I love a clean house, but I worship my privacy. I enjoy cleaning up at odd times, never as a routine. We use a cleaning service also.

D: What color do you suggest for the laundry room, a color that will be cheerful and lively on a rainy gray day?

A: What do you feel like seeing when you walk in here?

D: Yellow.

A: Sunshine, happy. Look at these swatches. It seems to me the yellow should be in this range. Would you like a periwinkle blue ceiling? White trim?

D: Sounds pretty. After it's painted, what can I do to add charm?

A: Do you like quilts?

D: I adore quilts. I have quite a few. I'll show them to you.

A: Would you ever consider hanging one on this wall? You can use Velcro on a strip of wood so it won't damage the quilt.

D: That would be great because it would soften the space. Let me show you the ones we have.

A: They are beautiful. How can you bear to hide them in this wooden chest?

Decorating is the art of arranging beautiful things comfortably.

RUBY ROSS WOOD

All rooms should begin as outgrowths of the owner's personality, then become lovelier, more personal, and more welcoming with each year.

BILLY BALDWIN

D: Let's pick one to go in the garden–reading room and another for the bedroom.

A: Don't worry about hanging a good one in the laundry room. It won't be exposed to direct light so it won't get damaged. Pick one you like because you'll enjoy it every day. I love the blue-and-white one, too. The large geometric pattern will be bold and dramatic.

D: This is so liberating. I love these quilts. I just didn't get around to finding a home for them.

A: Do you have any other treasures hidden away that we can unveil? Walk me through the house and show me all the objects you like and tell me why they are meaningful. I'd love to see your china and glassware and your flatware and table linens, also, if that's all right with you.

D: We do have nice things to set a pretty table. I'll set up lunch in the dining room.

A: Pick your favorite things. Let's make it a visual feast. While you prepare lunch, may I come join you so I can observe your rhythms in the kitchen?

D: Certainly.

A: While we're looking at your china, show me all your favorites. I want to see the patterns and colors that speak to you. Also show me what you rarely use. Tell me why.

D: Habit, I guess. Some of these dessert plates are too fine to put in the dishwasher so I rarely use them. I love them; each one is painted with a different flower. They are so beautifully detailed.

A: Would you ever consider hanging them in the garden room amid the botanical prints?

D: I'd love that. Let's do that. I have twelve. They will look so pretty hung as a collection in the garden-oriented room. I have so many other sets of salad plates and dessert plates. This is a wonderful use for them.

A: That room seems to be decorating itself. Some years ago, I attended a lecture by a couple who were going to India to be missionaries. They told the audience that all one really needs to

No one chair should be too isolated.

ELSIE DE WOLFE

Nothing is in good taste, regardless of its cost, unless it suits your personality and the way you live.

BILLY BALDWIN

be happy is sunlight, flowers, and books. You have that already. Sometimes the simple beauty of what we love is right in front of us and we just have to acknowledge it.

D: John will be home soon. Let's go in the garden and pick a fresh bouquet of flowers. I'm already feeling the joy of being able to walk through the new door from the garden-reading room, rather than having to go out the front door or climb over the terrace wall.

A: Your garden is enchanted. With the new door you can extend it so it hugs the house.

D: I want the whole house to feel as sensuous, light, and colorful as this sweet garden.

A: Does John like to garden?

D: He loves to garden. We spend hours together, gardening and listening to classical music. John loves music. In fact, he calls his study his music room. I'm going to let him show you his room.

A: I hear John driving up the driveway.

J: I've looked forward to meeting you, Alexandra. Thank you for helping us sort out how we want to live in this funny house. We love it but I'm sure Diane showed you around and told you what's working and what's not.

A: Yes, Diane and I have had quite an exciting morning. After lunch I want to see your study that Diane tells me you call a music room, and I want you to tell me privately what ideas you have to improve the flow of your life in this house.

J: We considered selling this house and looked and looked for another one we liked, but we always came back to this house because we realized it is so full of love. Bonnie and Michael were both born in this house. We've lived here for over sixteen years. It's convenient to the hospital, and the public schools are excellent. We've decided we want to invest our energies in fixing this house up. For the foreseeable future, this is our home. Diane, the dining room table looks so pretty. Alexandra, did Diane tell you this is my favorite room? I love this dining room. It's one of the things I fell in love with about the house, but we rarely use it.

I feel that it is infinitely better to use good chintzes than inferior silks and damasks.

ELSIE DE WOLFE

I believe in a mixture of everything, old and new.

BILLY BALDWIN

A: Why?

J: Because it's too inconvenient. It's too much work to bring the food in here from the kitchen. Diane loves to cook but she is busy with her deadlines and it always seems too much of an effort to eat here regularly.

A: After lunch when we have our visit, we'll talk about the dining room. We have some ideas to improve it, to make it more accessible. Now, are you ready to show me your study–music room?

J: Yes, come. This room means a great deal to me, Alexandra. It is truly mine alone. No one comes into this room without an invitation. As you can see, I love to read, from medical to spiritual material. Pick out some music and let's talk.

A: Is there anything that's not working for you in this space?

J: Yes, this armchair is too low. It's uncomfortable because I'm so tall. I wish it were two inches higher. Look at my knees.

A: Most chairs must be too low for you.

J: Most are.

A: Would you please sit at your desk so I can see you there? Are you comfortable?

J: Yes, because the desk is higher than most; it's thirty-one inches high. The chair is higher than average. I feel good here. Most often when I'm in this room, however, I sit in the upholstered chair and read. I'd like a large ottoman so I can put my feet up when I want to have a nap. If we're to select another chair, I'd like the back to be higher. I like to listen to my music, read, and have short naps. My hours at the hospital are long and I'm usually sleep deprived. I really do love this room.

A: What do you think makes it so meaningful to you?

J: That it's mine. I can come home from the hospital after operating all day. I like to dig in the garden. I enjoy sitting on the terrace and watching the swans on the lake. Sometimes, I listen to my music on the terrace and sometimes I like to listen to the wind, to the birds. But after the sun sets I enjoy having some quiet time in my room. It's a form of meditation for me. It bal-

It isn't the money you spend, it's the taste you use that makes a house distinctive, attractive, comfortable.

HELEN KONES

I do not think that the furnishing of a house or room should be approached with the same point of view as the purchase of a dress or a hat.

BILLY BALDWIN

ances me. I need this quiet time. It's very spiritual. I forget about my patients, about the sadness of those who don't live through an operation. I sit here and feel awe. I would grow thin inside if I didn't have this room. I guess it's my chapel.

A: The energy in this small space is amazing. I feel this is a holy place.

J: Yes, it is. It's profoundly important to me. I'd feel homeless without this room, Alexandra.

A: John, I totally understand. I only wish everyone could come to terms with their intimate personal needs at home as you have. Ideally, everyone should have a corner of the house that is theirs alone. It could be in the cellar for one person, or the garage, or even a laundry room. I know a woman who listens to meditation tapes in her laundry room while she irons.

J: Why do you think some people don't claim their own space in a house?

A: Fear of confronting their soul. Fear of being isolated from the activities of the household. Not having the confidence to value themselves. Lack of self-esteem is certainly at the core of this issue. Men are generally better at claiming their space than women. Diane and I have some ideas for her to have a study. We'll tell you about that later. Men have offices, women have their house. In theory, all the rooms should satisfy our soul, but not having a physical place where you can go to retreat, to be alone, to work, to collect your thoughts, would be torture for most spiritually enlightened people.

J: I agree. Having a home within a home is essential.

A: I've seen marriages break up because the wife didn't have a space to contain her interests and therefore couldn't grow intellectually and spiritually. For example, an artist married a man who turned her studio into his media center. Surely, it would be bad karma, if I were an artist, to have to paint in a dark room while my spouse watched the big game on the big screen. Everyone must have one

Something to sit upon—which must have beauty and comfort; something to look upon—which must reflect the personal taste of the owner; and something to put upon—which means tables of comfortable height, conveniently arranged.

BILLY BALDWIN

place in their home where complete privacy is respected. For women it should be more than a bathroom with a door that locks. That's one reason why women love to take baths versus showers, so they can read in the bathtub undisturbed. Women still find it difficult to sit with their feet up on an ottoman and read a book in their living room. A man wouldn't think twice. This is one of the reasons why I like to interview men separately from their wives. People confide truths they sometimes don't tell their spouses. I encourage every woman to have her own desk. This assures her a place to think and work. Without a desk, you are drifting around. I see you don't have a computer in your music room.

The art of measurement is universal, and has to do with all things.

PLATO

J: No. I never will. I use a fountain pen for all my desk work. It soothes me. I love the sound of the pen squeaking along the paper. I write poetry for fun and have my special paper to write on. I'm happy putting pen to paper. I like to write letters. I have a niece in medical school and we correspond regularly. I write my parents once a week.

A: John, I'd like to hear from you about how you feel about the way this house is working for you, Diane, Bonnie, and Michael. I want you to tell me what you like and what you dislike. You won't hurt anyone's feelings. Diane and I had a wonderfully frank discussion this morning. I believe there are some ways that you can greatly improve the quality of your day-to-day life in this house. I want you to tell me your story. I know about the past. Tell me about right now. Tell me about your dreams and aspirations for the future, say the next five years. Diane told me you are prepared to spend some money to renovate if that proves necessary. She told me you are prepared to redecorate, too. But I want to hear from you. Speak to me about your house and your life in it.

Every spirit builds itself a house, and beyond its house a world, and beyond its world a heaven. Know then that world exists for you.

EMERSON

J: First, I want you to know that Diane and I are willing to make loving compromises in order to achieve what will be mutually satisfying. I know there are men who leave these matters to their wives, but we are true partners. I care about the way the house looks and feels. I want to be hands on. I want to be part of the entire process.

A: Good. That's the way it should be. A home is alive with energy, evolving and changing to meet all the changing, evolving needs of the family. I've never understood how anyone could claim they were too busy to work on their own home.

J: The house has gown on us, Alexandra. It's not perfect, but it's open and airy. The kitchen is quite wonderful. Because Diane enjoys cooking, we spend a great deal of time together there as a family. Anything we do from now on I want to do with quality workmanship, to refine the house the best we can.

A: Have you and Diane discussed money? Do you have a time frame and a budget to spend so much over a certain period of time?

J: I'm prepared to spend some money initially, and then I'd like to establish a master plan to improve our home bit by bit, piece by piece. I'd like to begin collecting art, for example.

A: Good. If you buy one painting a year, in twenty years you'll have a substantial art collection.

J: My taste runs a bit on the more formal side than Diane's.

A: Tell me how you want your house to feel. What areas do you not like? What are the barriers keeping you from fully enjoying your rooms? What space do you use the most each day? What are the areas you rarely use? I notice you don't have a television in your bedroom or in your study. Do you watch much television?

J: Sometimes Diane and I like watching the news while she cooks dinner. We're not big television watchers. We're both readers. I read news magazines and glance up at the television, but I prefer print.

A: How often do you use the dining room?

J: We rarely use it, much to my regret. It is so lovely, but it is just too much work and too time consuming. We usually end up at our round kitchen table, seating eight. We use the terrace more than the dining room.

A: Tell me what you think about the way the living room looks and feels? How often do you use it?

J: Rarely. It's a waste of space. The room isn't welcoming. It's not comfortable. I think it looks rigid. I don't like the furniture. I'm receptive to changing the living room and I'm interested to know what you and Diane discussed.

A: I'm going to let her tell you in a little while. Let's talk about the dining room. What do you think it would take to make this room integrated, more accessible, so it is user friendly?

J: I don't know. If you know of a way we can use the dining room more I would be very pleased indeed.

A: Would you be willing to do radical surgery in order to make this space work for you every day?

J: I'm receptive to listening, Alexandra.

A: Diane knows how you feel. She and I spoke about wanting to incorporate this room into the kitchen. Right now, as I told Diane, it is anachronistic. It is a room designed for a family with servants. It's out of tune with the reality of the times. It can sit there like a dream unfulfilled, or you can open up the east wall joining it to the kitchen and use it all the time. All you'd have to do is move the dessert server on the west wall. The white shell sconces can also be relocated. You'll need to extend the wooden floor into the kitchen. This way, when you entertain you can use both tables. Your kitchen is already so attractive and open. You'd gain two more windows plus the French doors that lead on to the terrace. What do you think?

J: I wonder why Diane and I didn't think of this plan ourselves. That wall is the barrier—physically and emotionally. Can we keep our dining room rug?

A: Absolutely.

J: What else would we have to do?

A: Nothing, really. You demolish the drywall, relocate the electricity, and extend the sugar pine flooring to the kitchen.

J: Is the wood floor practical in a kitchen?

Laws of anatomy, physics, and human intentions force chairs to have shapes and materials that make them stable supports.

STEVEN PINKER

Quick decisions are unsafe decisions.

SOPHOCLES

Genius is the ability to put into effect what is in your mind.

F. SCOTT FITZGERALD

A: Diane asked the same question. We'll seal it with six or eight coats of polyurethane, making it washable with soap and water. We have a wooden floor in our cottage and we love it and find it easy to care for. We have a colorful cotton throw rug under the sink.

J: I think this is going to work; I can see it. We're really not losing much. It looks as though we're gaining light and an open space.

A: This won't be expensive. It can be done quickly. I know where I can get some wood for the kitchen floor.

J: My ideal would probably be to have an old-fashioned, traditional dining room. But by making concessions, we can have a working dining room. Let's get Diane out here. I'm excited.

A: Diane, let's now discuss the living room. Tell John what ideas we talked over this morning.

D: I explained to Alexandra that I really don't like the living room furniture. In reality, I confessed I don't like anything in that room. I couldn't see beyond what is there. Now, I'm excited because I can visualize a light, cheerful, welcoming, and happy room I'd long to spend time in. I want to completely redo the living room, turning it into a garden–reading room. Rather than having traditional furniture, I want natural rattan. I want it to feel like a garden. The windows could be made into French doors and we could have a winding path from the garden to the doors, bringing the garden inside.

J: Tell me more.

D: I can give the furniture back to Mother and she can pass it on to someone who would appreciate it. This room can become an inviting place for reading, visiting among ourselves, doing a puzzle, or playing a game. We'll build bookcases on either side of the mantel. I envision trellis and botanical prints, a dark-green floral chintz with pale-green walls. I can really see this room transformed, bathed in a more relaxed, more real light.

J: I'd love it if we could buy our first painting together to go over the mantel. I agree the room doesn't seem to fit our lifestyle. I want a family room, a friend's room. A place where Bonnie and Michael like to be, where friends feel comfortable, where people of all ages like to be together. A traditional living room might be too rigid, too limiting for us.

A: You will truly be creating a living room if you love being in the space.

J: What are your thoughts for the guest room?

D: Alexandra and I think this room could be my office. She suggested turning the twin beds into daybeds with bolster cushions and pillows. Your parents can stay here, but it won't encourage house guests. I'll have a proper room where I can work. There's light and a view. I'd love it if I could claim this space.

J: Do. It's yours.

A: Is there anything in our discussion that makes you feel uncomfortable?

J: I'm excited. I never thought I would feel happy giving up the old dining room. But I see it is actually a blessing. The space will be quite wonderful.

A: How do you feel about the living room transformation?

J: I never visualized it in this informal, indoor-outdoor way. I always assumed we'd have a living room that would be more formal than the rest of the house. This is the way my brain has been programmed.

A: How does your heart feel?

J: Happy to be liberated from a myth that was holding us back. Thinking about the people we usually have in this house, most people will feel more comfortable with a less rigid, less formal space.

A: I'm looking forward to meeting Bonnie and Michael. Here they are. Hello, Bonnie. I'm Alexandra Stoddard. How was art class? What are you working on?

B: I'm doing a watercolor still life. We're having an exhibition the end of the month.

A: That's wonderful. How many paintings of yours will be in the show?

B: Four or five. I'm not sure.

A: Do you love to paint?

B: I just love it.

What is invisible to the eye is felt—the atmosphere, the energy, the spirit.

I hope to be remembered as someone who made the earth a little more beautiful.
JUSTICE WILLIAM O. DOUGLAS

Honor to the house . . . so that there the intellect is awake and reads the laws of the universe, the soul worships truth and love, honor and courtesy flow into all deeds.
EMERSON

A: Do you have any of your paintings in your room?

B: Yes, want to come see?

A: I'd love to. I waited to see your room so you could show it to me.

B: This is my room. I painted this flower picture when I was seven.

A: It's so pretty. Can you actually remember painting it?

B: Yes. I went out in the garden with a small canvas and my acrylics.

A: It's amazing how we can remember, so well, doing something we love to do. When I was your age I painted our garden, too. My mother and I liked to paint together. I can remember, and that was a long time ago. Tell me about your room. I love the blue wall color.

B: Blue is my favorite color.

A: This is a particularly pretty shade. It is so cool it feels as though there is lavender in it. It's so refreshing.

B: My bed cover is reversible. One side has flowers and the other side stripes.

A: That's wonderful to have that variety all in one. Tell me about your desk. Do you do your homework there?

B: Sometimes. I do my homework all over my room, even on the floor. I like to draw at my desk. Here are some of my drawings.

A: Bonnie, you are so good at drawing. Are you going to continue being an artist when you're older?

B: I hope so.

A: You draw in your room. Do you also paint?

B: Yes, I use a set of colored pencils with water. I'll show you some of them if you want to see.

A: Of course I want to see. These are so wonderful. You love color. I can see you are an artist and this is your studio.

B: I wish there weren't carpeting on the floor. I'd really like to be able to be messier and be able to use acrylics and oils, but I'd get paint all over the place. When I work in art class, we wear aprons and they usually get pretty covered with paint.

A: If you didn't have the carpeting, would you still sit on the floor to do your homework?

B: I'd rather have a hard, washable floor so I can paint and not hurt anything.

A: What about putting a large canvas dropcloth down when you work?

B: That's a good idea.

A: If there were no carpeting, what kind of floor would you like?

B: Something washable.

A: There is a wooden floor under this carpeting. I never recommend wall-to-wall carpeting in children's rooms for this very reason. The floor is for building things and whatever creative projects go on in a space, the mess ends up on the floor. We can talk with your parents and see if they'll let you have the wood floor. We could paint it blue and spatter white on top. I've done this in red with yellow and white and it's great looking and washable. If you like the idea we can do it together. It's so easy and fun.

B: That sounds so cool. If I had a hard floor, I would set up an easel. I can't on this carpeting. It's too soft. Anyway, I don't like the color.

A: What else do you want to improve?

B: I'd really like more storage. My closet is stuffed. I need a place for my art supplies.

A: You could have huge square storage drawers under your bed that could roll out on casters. You could store your canvases, sketch books, and portfolios. That can easily be accomplished.

B: Do you think I need a bigger desk?

A: Do you?

B: The computer takes up so much space. I really wish I had a table where I could have more room. I'd like to be able to spread out my paints and brushes.

A: Maybe we can put the computer on a smaller stand and replace the desk with a table. What shape do you see? Where do you want to place the table?

B: In the middle of the room.

A: How often do you use the computer?

B: Maybe one hour a day.

Life is a serious attempt to make something of oneself, and one's surroundings.

ANGUS WILSON

Observe constantly that all things take place by change.

MARCUS AURELIUS

A: Do you feel you have enough book storage space?

B: No. My books are everywhere.

A: You're a big reader, just like your parents.

B: Yes. Michael is, too.

A: Maybe we could have shelves built under the window along the whole wall. This way you'll have plenty of space for your books and on top you'll have a ledge to display some of your favorite things.

B: I'd love that.

A: What do you like most about your room?

B: That I have all my things in it.

A: How long have you had your bunk beds?

B: Not long. Before, we had two beds in the room so I could have a friend spend the night, but the room looked too crowded. The bunk beds were Michael's. I gave my beds to Michael. They're bigger and so is he. His room is much bigger than mine. Have you seen his room?

A: Not yet. I want him to show it to me.

B: I love my bunk beds. I like to climb up to the top. That's where I sleep and read and do homework. It's cozy up here with all these pillows.

A: Let's go see Michael. We didn't talk about lighting, but we can do that later. Hi, Michael.

M: Hi. My mom has been looking forward to having you come. She's ready to make some changes. Dad, too.

A: Change is important. All too often people set up their house and it stays that way for years and years. We're all constantly changing and the house is stuck in the dark ages.

M: I need some help with my room.

A: What a nice large room. You're lucky. When did you and Bonnie switch beds?

M: A few months ago. They were too small for me.

A: How tall are you?

M: Six feet.

A: Do you like having two beds in your room? How often do you have friends over?

M: Once a week.

A: Do you like where the beds are placed?

M: I like having one against one wall and the other one against the opposite wall because it leaves me so much floor space, but they're harder to make.

A: Are they on casters?

M: No.

A: We can put them on casters. I like the way they don't take up space in the middle of the room, too. Do you want to add some bolster cushions and some throw pillows and use them both as sofas during the day?

M: That sounds good.

A: What activities do you do in your room? Where do you study? Where do you read?

M: I study at my desk and I also study and read sitting on my bed.

A: What are some of your hobbies? What sports do you do?

M: I play soccer and baseball. I'm also a swimmer. I like to ski in the winter. I play tennis in the summer and sail.

A: How much time do you spend in your room?

M: Not much. If the weather is good I'm usually outside. I like to shoot baskets in the driveway. If it is raining or snowing and I have some free time I like to go to the basement and make model boats. When a friend comes over we play Ping-Pong and pool. I spend more time there during the daytime than I do in my room.

A: It sounds as though you are extremely active. You have a lot of physical energy.

M: The only time I sit still is when I study or read, work on the computer, or watch television.

A: Where do you watch television?

M: In the basement.

A: How much do you watch?

M: Not much. I watch it when I'm working on my model boats.

A: Other than studying, working on the computer, and reading, are there any other activities you do in your room besides sleep? Do you play a musical instrument? Do you paint or draw? Do you collect anything?

What I must do is all that concerns me, not what people think.

EMERSON

When we lose the right to be different, we lose the right to be free.

CHARLES EVANS HUGHES

M: Not really. I'm not very musical. I sing for fun. I like art but I'm not artistic. Bonnie is. Did she show you her drawings?

A: Yes. She's gifted.

M: I collect photographs of my sports heroes, and as you can see, I have them around in Lucite frames.

A: Tell me about your bulletin board.

M: All this memorabilia is important to me. I put things on this board I want to save—letters, postcards, ticket stubs, photographs, quotations, newspaper articles. Every six months or so I have to weed it out because it gets so cluttered.

A: How long have you had this giant bulletin board?

M: About three years.

A: Where do you put the nostalgic things you take off the board?

M: I need a bunch of boxes.

A: Would a shoe box size be good?

M: Yes.

A: You can buy them at discount stores in bright colors.

M: I need a bunch. I have the old clippings and memorabilia in shopping bags in my closet. I'd rather have the stuff in boxes. It's fun to go back and relive events and certain times in the past.

A: This way you can have memory boxes. Or, would you rather have one old leather suitcase for everything? There are clear plastic folders you can use to subdivide the material so it's roughly chronological.

M: I think I like the suitcase idea. I have an old leather suitcase that was my Dad's and he's given it to me. I can use that.

A: Are you also a photographer?

M: Lots of these pictures were taken by me.

A: You are artistic. Being a photographer requires a disciplined eye.

M: I'm strictly an amateur, but I love it.

A: Amateur means lover. Where do you store your photographs and the negatives?

M: I've been putting them in the drawers of my desk but it's bursting. I need a system for organizing them.

A: Tell me what you like most about your room. What makes it special?

M: My bulletin board. My photographs. My books.

A: Are there things you don't like about your room? Things you want to change?

M: It is too dark. I need more light. I'd like a brighter color on the walls. I hate the brown paneling. It's too dark.

A: You can paint over the brown stain and your room can be any color you wish.

M: I'd love to have a white room. Shiny white.

A: What color ceiling would you like? Would you ever consider a sky blue? When the sun isn't out you can look up at the blue ceiling and feel as though the day is sunny.

M: Sounds neat.

A: What colors do you like? What colors do you least like?

M: I like blue, yellow, and green. I don't like purple and I'm sick of red.

A: What do you think of the beige carpeting?

M: It's okay.

A: Do you like it?

M: I don't like it, but it's okay.

A: What do you think the color will look like with white walls and a blue ceiling?

M: Terrible. It's that textured beige so it won't show the dirt, but I always feel it is dirty. It's really not okay. I don't like it.

A: Once your walls are shiny white they will reflect and bring light into your room, but at night you'll need lots of light in order to read and study. There are swing-arm wall lamps with a three-way switch you could have for each bed. You also need a desk lamp that provides more light. Do you have any other thoughts on ways to make your space work for you better?

M: If we get rid of the carpeting, what should we do to the floor?

A: What would you like to see?

Where the environment is stupid or prejudiced or cruel, it is a sign of merit to be out of harmony with it.

BERTRAND RUSSELL

If a man write a better book, preach a better sermon, or make a better mousetrap than his neighbor, though he build his house in the woods, the world will make a beaten path to his door.

EMERSON

M: I don't know.

A: Do you want the wood floor with a rug?

M: Maybe. Can we decide after we see the room painted white?

A: Yes. Is there anything you can think of that you want to discuss about your room? If not, let's go downstairs and join up with your parents and Bonnie.

Just as a picture is drawn by an artist, surroundings are created by the activities of the mind.

THE BUDDHA

Michael and I went downstairs to see Diane, John, and Bonnie. We all congregated on the terrace and talked about the day. It was lively and productive because we all shared our opinions and made our points of view known. Bonnie and Michael were excited about the plans to transform the living room into a fresh, comfortable place. They thought the idea of knocking down the wall between the dining room and the kitchen made sense. We discussed transforming the guest room into Diane's study and also talked about creating a sitting area in the master bedroom. Diane and John were receptive to taking up the carpeting in Bonnie and Michael's rooms. Initially, John resisted painting the stained paneling in Michael's room, but when I reminded him that it was only cheap plywood, he agreed it wasn't going to diminish the value of the property to paint it. They also agreed to paint the paneling in the basement white to maximize the light from the small windows.

Inspiration cannot be willed, although it can be wooed.

ANTHONY STORR

A personal inventory, such as the one I conducted with this family, in which a detailed list was made of things that are working and things that are not, is invaluable. We have to look at the reality of how we spend our time, how we feel about ourselves, how our spaces are serving our own best interest. The myth of the dining room as the space where this family dined was a fiction or half truth. The truth is that this is a modern-day family where both the husband and wife are busy professionals. Their time at home together as a family is precious. Bonnie is a gifted artist and needs her bedroom to double as her artist's studio. Michael is an athlete who is bright, hard working and applying to top colleges. His room should be lighter, brighter, more cheerful at night and in bad weather. Their living room has been put together with hand-me-downs, however sentimental or valuable. This room has never been a living space for this family.

To help John and Diane eliminate their budgetary concerns while still meeting their dreams, we set up a budget for immediate needs to be met. Reviewing our notes, we prioritized each project. We ended up doing the children's rooms right away. Diane and Bonnie painted the floor and enjoyed their mother-daughter time together. Once the dingy wall-to-wall carpets were removed from the two bedrooms, it became clear that the carpet should be removed from the stairs and the upstairs hall as well.

Michael's floor was too dark. Rather than having an area rug, he selected a blue, green, yellow, and white plaid wall-to-wall carpeting.

We did the renovation in the dining room and installed the French doors in the living room immediately. When we looked at door designs together, John and Diane loved the idea of Palladian windows rising above the French doors to add grace and light to their new living space.

We immediately replaced John's upholstered chair, added an ottoman, and put his old chair in Diane's new office study.

The garden-reading room has a painting over the mantel that John and Diane selected from a gallery in Boston, the first in their collection. The room took about a year to put together, but it was worth the time and thought. Now the family gathers there before dinner every evening. The room is open, light, and airy, more like a sunroom that welcomes you with open arms.

The sitting area in their bedroom enables John and Diane to spend more time alone together, especially when the children have friends over in the garden–reading room.

The big surprise was the dining room becoming the favorite place for breakfast, lunch, and dinner! Several times a week John comes home to have lunch with Diane in this transformed space. Now it fulfils everyone's dream.

I felt satisfied that I had learned the truth about this family—where they are now and where they want to be in the months and years ahead. It's far better to dream of everything you want than never to dream at all because you are afraid it will be too expensive or impossible. Having a plan, setting goals, focusing your energy on your true feelings, identifying your needs and wishes, knowing what you've outgrown or what no longer works for you, is the only way to set yourself free at home.

Diane and John's home reflects a number of contemporary decorating concerns, including budget, private spaces, time, outmoded expectations of rooms, changing needs, and fears. I have found that these issues come up repeatedly in different guises with different clients.

So-called inspiration is no more than an extreme example of a process which constantly goes on in the mind of all of us.

ANTHONY STORR

The Empty Living Room

Years ago, a young couple consulted me about what to do with their living room. They needed to spend their money on urgent necessities—paying the mortgage, buying beds and kitchen essentials, and maintaining the house. They had to close in the yard for their dogs. They needed a new clothes dryer. There was work to do in the bathrooms, as well.

I advised this young couple to buy some deck furniture and bring it indoors when the weather turned cold in the late fall. This way they were able to buy some nice outdoor furniture for their deck—their summer living room—and use it indoors in the winter months until they could afford to begin furnishing the living room of their dreams.

There is no greatness where simplicity, goodness and truth are absent.

LEO TOLSTOY

We can't just plunk furniture around a room and expect to have the space come alive. There has to be some emotional integrity to what is selected. In the case of using inherited furniture we don't like, it can become a trap. We feel guilty not using it, but it is wrong for us. It is also tempting to buy "just-for-now" pieces (cheap furniture that is not well made or well designed), purchased as a stopgap. It was better, in this couple's case, to invest in some good-quality deck furniture and ask it to do double duty for a while, than to compromise on furniture they would probably throw away at a later date.

Formal Versus Informal

As it turned out, it was helpful for this young couple to have their outdoor furniture in their living room for several winters because it made them realize how simply they really wanted to live. The feeling of relaxation, of unpretentious grace, led them to create a living space that was informal, not that different from the feeling of their patio furniture. Their experience of living with casual outdoor furniture informed this couple about what feels most comfortable to them, and helped them not to fall victim to creating a room for show rather than a room that they felt comfortable living in *every* day.

I have many clients who love their formal living rooms and who use them day and night with great satisfaction and enrichment. On a scale of one to ten, one being informal and ten being formal, I consider our New York apartment living room about an eight. It is unpretentiously elegant but in no way conventional. It is truly a living room. Both Peter and I spend several hours in this charming space each day when no one else is in the apartment. Peter has his desk there and I have my favorite piece of furniture in front of the window—a marble-topped, carved, fruitwood Regency table where I sit, meditate, and write. This one object, a table, bought in Grasse, France, in the early sixties, has taught me about psychic energy. Because I love the way this table feels and looks I am drawn to it, wanting to sit at it, caress the cool marble, examine the curves of the carving.

We are all visionaries, and what we see is our soul in things.

HENRI-FRÉDÉRIC AMIEL

The idea is to seek a vision that gives you purpose in life and then to implement that vision.

LEWIS P. JOHNSON

My Favorite Table: The Objects We Love

Far more important than its beauty is the emotional hold this table has over me. It was a real stretch to spend several hundred dollars to purchase this eighteenth-century find. I'd saved up change in a mayonnaise jar for years to be able to go to France. Although at first I walked away from the antique shop without committing myself to buying it, I couldn't get the table out of my mind. It spoke to me profoundly. There was a strong connection I had to pay attention to and eventually did. All these years later, writing books at this table, breaking bread with family and loved ones, sitting at it at the happiest times of my life as well as the saddest moments, my life's reality has brought this table to a living, breathing presence.

We can feel life's richness in the things that are so full of memories and association. They symbolize the most beautiful, most intimate experiences. Estimating conservatively, I've sat at this one table over twenty-five thousand hours, based on an average of two hours a day, seven days a week. Sometimes I am away at the cottage in Connecticut or traveling, but when I'm in New York, this table is put to happy hours of service. I'm sure I've actually logged in fifty thousand hours at this sweet table—so far. One winter I moved it in front of the fireplace, put a lamp on it, along with a dictionary, and spent every evening there the entire winter writing *Living Beautifully Together*.

The table gives off a loving energy. All I have to do is be there. Sometimes I clean the marble before waxing it and feel I am praying. Other times I place on it a flowering plant I've just watered and feel the blessings of nature as I gaze at the blossoms against the beauty of marble and wood. I love to set this table that seats six. How lovely to be able to have the grandchildren over for supper in the springtime when the west light bathes the room in a pink glow.

I remember the first time my mentor, Mrs. Brown, came for dinner, we ate in the living room at this special table. I can recall romantic breakfasts for two, family suppers, and fun small dinners, as well as our traditional annual lobster supper with a couple we adore.

A thing is worth precisely what it can do for you; not what you choose to pay for it.

JOHN RUSKIN

Trust is that prompting within you.

EMERSON

The reason our living room is elegant to my eyes is not that it is filled with expensive antiques or is conventionally elegant, but because it is filled with objects gathered over many decades, appreciated more each year. We have three tables I bought at auction that were owned and loved by Mrs. Brown. They are all of a different scale and design but each is delicate and refined. They give out a sweet nostalgia, as does a round silver frame holding a picture of us taken on her ninety-fifth birthday, seated together on her living room sofa in her apartment.

Mrs. Brown, born in 1890, used her living room. The afternoon we were photographed, she had a crackling fire, champagne, and smoked salmon sandwiches, and the company of her good friend Horst, who would memorialize the event with his photographs. There were laughter and lots of stories, so many happy memories of good times shared.

There is some of the same fitness in a man's building his own house that there is in a bird's building its own nest.

HENRY DAVID THOREAU

A Living Room Should Be Alive

Why is it, do you think, that people have the most trouble coming to terms with themselves in their living room? I believe this room is thought of as an entertaining space, a place where we have cocktail parties, tea parties, and receptions. In other words, it is created for 4 or 5 percent of our home life. This kind of a room is certainly not a living room, because living, breathing people, flowers, and plants are not empowering it with psychic energy every day. A dormant space has no charm, no vitality, no living energy. It sits there.

You can't expect to turn energy on in a space simply by turning on the lights. There have to be emotional attachments, such as those pretty roses in a bowl you want next to you as you read the morning paper. This being said, light does help: If one of the seven locations where you tried reading the newspaper wasn't your living room, try an eighth location, but you might find you'll have to drag in a standing halogen lamp because most living rooms are too dark to read in.

If you can't sit on a comfortable chair with good reading

The last proceeding of reason is to recognize that there is an infinity of things which are beyond it.

BLAISE PASCAL

light in your living room, you have a dysfunctional room. It's old-fashioned to believe the myth that a living room is only for conversations, not for reading. Because Peter and I enjoy reading and writing, our living room has excellent halogen reading lights next to chairs, as well as table lamps and several powerful standing lamps.

There's nothing static or reserved about our living room, because it is set up for how we actually like to live. Peter and I both work a great deal in our living room. Peter does his legal work at his desk. He has old leather suitcases on the floor under an antique table, stacked one on top of the other, to hold his legal documents. He pays bills at his desk. He writes letters, reads, has visits with clients, family, and friends. We have tea and refreshments and we often eat breakfast, lunch, and dinner there. The more daily activities we can do in an easy flow, the more we'll want to use a space.

Ask yourself what you enjoy doing at home. Write in your notebook ten or fifteen things you like to do as well as things you have to do but want the activity to be pleasant. How many of these things can you accomplish in your present living room? If you have a family with young children, it seems logical you'd want them to feel comfortable playing with their toys in this space. There are great-looking wicker baskets with flat lids and handles that could easily be incorporated into the decorating scheme of a room, for toy storage. Our young friends who come to visit us often bring their children with them. I think it would be wrong not to be able to visit in this space, unless you're dealing with an undisciplined two-year-old, and that's another story.

We have two living spaces in our cottage in Stonington—one in the front of the house and one in the middle, separated by a large opening with bookcases on either side. In the center of the two spaces is a generous round French farm table where we can sit and read, do paperwork, write letters, or write our books. The clutter that accumulates with use is inevitable and we weed it out every few days or so, but our rooms are there for us, ready for our instant gratification. I believe this is the way living rooms should be; otherwise we should call them something else, such as still-life rooms.

I collect my tools: sight, smell, touch, taste, hearing, intellect.

NIKOS KAZANTZAKIS

In liberated moments, we know that a new picture of life and duty is always possible.

EMERSON

Having potted plants in the living room draws you toward them because most of us are nurturers, and caring for plants is a way of caring for yourself. On top of a high, painted cabinet in our cottage, next to a front window, I placed a large white geranium in a periwinkle cachepot that our daughter Alexandra gave me as a gift. It is lined in acid green, and you can see the rim as you look up at this graceful plant. I love the fact that the plant is alive, and when I come down the staircase, I can peek at it; often I turn it a few inches so it gets a different light exposure, and I put my finger in the soil to see if it needs water.

On the round table and on a coffee table, we have two terra-cotta pots brimming with dozens of pansies—dark purple, fuchsia, yellow, pale pink, and white. They reach out in all directions toward the light. They delight us. To make watering easy, and to protect the wood table surfaces, I have two large blue dinner plates underneath the pots. To keep them from becoming too leggy, I snip some pansies off and put them in bud vases to cheer up a kitchen or bathroom sink or end table. Purchased for a few dollars at the local grocery store, these pansies bring us hours of pleasure each day.

Have nothing in your houses that you do not know to be useful, or believe to be beautiful.

WILLIAM MORRIS

It's Time for a Change

Just the other day a friend called me from Knoxville. We had a great catch-up and ended up talking about our families. Becky told me her good news. Her daughter has one-year-old twins, and she and Joe have four grandchildren under four years of age. "Alexandra, I have such an urge to turn our living room into a family room so our grandbabies can have a large place to play together. Our dining room is lovely and wonderful, but we need that room to be a little more comfortable, too. We don't use either of these rooms right now and it's such a shame." "Wow, Becky. What are you going to do about it? Are you going to bite the bullet and turn them into everyday rooms for your family?" "I want to. I think we will!"

Antique furniture brings a quality to a room that nothing else does. Some modern furniture, carefully selected, is good and becomes the antique of the future.

BILLY BALDWIN

By stirring up the pot, by looking at the bare truth about our feelings about home, exposing areas as being impractical, dull, pretentious, extravagantly showy, or ostentatious, we can then turn the energy around. No one can do this work for us because it has to be done from within each human heart. Home is the place where we work with our hands to improve our daily life for ourself and our family. We will never arrive at a place where we will stop our journey, our adventure. Every day we can see life not only with fresh eyes but also with a more sensitive heart. There is always stimulating work we can do in our home.

Doing Your Own Work at Home

Our home should be the safe, private place where we can discover and rediscover our passions, what interests we want to pursue, what enthusiasms we've found fascinating. And once we are in the swing of this positive psychic energy, we will embrace working at home. We'll want our rooms to house our growing interests. Home becomes our schoolroom. Directly working for others is one way of serving, but another equally valid way of giving back to society is to create meaningful work on our own, doing things that we love to do that will, over time, develop our gifts into something we can share with others. Whether you write, paint, do computer programming, sew, sing, dance, do carpentry work, or quilt, what you create out of love will affect others positively.

Many people need to go to an office to do their work. However, some of us are fortunate enough to be able to work at the kitchen or dining room table. A big part of communicating with our self is making changes in our spaces that free us to more easily pursue our interests that go beyond our love of family and home. Each of us is an individual with unique talents, gifts that need to be explored for us to feel real fulfillment in our short lives. More of us are working at home, finding it more convenient and cost and time efficient. And it provides a spirit of place where we are in touch with who we are and focused on what work we want to do.

How many different spaces in your house have you set up for your work? Do you have your own room? Whether it is in the attic, the basement, the room over the garage, or a spare room, try to claim a room or a space just for your work. The more seriously you take your work, the more thoughtfully you will set up this area. The space eventually will inspire the work, rather than thwart it. Ideally, this space should be yours alone, one corner of the world you claim for yourself, even if it is only a desk in the corner of a room.

It is far more important to have three rooms that are beautifully done and beautifully run than to have ten or twenty that are dreary and neglected.

BILLY BALDWIN

Taking Stock

I used to love the Latin saying *carpe diem*, or "seize the day." Now, I believe we should think in terms of "carpe momentum," because home is the breathing in and breathing out of loving energy, moment to moment, all the days of our lives. Go from room to room with your notebook. Write everything down you see and feel. You don't have to tell someone else your shortcomings or your unrealized dreams. No one will see your notes unless you choose to share them. The time you spend looking as well as feeling around will not be wasted. Invariably you'll come to a deeper understanding of the possibilities for improving how you are living at home. Identifying how you feel about yourself as you perform certain activities at home is key to any realignment of your spaces.

The responses we make to surroundings and events determine the characteristics that make each one of us a unique, unprecedented, and unrepeatable person.

RENÉ DUBOS

What's Bogging You Down?

If you really loathe ironing, is it worth the money to have shirts done by an outside laundry service or sent to the local dry cleaner?

If you really don't like doing the wash, that's what Laundromats are for, and someone can fold the clothes neatly for you for a little extra. If you really don't like to watch television, you can make it a habit to forgo watching it except on special occasions. If you really want to grow spiritually, you may have to give up another less-valued activity in order to gain time.

Before reading on, identify all the things you don't enjoy doing. There are ways to make table setting more efficient and appealing. There are ways to make cooking more enticing. By having handsome china, crystal, glass, and flatware, as well as table linens you love readily available, setting an attractive table becomes a grace note. If you want to live beautifully but can't be bothered spending time ironing napkins, there are always kitchen dish towels that look and feel great right out of the dryer. But if paper works best for you, it doesn't have to be plain white. You can collect a bunch of different colors and patterns that will add zest to any meal.

> *I try to design rooms around their architecture or to create architecture where none exists.*
>
> ELEANOR MCMILLEN BROWN

What's Best for Your Needs Now?

If you find you really aren't enjoying cooking, there are ways to gather fresh foods that don't require a lot of preparation time. Let others make your homemade chicken soup to free you up to do some gardening or baking. In other words, everything you do at home should be done with a new consciousness. You are going to do certain things anyway; they must be done. How can you change your attitude about doing these daily necessities? You can rearrange how these necessary tasks are accomplished in order to use your energy positively, constructively and concretely.

> *The wall is the background of the room.*
>
> ELSIE DE WOLFE

Maybe this personal inventory will help you to see that it is time to downsize and have a smaller house with less land. Or, maybe you'll see that you need more space for your family and it's time to buy a bigger house, giving up a little gem for a less-than-perfect larger house that you can renovate and love over the years.

Remembering Edith Wharton's advice, "The better the view, the less need for window treatments," perhaps you'll see you don't want living room curtains at all. You'd rather spend your money planting the terrace and putting lights outside in the trees to bring the illuminated garden atmosphere inside, making it an integral part of the indoors. Or maybe you'll feel a need for indoor window boxes in your apartment so you feel grounded in the good earth, not sacrificing having a garden just because you live on the tenth floor of an apartment house. Perhaps you'll look around your house and come to terms with the fact that it is dull and a little on the sad side of life. You'll be able to burst the spaces into the light, selecting cheerful uplifting colors you now adore. How many years has it been since you refurbished your paint colors and fabrics? If you live in a city, colors lose their life every five or six years. Whenever you re-cover a sofa or chair, tuck a snippet of the fabric inside a pillow or under the seat cushion. Later, comparing the fabrics, you'll be surprised how the re-covered chair's colors have faded and become grungy.

Once you face the truth about your needs, you might have to make some changes in your daily habits to bring more balance and harmony into your home. You might want to sit at the table more regularly with your family. You may learn that you don't spend enough time openly listening to your spouse or children.

Money Is a Tool

One of the most unnecessary conflicts in a household is any misunderstanding about money. Money is not the problem; our attitude about it is. There has to be a meeting of the minds about how you spend your money. "Whatever it takes" isn't concrete enough. You have to communicate what you value and where you should make your emotional as well as monetary investments. Are you putting your money into things that improve the quality of everyday living for

Small rooms are the most intimate. But to get a room that sizzles with personality, you've got to take risks.

BILLY BALDWIN

There never has been a house so bad that it couldn't be made over into something worthwhile.

ELSIE DE WOLFE

you and your family? Would it be better to entertain business associates at a restaurant, a rented space, or a club if you find that special events at home are a sacrifice for your family? Spending money on beautiful objects and art is not a waste of resources; these are, I think, the things that inspire us to love life more abundantly.

Rather than redo the kitchen, it may be enough to move the children's swings nearer to the kitchen window so that you can see them at play as you rinse the lunch or dinner dishes. Instead of costly renovation of a basement laundry, you might decide to have an electrical outlet put in the backyard so that you can iron out of doors, hanging up your linens on an old-fashioned clothesline as you watch the children. You can also play favorite music or listen to sermons or inspirational tapes while you spray-starch your tablecloths and napkins. An electrical outlet outside could be used for a radio, a fan, or an iron; it allows you the freedom to do what the spirit moves you to do, regardless of whether you are alone in a happy trance gardening to Bach or seated under an umbrella enjoying a cool breeze from a fan when there may be no cool air circulating on a hot August afternoon.

If adding a sitting room to your bedroom is too costly for now, you might discover you want a hammock under the shade of the maple tree in your backyard, where you can garden and then have a nap with your spouse on Saturday afternoon. Or, you might want a romantic white paddle fan over your bed to make summer nights cool without the hum of the air conditioner, so that you can read or dream together in comfort. No one else feels exactly the same way you do.

As your awareness of your self unfolds, let your home be enriched by your thoughts and actions. By being more aware of your life's patterns, you can be receptive, more flexible, learning and growing to become a healthier, happier, more spiritually enlightened person. If home is the center of our being, then it is important that in this personal oasis of our earthly life we enjoy happiness every day. Let's examine being happy at home.

CHAPTER 3

Fifteen Essential Elements of Emotional Comfort at Home

Go confidently in the direction of your dreams!
—HENRY DAVID THOREAU

How welcoming is your home? Does it incorporate all the elements that you identify with? Does it accommodate your specific needs? If you want a hot bath by candlelight, what are the little ways you can make this a more meaningful ritual? We should think about putting ourselves in as comfortable a situation as possible as often as we can.

Our home can be a sacred place. We will be happy at home when we are true to ourselves. Home is fertile ground for us to grow into our essence. What are the essential elements you need for your well-being? Beyond the basic needs of food, clothing, shelter, and the need to love and be loved, we should identify the basics that make a house our spiritual center, our true home. When we are able to identify and incorporate these components into our physical surroundings, we will be in closer touch with who we are and what

Light is light; it does not ask for more light.

J. KRISHNAMURTI

our needs are for our well-being. By identifying these essential elements we will be defining our ideal home. What is the best way for you to live under your current circumstances? How can you better enjoy being at home?

In this chapter I'm going to list the essential things I value that make me feel happy at home and that bring me emotional comfort. You may want to make some notes in your notebook the way I have, in order to fine-tune your own. This way, you can work to improve the areas you've defined as important to your sense of wholeness, comfort, and happiness.

Positive Energy

Every house or apartment has an energy, a personality, and integrity. Houses have character, not just in the interior and exterior architecture, but in the ways we use and enjoy them day to day. Houses are alive; they breathe the life and health of their inhabitants.

What is the personality of your house? How does your house make you feel? Does your house have a name? You don't have to have a plaque out front to give your house a name. Even if you don't tell anyone, write down a name in your notebook. Let it be the logo for your home.

Even houses with problems can have positive energy. As I've often said, once you own a house, there's always something that needs to be repaired and you'll never be bored. This is especially true if you own an antique house as Peter and I do. All our labors are surely out of love. Yet our house should never be a work trap, and the problems we encounter, some catastrophic, others heartbreaking, are, properly viewed, part of the blessings we derive from having a house we feel is our true home.

A House Can Be Fixed

Early one morning as I approached the kitchen in our cottage, I thought I heard a fountain, only to discover a flood. Our kitchen, freshly renovated following the repair of a burst pipe, had another disaster caused by a northeastern storm. Buckets weren't sufficient to contain the water.

I felt a pain in my chest, aching about our sweet old house's recurring problems. After calling the contractor, we had to leave our cottage that morning to take a train to New York because Peter had jury duty. I was probably spared, having to walk away that morning. I really wouldn't have wanted to see the operation. After the storm subsided, the entire newly installed ceiling was chopped out and replaced. By the time I returned, things were nearly back to normal. Do these situations make me love the house less? Absolutely not. We've learned from leaks and floods to keep the energy in our dear cottage positive. Getting upset over problems you have no control over is normal. But we must try to face whatever realities occur and move forward. We are not the only ones who have house problems. Everyone has painful experiences. We are not alone.

We should use our precious energy quickly to attack the problems at hand. The better the energy in the house, the more happiness you'll feel day to day. The little petty inconveniences such as the clogged toilet, the brown front lawn, the diseased trees, the mildew, can all be fixed. In many cases, we'll have to work extra hard in order to be able to pay for the repairs if we are unable to do them ourselves. We may feel that certain situations are the last straw, but they never are. There will be another surprise around the corner. This is life.

I can see more and more clearly that I will have to work very hard to render what I am looking for: the instantaneous impression, particularly the envelope of things, the same all-pervading light.

CLAUDE MONET

The light of any lamp dispels in a moment the darkness of long eons; the strong light of the mind in but a flash will burn the veil of ignorance.

THE BUDDHA

A Pigeon on Your Desk?

One sunny day, Peter told me there was a pigeon on his desk in the living room in our apartment. I avoid pigeons; they carry germs. I felt disgusted. Peter told me the windows were closed tightly and it hadn't flown down the chimney, as there were no telltale ashes. We opened the windows wide and shooed the pigeon out, but it was messy. I cleaned up, including washing the windows, and we went for a walk around the reservoir, enjoying the cherry blossoms in full bloom.

Rather than dwelling on something unpleasant, it is often wise to leave home, enjoy the sun while it's out, and not think about the problem. But the story wasn't over. Weeks later, Alexandra came up from Washington with her husband, Peter Scott, and they stayed in her room. That's when we learned that the pigeon apparently had entered through her bathroom window, which someone had left open, and, because we had been away for several days, had camped out in her bedroom, on her window ledge. It also sat on a lovely antique quilt at the foot of the bed, making a mess. We washed the quilt three times, sprayed it with lemon cologne and put it back on the bed. We scrubbed the window ledges with Soft Scrub and bleach, poured some boiling hot water and ammonia on the window outer ledge, scrubbed it clean, closed the window, and lit a scented candle to remind ourselves that the pigeon was, we hoped, gone forever.

Identifying Unfortunate Situations

Jot down on a sheet of paper some of the most horrendous things that have happened to you in your home that were not in your control. Look at this list of unfortunate situations. They no longer have any power over you because they're in the past. Rip up the paper and throw it away. I'm more mindful now not only to check the windows I can see, but to check all the windows in the apartment. Not a bad idea for safety and dirt, to say nothing of our health. I'm sure you have more dramatic stories, but in all instances, we must move on, continuing to love ourselves and our home. Whatever happens, be grateful because it could be worse. Most of our time at home can be stress free if we don't fight the problems. Most of our times can and should be happy.

The further I am from everything man-made, the more in touch I am with the light.

The Atmosphere We Create

Feeling light within, I walk.

NAVAJO NIGHT CHANT

The optimistic thoughts in our minds and the love in our hearts will give off an ambience that becomes the mood of the house. If you are in a bad mood, it will depress the atmosphere. While no one can maintain a happy, positive attitude all the time, our home should be treated with respect and reverence that honor the dignity of its hallowed four walls. Far better to go for a walk in the beauty of nature than to become discouraged or overwhelmed about the maintenance of the house.

We should try to let go of control. There are and will always be situations beyond our human powers. Not only will we encounter challenging circumstances with our house, but we will also have disappointments with the relationships we have with family, friends, and colleagues at work. Let these moments unfold and keep your energy constructive in order to have the strength and the determination to turn things around. Don't let any happening drag you down and rob you of your capacity to be happy at home.

Visualize a lit candle inside your soul.

JOAN BRADY

Think of your home as a place of healing. Light a candle. Play some favorite Mozart or Beethoven. Bake a Shaker lemon pie, clean out a messy kitchen drawer, sit in a favorite chair and read to a child, or have a nap, but don't blow any situation out of balance because becoming unglued creates—magnifies—the problem, not the resolution. The most important thing is to take personal responsibility for our own feelings. We have the power to redirect, to rechannel our energy by the thoughts in our minds, no matter what setbacks or disappointments we may face.

Instant Gratification

I find it useful when I'm not at my best to do something constructive around the house in order to focus my mind on a project that will result in something uplifting. Whether I iron a blouse or paint something a fresh color, even if it is only an old wicker wastebasket I transform into a yellow-and-white check design, I have instant gratification. I can wear the freshly ironed blouse, and the wastebasket under my pine desk in the bedroom pleases my eye. Whenever our mind is concentrated and we are in the swing of an activity with its own rhythms, we tend to forget about our aches and pains as well as our troubles. Whatever it takes to let go of the angst is worth the time and inner resolve, no matter how painful. The reward is our return to having positive vital energy.

Vital Energy

If you keep your energy positive, you are encouraging others to do the same. No matter how others act, you are in charge of your reactions. Rise to the highest place in your consciousness and take a deep breath. For five minutes, pay attention to your own breathing and nothing else. We should try to listen with an open heart and not judge.

No one wants to be around someone who drags them down or in a house that has negative energy. Pay close attention to how people and places make you feel and trust your instincts.

We will be affected, for better or worse, by the energy of our home and we should try, the best we can, to keep it healthy, life affirming, and loving. We animate our inanimate space with our vital energy. No normal, healthy person stays stuck for long.

The Chinese word for vital energy is ch'i. Accentuate the ch'i of your home as well as your own. You will see that by raising one, you raise both, because the energy reverberates like a hummingbird. When your home has an abundance of vitality and good vibrations, not only will you feel happier at home, but everyone who you welcome inside your front door will feel this uplifting atmosphere. As you work to improve your own ch'i, look around your rooms. Whenever something doesn't feel right, be guided by common sense and change it to make a more harmonious space. Lighten a dark corner with a mirror. Soften a hard angle with a plant. Cheer up a sad disinherited nook by creating a desk area that will be both practical and attractive. Often the smallest change can make a huge difference. A painting might be too small on one wall, but when you relocate it to a smaller wall space, it looks perfect. A chair seat might be too low, but when you add a cushion it perks it right up and sits you where you want to be, higher up, closer to the table, while also adding comfort to your fanny and color to cheer your spirits.

The Shakers believe light to be heavenly, illuminating their interiors, allowing us on earth a touch of Divine goodness. I always feel happiest in light, bright rooms. How important is light to your sense of well-being?

Shiny surfaces reflect light— wood, leather, lacquer, silver, brass, and porcelain.

Light

Why have modern scientists, until relatively recently, largely ignored the connection between our environment and our behavior, even though we have observed the link between optimum health and our surroundings for thousands of years? We evolved as Homo sapiens in the sun. Our physiology and behavior can be looked at from the viewpoint of light. As far back as the second century A.D., doctors prescribed putting people in the warm rays of the sun. Why have we over-

He whose face gives no light shall never become a star.

WILLIAM BLAKE

looked the most obvious reality: that the sun elevates our psychic energy? While we don't know precisely how light affects our brain or our behavior, we know that light is our energy source and should be understood as a major priority at home.

Light Deprivation

Since the Industrial Revolution in the nineteenth century, when Westerners turned from the rhythms of nature, we haven't focused on the fact that being inside with the lights on gives us less light than being outside in the rain. One third of us suffer from mood and sleep problems. While there has always been a segment of society who suffered from melancholia and lethargy (and while recognizing that light deprivation is not the sole factor that causes depression), we now know for certain the importance of having more light, especially during the winter months. If you are an active outdoors person, you will benefit from twice as much light as you would have if you were stuck in an office or housebound. An office worker experiences only an average of half an hour or less of sunlight each day. Understanding how sensitive you are to light deprivation is a significant step toward living in a more ideal atmosphere at home each day—fall, winter, spring, and summer.

On a scale of one to ten, with ten being extremely sensitive to lack of light, rate your need for light. I am a ten. Light is my vital energy. It fills me with optimism as I enjoy the rhythms of my day. I follow the light from one end of the house to the other. When we are in tune with our biological rhythms, in the flow of vitality in sunlight and conserving our energy in the darkness, we are attuned to our internal twenty-four-hour clock known as our circadian rhythms. Seasonal Affective Disorder, or SAD, is a form of depression, caused by light deprivation. It can be avoided, even in climates where sunshine is rare.

Here is an experiment that will allow you to pause and think about how light affects your mood and attitude. Toward the end of June as the summer solstice approaches, try to experience the sunrises and the sunsets for two or three days straight if you are fortunate to have clear weather. Wake to the sunrise even if you have to set an alarm, and, after the sun sets, go to sleep. If you can do this while camping, this is ideal, but you can try it at home. This will make you more conscious of the effects of light on your well-being.

I feel humbled every day to be able to spend so much quality time in our cottage in Connecticut. Our village is situated on a peninsula with the sun's reflection on the water bouncing dappling light into our house, winter and summer. Even though we are cheek-to-jowl with other houses and have only one seventh of an acre, we think of our dear cottage as the house of light.

We have tried our best to maximize the available natural light as well as to supplement it as much as we can. We have an abundance of light sources in our cottage living room so that we can read while sitting in a chair, flopped on a sofa, or seated at a table. The six windows have sheer white café curtains that don't cover up any glass. We have pictures lit from the ceiling as well as decorative lamps on all the tables, including the round table in the center of the room. Where there are no tables for lamps, we've used standing halogen lamps. We even added strips of light under a hanging shelf that displays porcelain fruit and vegetables and decorative plates. We've placed the upholstered furniture where it gets as much natural light as possible. The swivel chairs help us to adjust ourselves to receive more light while reading. If the success of a room is judged by how often you are drawn to spend time in it, having a wide range of lighting options is a great start toward success. We should all be able to read the morning paper in a comfortable spot in every room in our house, without eyestrain. As you tried different locations for reading the newspaper (Chapter 1), I'm sure it became clear to you that some locations were great when there was natural light,

As we let our own light shine, we unconsciously give other people permission to do the same.

NELSON MANDELA

My candle burns at both ends; . . . But, ah, my foes, and oh, my friends—
It gives a lovely light.

EDNA ST. VINCENT MILLAY

Among the several kinds of
beauty, the eye takes most
delight in colors.

JOSEPH ADDISON

but in bad weather they weren't useful for reading because of inadequate artificial lighting. Having a dark color on the walls of a study can give a cozy feeling, because you're concentrating on reading and writing. With strong focused lighting, this atmosphere allows us to pay attention to the work at hand without distractions. But if all the rooms in a house are dark, the atmosphere is depressing.

In the forty years I've seriously studied the links among light, behavior, and emotions, I've concluded that a great deal of unnecessary sadness is caused by a lack of essential light. We can and should do something about light awareness in our lives at home now. Because we have no control over the weather, we should have ample light in the rooms where we spend so much time, especially when it's dark and nasty outdoors. Last spring there were bad storms in Connecticut and it rained hard for six days. Our cottage became our world. Not only did we light a fire to make us feel more cozy, but we also lit candles and turned on all our lights, including strong halogen standing lamps. With white walls and white curtains, our cottage is bright and cheerful when the sun is out, but during this stormy period the rooms were dark and we needed to lift our mood with lots of strong artificial lighting.

Your Moods and Your Rooms

We need songbirds and
church bells and the smell
and sights of spring green to
keep us human.

RENÉ DUBOS

Our walls are barriers blocking the sun. We have too few windows and doors that open rooms to the natural light. When you are inside on a sunny day, you are experiencing only 10 percent of the light you would have if you were out of doors under an umbrella or the shade of a tree. Few of us have enough windows and doors to bring in adequate light. The best ways to brighten a dark room are:

- paint the room brilliant white with high-gloss white trim
- always have clean windows

- place a mirror opposite a window or on a wall adjacent to the window
- install halogen ceiling track lighting
- use floor can lights
- use standing halogen lamps
- keep all wood tones light
- use picture lights for paintings
- install strong light strips under counters, bookshelves, and cabinet shelves
- light candles
- polish wood, brass, silver and marble objects
- don't forget your touch of yellow!

Add up how many light sources you have in each room. Experiment with different light effects.

Light the lights.

Write in your notebook your moods at different times of the year. Do you experience shifts in your energy in the fall, summer, and spring months? What time do you tend to want to wake up on a sunny day compared to a rainy one? How much sleep do you need in the summer compared to the winter? When you take a nap, what time of day is it, and what is the weather usually like? Do you tend to eat nervously because you feel low? When you eat out of doors, do you tend to eat healthier food than when you're in an airless room with no windows? Do you tend to gain weight in the winter months? How much, on average? Most people gain approximately five pounds in the winter, but people who suffer from SAD or light depression tend to gain twice as much weight. Are you a morning person? Does it depend on the light? Do you sleep with black-out curtains or do you awaken to the sunrise?

Do you live in a house, a townhouse, or an apartment? What floor is your bedroom on? Does your bedroom face north, south, east, or west? If your bedroom faces east, you will probably get up earlier and need less sleep than if your bedroom faces west. Do trees block the light? Because architects and designers are becoming increasingly aware of the importance of light to our sense of well-being, they are

Keep your face always toward the sunshine, and the shadows will fall behind you.

ANONYMOUS

arranging rooms with windows, skylights, and glass doors that bring in and borrow more natural light.

How much natural light do you have in your bedroom? What colors surround you when you awaken in the morning? Do you live where you can watch the sunrise and the sunset? My Zen writing room faces east, and I love going there early in the morning to watch the sunrise. I feel I am enclosed in a luminous envelope. Our living rooms in our New York apartment and our Connecticut cottage both face west, where we can ritually watch the painted sky work its magic. One of the sad losses of foul weather, aside from the loss of light, is being deprived of the beauty of sunrises and sunsets. When you take vacations, what climate do you seek? What time of year do you tend to want to get away? I'm from New England where we often have dark, dreary winters. Because of light deprivation, Peter and I tend to get a winter cold or even flu, but for the most part, we can avoid being sick in the summer months.

> *The real point is to know how to use colors. I use lead white, cadmium yellow, vermilion, dark madder, cobalt blue, emerald green, and that is all.*
>
> CLAUDE MONET

Light the Lights

Think of light therapy as a counter to bad weather, to the darkness of winter, and to our own built-in temperament, as well as to the stress of everyday disappointments and frustrations. Keep the curtains open at night. Once the lights are out there isn't a privacy issue. The bathroom can have a night light on and the door can be left ajar. I'm enormously grateful for the advances in technology that so recently brought us the white light of a halogen bulb, and I mix it with incandescent light. I rip fluorescent lighting out of clients' houses because I personally feel this illumination is extremely disturbing; it is not a continuous light but an intense flickering that can cause jittery nerves. While studies have not proven the harmful effects of fluorescent lighting, I do not recommend it to my clients, no matter how energy saving.

> *The purest and most thoughtful minds are those which love color the most.*
>
> JOHN RUSKIN

The More the Better

We still don't know for certain what kind of artificial light is best at home. All we know is, the more light, the better. If you are near the source of light, you will benefit far more than if you are at a distance. If you are at the light source, you have 100 percent intensity from the illumination. If you walk away several paces, you will have much less intensity. If you go twice that distance, you won't experience 50 percent intensity, but as little as 10 percent. This suggests that it is wise to have many different light sources in a space in order to benefit from the energy. While a chandelier over a dining room table is elegant and romantic, by adding two pairs of candlesticks, a pair on each side of a centerpiece, the flames will be nearer to the persons seated, providing more vital energy, ch'i. You can place a small votive candle in front of each place setting as an alternative to candlesticks. Experiment with different kinds of decorative candles. Your centerpiece could be several colorful candles creating a light composition.

Experiment with several light sources in preference to one. If you have a long hall table, try placing a pair of lamps on either end rather than one lamp in the center. If you have a dark corner in a room, consider placing a can light on the floor to wash light up. Take a careful look at your art. Artists either paint out of doors in natural light or have bright lights in their studio. Their paintings are meant to be illuminated so that the viewer will appreciate their natural ambience, detail, and subtlety. Try to have as wide a range of light sources at home as possible in order to emulate the illumination and intensity of the vital energy of a summer day.

Found most beautiful green stone. Come immediately. Zorba.

(A telegram sent to Nikos Kazantzakis one thousand miles away)

Color is wavelengths of energy.

Yellow is capable of charming God.

VINCENT VAN GOGH

An Epiphany of Light

When I am in a space that is pure, clean, fresh, and brilliantly lit, I draw in a deep breath in a state of exaltation. When this phenomenon happens in a man-made environment, the place is touched with a spiritual energy that is both rare and awesome. Most often I have these feelings of epiphany in dappling sunshine out of doors, usually at a beach or in a garden setting. Last summer I was lunching in a garden in Southern California with an enormous flaming fuchsia bougainvillea as a natural umbrella overhead. I was agog. Looking up at an intense, cloudless, heavenly blue sky as the backdrop for the riot of shocking pink blossoms lifted me up higher and higher as I kept taking in air, until I realized I was literally breathless. I'd had a moment of transformation, where the beauty and the intensely piercing clear light from a strong sun opened me up wide. A cool breeze touched my body, gently dropping several of these brilliant pink blossoms on the dazzling white tablecloth. These are times when we experience heaven on earth. This moment in this particular garden was one of them for me, and was all about light.

One evening recently I was placing some votive candles in small, clear-glass bowls on a freshly waxed favorite French Provincial table. I put some on top of leatherbound books and two on an old brass scale, and lit them. The mirrored wall behind doubled the light and created a dazzling romantic mood with everything reflecting, twinkling, and shining. I felt as though I had transformed the darkness of night.

Blue color is everlasting, appointed by the Deity to be a source of delight.

JOHN RUSKIN

The sun and stars are mine; if those I prize.

THOMAS TRAHERNE

Solar Energy

The best energy is solar. Use the sun to heat and illuminate your house. Larger windows, glass panes in doors, French doors, bay windows, and skylights all bring more light inside the square boxes where we live. If you bevel the edge of a pane of glass, you intensify the light, giving a reflective sparkle. The cleaner the glass, the more light it gives off, as well as seamlessly connecting you to the atmosphere out of doors.

There is emotional significance to all colors. What are your five favorite colors?

Light Evaluation

Look around your house or apartment after you've been outside on a sunny day. Before turning on any lights, what do you see? How do your rooms feel? Walk slowly from space to space. How dark are your rooms? You can have two similar-size spaces, but because of the location of the windows, one room could appear substantially darker than the other. Maybe you'll be pleasantly surprised that your spaces are flooded with light, and you don't need to put on too many lamps to make them feel cheerful and light.

Now walk back through your house, one room at a time, and light all the lights, one by one, if they are not on a single switch. Jot down in your notebook how many light sources you have in each room and how much illumination each lamp or fixture produces. Are your lamps on three-way switches, for example?

After you've completed this exercise in all the rooms, ask how many lightbulbs you found that were burned out. Do you have new ones to replace them? What is the extent of your lightbulb storage? We should all have a reserve of three or four bulbs for each wattage and socket type. As we know, often bulbs burn out in tandem. How do you rate your light, both natural and artificial, room by room? Do you have any fluorescent lighting in your house? How does it make you feel? Perhaps you have some underneath the upper cabinets in your kitchen. If you do, and you want incandescent lighting there, you can easily change the lighting to a strip fixture with small bulbs, which are easy to change and install, and which give ambient light.

Look for the stars, you'll say there are none;

    Look up a second time, and, one by one, you mark them twinkling out with silvery light,

    And wonder how they could elude the sight!

WILLIAM WORDSWORTH

The next stormy, dark, dreary day, come in from the rain and repeat this same exercise. Note the difference in the way your rooms look and feel. But even on a sunny day, you will probably feel most of your rooms are dark. We turned on six lamps in our living room on a sunny day in order to feel the sunshine indoors.

Light Boxes

The heart is like a window.

STEPHEN MITCHELL

Taking an honest look at the light in your rooms helps you to understand more about your emotional needs. Evaluate what rooms you're drawn to most. Are they the lightest, brightest rooms in the house, or the darkest? What do you tend to do in those rooms? In my shiny wine-red room in the apartment, I prepare slide lectures on a series of large light boxes. Hours of uninterrupted time go by in the glow of lots of light and the pleasure of looking at pretty pictures of gardens, trees, sky, water, houses, room interiors, and favorite artists' work throughout history. Turning off the light boxes at the end of a three- or four-hour session is like plunging myself into the dark, even though there are four 150-watt ceiling cans and a student lamp on the counter. Obviously, I am in a space with the light equivalent of being out of doors in the open air with the sun shining. And I can be exposed to this heavenly light on the darkest days in February or at night when it is pitch dark outside.

You must not blame me if I talk to the clouds.

HENRY DAVID THOREAU

Light is a spa for the soul. A photographer friend discovered his low spirits were caused by long hours spent in his darkroom. Light boxes are a known cure for SAD. Perhaps you could buy a light box at a camera supply store or an art store.

When Light Hurts the Eyes

In the disorder called photophobia, patients suffer from ocular problems that make bright light painful to their eyes because of the glare. If you have any kind of sensitivity to light and you want to turn off the lights, see a lighting designer immediately, because you can have good illumination without the glare. Experiment to find the light intensity that lifts your spirits the highest. Always make the conscious connection between your mood and the available illumination. Do you sit near a window on a sunny day, facing out of doors, or do you go outside to read? Do you ever find yourself pausing near a plant light because it soothes you? Do you live in a sunken area of land, going lower as you approach your house, or do you live on a high point of land? The location of your house will affect the quality of light you will have, regardless of the regional climate patterns.

Mirrors

Mirrors create magical effects in small spaces, visually doubling the size and illumination of a room. If you feel more comfortable in light, bright, airy spaces, consider using mirrors architecturally in large panels on your walls. Mirrors attract light and reflect energy. Whether you display decorative mirrors in attractive frames or install mirrors in walls to fool your eye into believing a space is larger and brighter, they can cast a happy spell on a room and on your mood. Mirrors draw you to them because they help bring a room alive. Whatever moves in front of them is reflected in the glass. They always seem to twinkle, to smile back.

In our tiny enclosed backyard we installed a mirror on a wall before having white trellis installed in front. The idea was to have the reflection from the harbor bounce into our little space behind our house that only has a sliver of view of the boats in the water. Not only did the mirror bring sparkle to our outdoor private space, but the ivy was drawn to climb up the trellis and now, after eleven years, it almost completely conceals the mirror. Yet, like facets of a diamond or a piece of mica, the tiny glimpses of

On a clear day you can see forever.

ALAN JAY LERNER

It costs me nothing for curtains, for I have no gazers to shut out but the sun and moon and I am willing that they should look in.

HENRY DAVID THOREAU

*Privacy is central to our
happiness and harmony at
home. If you don't have privacy at home, where will
you look for it?*

*Allow yourself uninter-
rupted time when you can
process your experiences.*

mirror behind the ivy look like twinkling stars in the sky. The effect is quite magical, as though we are looking through pinpricks into eternity.

Shine

One of the great ways to bring more light into your home is to pay attention to what shines. Whenever a surface shines, it reflects something else. A pair of shined shoes reflects light the way patent leather does. A glass-topped table reflects the objects on it the same way a lacquer table does. Shiny smooth walls act as a mirror. You can see impressionistic images in them. If a wineglass is cut crystal, the reflective effect is intensified. We have a habit of always leaving one picture light on in our apartment to welcome us or a family member returning home. Because of the shiny pale-pink walls, as well as two large panels of mirrors on either side of the mantel, one 60-watt tubular-bulb picture light casts a pink glow on the whole room, giving us the feeling of security and comfort, saluting us on our arrival home.

Candles and Fires

*Light, air and comfort—
these three things I must
always have in a room.*

ELSIE DE WOLFE

Bring more vital, psychic energy to your rooms; light candles in the daytime as well as at night. Make a ritual of lighting a candle to illuminate a tabletop or place one in the front hall to welcome a spouse's return from his commute from the office. If you have a working wood-burning fireplace, use it. So many of my clients can't be bothered or feel it's too messy, and the focal point of their living room becomes a black hole. A roaring, crackling fire pours energy into the space, and you would use the room more because people are instinctively drawn to the energy of a real fire.

If you can't have a wood-burning fire, you might consider having a gas jet installed. Some people prefer a gas jet because it helps to get the fire started and also can offer light even when they don't throw on wood logs. Forget how much work it is to gather the wood and lay a fire. Think of your memories of sitting by a fire. Go back to your childhood experiences when you roasted marshmallows over a fire on a mountaintop on a camping trip. Recall how you felt. I happen to be a fire lover, not only because of the light but because I become mesmerized by the patterns of the flames. I look into a roaring fire and meditate. Being able to have fires at home makes me extremely happy. We gather to sit and enjoy conversation and companionship as a family and with friends. Fires create a place for intimacy and romance. If we love to be by a fire in a favorite restaurant or inn, having our own working fireplace at home is a real luxury.

> *Eating outdoors makes for good health and long life and good temper.*
>
> RENÉ DUBOS

Color

Light is important because it also introduces color. We need light to live but we express ourselves through our personal color preferences. Color and light are wavelengths of energy, revitalizing us each day. Scientists have learned a great deal about the effects of color on our behavior; each of us has favorite colors that have happy associations and other colors that we find depressing. What's right or good for you could be all wrong for me because of our personalities, chemical makeup, cultural traditions, and environment.

Color Taboos, Color Liberation

Last year I had an interesting conversation over lunch with clients who had just bought a townhouse on Nob Hill in San Francisco.

We began talking about color because I was wearing vibrant char-treuse-green silk slacks and an acid-lemon blouse. Peter was raised during the Depression and was trained to wear colors that wouldn't show the dirt. Because the brown tweeds he wore were the same shades as dirt, he felt let down by the drabness. (When he was in Bermuda on a vacation with his family when he was fifteen, he bought a madras blazer in shades of purple, turquoise blue, and yellow, liberating himself from his drab tweeds.) At lunch we all spoke of our upbringings, when none of us was allowed to wear bright colors. As a young girl, I wore a camel-colored polo coat or an equally drab trench coat. My mother never wanted me to call attention to myself.

To break free as a teenager, I wore bleached white tennis dresses all summer with brightly colored sashes, and colorful bathing suits. My real color liberation occurred when I turned six-teen and traveled around the world with my aunt, Ruth Elizabeth Johns, an international social worker. When we landed in India, the intensity of the light and the vibrant colors of the saris worn by women made me painfully aware of how mousy my clothes were, as well as of how little pleasure they gave me. I liberated myself by wearing brilliant fuchsia, yellow, orange, and green silk saris for the month we were there. When we went on to Burma and Hong Kong, I had a few silk dresses with mandarin collars made in intensely chromatic shades of hot pink and acid green. Ever since, I've never been able to go back to the dull neutral color palette of my childhood. It just wasn't me.

I am passionate about pretty colors because of the way they make me feel. I do not deliberately wear vibrant colors to call atten-tion to myself; I wear bright colors because they express my spirit.

I feel most myself when I wear clean, bright colors. Often people comment, "Alexandra, you're lucky you can wear those bright colors." I don't select colors that look good on me. The colors I'm drawn to and feel good wearing are the ones I intuitively select. We can extend this color awareness to the rooms in our home. Colors that make us feel buoyant are the colors we want to surround ourselves with, wher-ever we are, whatever our circumstances.

Painters understand nature and love her and teach us to see her.

VINCENT VAN GOGH

I Love the Color Green.

Peter, for some unknown reason, doesn't like the color green except in nature—grass, trees, flower leaves, mint, basil, limes, lettuce, and vegetables. He loves bottle-green shutters on an old New England white clapboard house, but even on Saint Patrick's Day, he won't wear a touch of green for the Irish. I love the color green. Strangely, my mother's last name was Green; my maiden name was Alexandra Green Johns. I wear a great deal of green and am crazy about any form of chartreuse. At a Staples office supply store, I spotted a Day-Glo-chartreuse plastic clipboard that gives off a bright light. I love the idea that for a few dollars, the same price you'd pay for a dull brown clipboard, you can have a favorite color to keep your papers in order and put a private smile on your face.

> *Earth laughs in flowers.*
>
> EMERSON

I still have a chartreuse ball I found in a plastics store in the early 1960s that I love to toss around when I'm on the telephone. I also enjoy using a chartreuse highlighting marker when I'm marking articles for future reference. The intensity of the color gives me a kick, far more fun than using a lead pencil. I feel discouraged when I'm put in a neutral environment, so I always bring some colorful personal objects with me when I travel; I rarely find a hotel room decorated in fresh, clean, garden-bright colors. I purchase fresh flowers, and they always cheer up a dull, drab space. I have a flower-patterned baby pillow, several colorful clipboards, pens, a stationery box, and some pretty postcards I put around the room. Looking at a vibrantly colored Matisse or Monet takes my mind away from the dreariness of the lack of pretty colors.

The colors you love are intimately yours, and you should be able to enjoy them in as many ways as your imagination allows. You have to look within your soul to bring out the colors you adore, paying no attention to color trends. Before reading on, write down in your notebook as many colors as you can think of that you enjoy. If there is one predominant color you love, one that is most you, write it down, and then write next to it all the shades of it you most like. Suppose your favorite color is blue.

Are your favorite shades cool purple-blue tones, such as periwinkle, or more yellow shades of robin's egg or turquoise? There is no reason in the world that you can't find a wide variety of uses for these colors in your home.

After you've listed lots of different favorite colors, on another page in your notebook, list the colors you loathe. Don't concern yourself whether the colors you detest are favorite colors of your spouse or a child or a best friend. This list is for your private notebook only. I lost a client once because she had told me she hated orange. Apparently, I showed her a chintz that had a touch of orange in it. She went into a rage. I still wonder how anyone could hate orange so vehemently. But that was who she was.

On a withered tree, the flower blooms.

SHŌYŌ RŌKU

Cheer Yourself Up

Surrounding yourself with favorite colors that have happy associations can greatly lift your mood. Painting a bedroom hydrangea blue, for example, can make you feel wonderful every time you're in this space, providing emotional comfort and contentment.

On a scale from one to ten, do you feel you are highly sensitive to color? By being in tune with colors that lift our energy to exalted levels, we're able to reduce stress, actually becoming more emotionally balanced because our immediate surroundings speak to us in intensely personally meaningful ways.

I perhaps owe it to flowers for having become a painter.

CLAUDE MONET

In general terms, the warm colors—reds, oranges, and yellows—are stimulating; because of their energy, they raise our blood pressure and appetite. When used in the wrong atmosphere they can cause aggression. My mother never had any blue in the houses of my childhood because she felt blue was a depressant; when people were sad they felt "blue." While blue is a cool color, along with green, it can calm your nerves and lower your blood pressure, making you feel more meditative. For me, however, whether a color is a warm one or a cool one is not important. Blue is one of my favorite colors because it connects me to the heavenly sky above and the deep-blue sea below. Blue expands my soul. I love all clear colors. I never like colors that are muddy. Obviously, I am not in the majority but in the minority. Look around. I have no idea where I inherited this dread of muddy, murky colors, but I don't see them in nature. I feel deprived when I'm not surrounded by flower colors, by the blues of clear sky and fresh water, by the healthy greens of grass and trees.

Break a Habit of Color

A client confessed to me many years ago how much better she slept, how much more energy she had, after I encouraged her to paint the dark-brown beams in her bedroom pale heavenly blue. It was a struggle to persuade her husband to let us paint over the old brown beams, but he became a convert after the transformation, admitting that he had often felt as though the brown beams were going to fall on him when he lay awake and looked up at them from his bed. If you feel that beams or wood paneling are dark and drain your energy, be irreverent; paint over them with a primer sealer and any light-colored paint.

We are united with all life that is in nature. Man can no longer live his life for himself alone.

ALBERT SCHWEITZER

Usually when we live in a dull atmosphere, we get used to it, not even noticing our immediate surroundings after a while. In much the same way, we don't notice the smell of our house, but others do; we aren't always aware how draining our rooms can feel to others. If you live in an apartment with little natural light, or if the rooms are small, you can lighten up the colors to open up the spaces. Bleaching dark floors does wonders to cheer up a dark room. Using lighter wood tones is another way to brighten up a space.

Be Not Afraid

As noted in Chapter 2, when we reconsider our homes, we agree not to precompromise. If you are afraid your spouse won't let you paint over the ugly, heavy oak doors and door frames, offer to move if necessary, because you know that the dark atmosphere makes you feel dark in your soul. When you are authentic, aware of the interconnection between the colors around you and your feelings of hope, contentment, and enthusiasm, don't let others who are not as aware as you are have the power to dictate to you how you live. Just as certain people's personalities depress you, there are certain environments that make us feel ill at ease, even sick. Color can transform the whole energy of a room.

The richness I achieve comes from nature, the source of my inspiration.

CLAUDE MONET

Often I have to act as an arbitrator between the tastes of the people who live together in a house. I listen to both sides of a spousal disagreement or to a parent/child altercation. The usual conflict is that the husband thinks that stained wood paneling and doors look more important, more formal, than a simple white-painted finish. Women tend to like lighter, brighter-feeling colors that create a fresh airiness in the rooms, rather than the dark spaces that seem ponderous.

Color Awareness

Whether you wear your favorite colors, decorate with them, or plant them in your garden, the more exposure to colors that make you feel good, the better. Color awareness is one of the cheapest and easiest ways to transform your energy to a more profoundly content frame of mind. Use every opportunity to play with colors you adore. Experiment with different favorite colors you enjoy using together. Some color combinations I love are blues and yellows; pinks, greens, and yellows; blues and reds; and purples,

blues, and pinks. Walk around your house with your notebook open to the page with your favorite colors listed, checking off each one when you see it somewhere in your house. Look inside closets and drawers. I laughed when I did this exercise because not only do I have a chartreuse plastic ring I love to wear but I also found a Slinky, Day-Glo plastic cups, plates, straws, notepads, colored pencils, sheets of paper, and jars of craft paint in this silly color I love. I have tote bags, a suit, silk slacks, shoes, a blazer, several silk scarves, ribbons for my hats as well as for wrapping presents, in this color as well. And there are silk, cotton, and paper napkins, paperclips, elastic bands, marbles, and patterned leather boots in this funky chartreuse color that gives me energy and makes me smile.

Color Inventory

Continue your treasure hunt until you see every favorite color somewhere in your home. If you're so inclined, write down where you see each shade, in what objects around your house. I have a rug in the laundry room and a plastic dustpan and brush in chartreuse. Why can't we indulge ourselves with these little luxuries when we know we're not irritating other people with our addiction to certain colors? Even if you have to paint the inside of a drawer some favorite shade of blue because you don't know where else to put it, think of how happy you'll be each morning you open the drawer to reach for your socks.

My heart leaps up when
I behold
A rainbow in the sky.
WILLIAM WORDSWORTH

Backtrack through your house with the notebook opened to the page identifying colors you hate to look at, seeing if they are anywhere in your house. I make a concerted effort to be sure there is no taupe in our house. If you do spot a few colors you loathe, make a note where you see them. Write down how you intend to get rid of them. It's worth the money to admit you made a mistake when you upholstered a pair of side chairs in a color you've grown to dislike. Recognizing that you've made a color error is a sign that you know what's you and what's not. Rather than being hard on yourself, change the color.

Life is too short to live and die with your color mistakes. Whether they're towels, sheets, or a sofa, the wrong colors in your house could make you uncomfortable, even anxious. While colors we love have tremendously beneficial effects on our mood, attitude, outlook, and health, colors that depress us are harmful to our sense of harmony as well as peace, and should be removed from our home, whatever it takes.

The more in tune and in touch we are with ourselves, the more we'll value having everything in our home be an outward echo of an inner vision. Using color in life-affirming ways frees us to live a more productive, happy life at home. Goethe, the German philosopher who wrote a definitive book on color theory, lamented, "It is a pity that just the excellent personalities suffer most from the adverse effects of the atmosphere." He was also including himself. The more committed you are to surrounding yourself with personally appealing colors, the more you have to protect yourself from being frustrated and irritated by colors you detest. Don't spend too much time in gloomy places with colors that cause you to feel tense and edgy.

I have always loved the sky and the water, greenery, flowers. All these elements were to be found in abundance here on my little pond.

CLAUDE MONET

A View

A Room with a View

Describe the views from the windows of your house or apartment. What is your favorite window? What do you look out on? Windows bring light into our spaces, and we're fortunate when we have some uplifting views from the windows where we live. This is not always possible, but certainly our dream house would have pleasant views to feast our eyes. Views offer us inspiration and vision. What is the first thing you do when you go to a motel or hotel? I always head straight to the windows and open the curtains. Even if I am overlooking a parking lot, I'm able to look up at the sky and see some clouds or the changing light.

How Much Do You Value a Good View?

On a scale from one to ten, one being unimportant, ten being extremely important, how do you feel about having an inspiring view from at least some of your windows? Does having a scene or vista beyond your window make a difference to your sense of happiness and well-being? If you live in a city, what do you see? If you are in the country, what do you look out at? On a fresh page in your notebook, write down some of your favorite views from your childhood until now. What makes each view so memorable? Were some from your own house, others from trips you've taken? I clearly remember seeing my own garden from one of the windows of my childhood bedroom at our farm in Upper New York State. From another window I saw cows grazing and our beloved old horse, Comanche Chief. It was these early impressionable years that made me aware of the powerful significance of seeing nature. Even in a city, you experience differences in light or see some flowers or trees, but if there is nothing to see but man-made buildings, you always have the option of looking up, becoming one with the sky.

Nature is greatness, power, and immortality.

CLAUDE MONET

As you recall earlier vistas, you may remember a flower garden from your childhood that moved you to reflect on life's greatest wonders, or you may recall a waterfall, a lake, a pond, or an ocean. You might have experienced a valley, a canyon, or incredibly high mountains, or you might have had a view high up on a hill over-looking a lake with houses and small towns at one end of the lake. Identifying the most memorable views from your past helps you to reevaluate the significance of a good view in your house now. When you plan a vacation, do you tend to go to a hotel or inn that will probably have a good view? Would you pay extra money when you fly to Florida or to a tropical resort in order to have a view of the water? How much of a priority is it to you and your family?

I remember being fooled into booking a hotel room that not only had no view but was located on a dark path in an area with lots of mosquitoes. The travel agent presented this as "a garden room" versus a room with an "ocean view." Trying to save money, we agreed to overlook a garden, rationalizing that we'd be looking at the ocean for the rest of the day when we were at the beach. Were we wrong! The garden merely meant we were not near water. The area where our bungalow was situated was far too dark to grow flowers. Fortunately, we were able to minimize our losses by relocating to a room with an ocean view before we unpacked, thus maintaining our cheer. We had flown to a tropical island to be in the light, to be surrounded by the magic of the turquoise water, only to discover we could have been at the bottom of a dreary deadend street.

Every flower is a soul blossoming in Nature.

GÉRARD DE NERVAL

My Favorite View

When I'm asked to name my favorite window in our cottage, I go immediately to a window overlooking the harbor where I see the sailboats come and go, as well as spectacular sunsets. We don't have a wide, expansive view of the water. When we were house hunting, we wanted a wreck of an eighteenth-century house we could fix up ourselves, we wanted it to be right in the village of Stonington, and we wanted to be able to peek at the water and boats in the harbor. We treasure our little glimpse of water and don't pine for more. Our house is twenty-five feet above sea level, making it relatively safe during hurricane season. Being right on Water Street, able to see the fishing boats in the harbor, is very special, but we don't need to have a perfect view in order to have a daily connection to nature. Our New York apartment has an expansive view east from the one kitchen window. Because it is at the back of the building, we were

A nobler want of man is served by nature, namely, the love of beauty.

EMERSON

given permission to have a large picture window installed. In the morning we see sunrises through high-rise buildings, at night we can stargaze by turning off the kitchen lights. This huge window admits light into the room and, more important, it provides depth. We see out for miles. In a crowded city, this is a luxury.

Creating a View with Mirrors and Furniture Placement

Our living room windows overlook a brick apartment building, but half a block north is a classic Georgian Presbyterian church. By mirroring the south wall spaces on either side of the mantel, we have not only gained the illusion of two more windows and twice as much light but we now get a clear view of the brick church. Even if your windows don't directly look out on something attractive, by experimenting with mirrors you might be pleasantly surprised at the views you can create. I have clients who live on the fourth floor of an apartment building on Fifth Avenue. Their living room and dining room windows overlook a reservoir, but the one window in their bedroom is off center, catching only a small slice of this spectacular view. By installing mirrors in the top and two sides of the recessed window space in the reveal, they can clearly see the reservoir from this window.

Your view should always be the first consideration when deciding on a floor plan for the furniture. Think of your view as your lifeline to nature and beauty. In our bedroom in New York, it is extremely important to us to see the sky and the church's steeple, so we located our queen-size bed near the windows. I remember my grandparents' bed being placed at an angle in the corner of their bedroom at their beach house on the Delaware shore in order that they might soak in the whole sweep of the beach. Rooms should, if possible, accommodate a view. Somehow we hunger for a room with a view.

Identify ourselves with the divine element which in fact constitutes our essential nature.

ALDOUS HUXLEY

The Deprivation of Being Without a View

Whenever possible have something growing or blooming in every room.

I've seen clients set free who once lived in a crowded city in an apartment on the ground floor where they had no view or light. The apartment's windows were depressing because they overlooked an airshaft from other buildings surrounding theirs. The couple kept the curtains closed day and night. They woke up each morning not knowing what the sky looked like. We all rationalize our particular situations, often in denial. Because both husband and wife worked, they felt it was all right not to have a view because they were never there during the day. But what about weekends? It was in June, when the days were longer, that this couple particularly craved the light and connection to nature. They finally decided they'd rather live outside the city, commuting on a train, where they'd at least see a sunset and some sky and trees. They bought a cottage on top of a hill, one hour's commute north of New York City. They are thriving with wonderful views, lots of light, communing with nature. They say the lack of views from their dark apartment was a deprivation keeping them from enjoying the therapeutic benefits of nature. They now enjoy the commute, using the time to read and do paperwork, so that they can sit out on their deck when they get home and absorb the beauty of the tall trees and the expanses of sky.

Flowers are the sweetest things that God ever made, and forgot to put a soul into.

H. W. BEECHER

Creating Illusion

To soften a harsh city view in front of a picture window, we have a large, tall ficus tree in our New York apartment kitchen. We had an eight-inch-deep ledge built in front of the window, ideal for growing basil and mint or for a display of African violets. You can install an inexpensive, indoor, wooden window box with a plastic liner, brimming with pansies or shrimp-colored geraniums. If you have an impossible window with nothing attractive to look out on, rather than seeing something ugly that will make you sad, it is best to hide it. You can cover the window glass with white vinyl shades and, in front, install light strips on all four sides of the window. To hide the lights and to give the illusion of a garden, hang shutters and keep them closed, but leave the slats open to admit the light. If you have a window ledge or an indoor window box, the lights will help plants to blossom. You will be creating something charming from something unsightly.

Something Important for Your Soul

In your notebook write down your feelings about the view from your windows. If having a view is extremely important to you because of your love of nature, you should then be willing to make the necessary sacrifices in order to satisfy this basic need. Having a view of sky, water, a mountain, a lake, a field, a meadow, a canyon, or a garden could make a major contribution to your life at home. If paradise is a place of ideal beauty and loveliness, having a view of nature from your window could turn your home into a paradise on earth. Whether you oversee rooftops or a church, cows grazing in a meadow or pretty trees, having a meaningful view is fundamental to your happiness and well-being at home.

Privacy

U.S. Supreme Court Justice Brandeis believed privacy is the right most valued by civilized men and women. The right to be alone, secluded, uninterrupted, is the greatest luxury. Privacy is ideal at home. Our home is not an open house. All of us should have boundaries.

How much do you value your privacy? On a scale from one to ten, ten being an extremely private person and one being someone who is happiest when there are a lot of people around, rate yourself. How is your household set up currently to accommodate your privacy needs? Do you have an in-law living with you? Do you have an elderly parent living at home? Do you have children at home? Do you have live-in help? Do you have a secretary or assistant who comes to your house or apartment during the day? Do you have someone who comes to help you clean and maintain the house? How often? Do you have a guest room? How often do you have guests? What does it do to your usual schedule to have houseguests? What is the average length of their stay?

I consider privacy as necessary as clean air and a healthy diet. Privacy is our time to be by ourselves, to listen to the rhythms of our own heart, to balance all the outer-directed activities with a look inward. Yet, even when we know at our core how essential privacy is to our well-being, we often get off our path. Feeling obligated to others or simply not setting up proper boundaries, we give up our privacy in little ways until we live in a house, not a home.

Being Alone

Take a close look at your feelings about privacy. I love being alone and need time by myself every day. I don't get dressed until I've spent several hours alone meditating and writing. I wander around the entire house, including the tiny secluded walled-in backyard. I don't answer the door or the telephone. My private time is my time. I resist any kind of intrusion. I like to be in my own world every morning and would feel hollow in my soul if I didn't enter into this sacred space within.

From my experience making house calls, I see a great lack of privacy. If you are on a spiritual quest, working on deepening your appreciation of the great mysteries and meaning of your existence, chances are you need more privacy than most people. But all of us need time and space to recognize our own feelings. Time in our private spaces is the greatest healer.

I believe each of us has to reclaim our privacy. We have to take a close look at our ideal, not giving up our hope for a better life. Without privacy, our lives will be a series of frustrations. Enlightenment is not automatic; it doesn't just happen. Everything is changing so rapidly. There is growing confusion and congestion everywhere. By taking a fresh look at our home we can make some liberating minor and even major changes.

A Door to Close

What are the factors that are undermining our privacy at home? What are our frustrations? When are you intruded upon? Do you have a private room with a door to shut where you can retreat from the interruptions of the rest of the family? What are the forces that keep us from accomplishing our goals? What are the demands on our energy that take us away from our center? If we can't have regular moments of peace where we live, where can we go? Where can we hide? Even a spiritual retreat or a spa has a regimen, a schedule to keep. Home does also, but who is in charge? By writing in your notebook all the conflicting factors that frustrate you, you'll be able to set up some firm boundaries and establish some house rules.

> *Natural law is as valid as ever.*
>
> SØREN KIERKEGAARD

Balancing Our Energy

It was after we bought our cottage in Connecticut that I realized I no longer enjoyed going to an office. We travel a great deal, and when we'd return to New York, we loved our apartment, but longed to go to our house in its quiet village on the water. Having to go to an office with no privacy seemed unnecessary and even burdensome. After having been with others on the road, we needed to balance our energy in privacy. I found that as an interior designer, clients wanted me to go to their houses and would rarely come to my office. I knew I needed more time alone, both at the apartment and the cottage, so I eventually gave up the office. Because I worked from home when the children were young, I have two rooms ideal for a home office. The mistake I made was to use them for others rather than for myself, as I had originally.

One room was created for me to prepare my lectures. I have a series of light boxes on the counters, and in three-ring binders on shelves, I store all my slides labeled by subject matter. The other was my writing room, with shelves for my books and notebooks and a door to close, soundproofed from the noises on the other side of the door. For eight years after giving up going to an office, I created a home office with several employees. The only problem, seeming so obvious to me now, is that I gave up Peter's and my privacy. We scaled back, doing more of the office work ourselves so we could enjoy true privacy. Since our children have left the nest, we can now reclaim our home more fully than we ever had before. After I cleaned out both offices and spent some time using these spaces again, I felt a newfound freedom I had mistakenly sacrificed. These rooms are there for me, ready to receive me whenever I walk through the door. I can work on a lecture at eight o'clock in the morning in my nightshirt and I can write at the kitchen table. The privacy has meant the world to both of us. I will never give up this space again.

Yet all in order, sweet and lovely.

WILLIAM BLAKE

We Pay a Price

There is a price we pay when we have others come into our home to help us, especially when it is full time. Whether you hire a nanny or a baby-sitter, a cleaning woman or an assistant, these people are human beings with their own needs. They have a presence, a watchful eye, and they move about freely in the space. You are not alone, nor are you all one big extended family. No matter how blessed you are to have their help, it is awkward. Do you sit and eat your sandwich at the kitchen table with your cleaning woman? Do you and your husband sit at the dining room table enjoying your lunch while your secretary is in the back office slaving away? Do you ask her to join you? Every day? On occasion?

I made the mistake of hiring a bookkeeper who came to the apartment to work. No matter how capable she was with numbers, she felt compelled to make continual small talk, complaining about the heat or the cold or whatever came to mind, causing me to hate being at home when she was there. When we have tension or friction or just plain lack of privacy at home, we survive by escaping. This is sad but true. Some people work late at the office or schedule unnecessary business dinners or even business trips. Other people go to a club or to a pub or a coffee shop on their way home. Whenever there are benefits, we can be grateful, but this does not mean we may not also be making sacrifices too costly to our sense of well-being at home.

The chief forms of beauty are order and symmetry and definiteness.

ARISTOTLE

Time Alone Together

The issue of privacy is central to a healthy marriage. Because I married Peter later in life, we both had children from previous marriages, making privacy difficult. Most married people have a few years alone before they begin their family. We didn't, but we feel we have a new lease on life now that we have the apartment back as our sanctuary. We're able to spend quality time alone, peacefully working.

We shouldn't be too quick to have someone come live with us, even if we need extra help with the children. I see so often such an intimate relationship between the mother and the mother's helper that the husband feels he is a guest in his own home when he returns from work or from a business trip. If your husband wants to go to the refrigerator to get a drink, he shouldn't have to get dressed to do so. Home is where we shed our public persona and become intimately ourselves. Home is where we unwind and relax. In our compassion and desire to make others feel at home, we limit the potential for our house to be our retreat where we take time to nurture our soul and heal ourselves.

There should be clear boundaries to keep the house a private haven for a marriage. There might be simple things you can do, as easy as having a lock on your bedroom door to guarantee freedom from someone walking in on you unexpectedly. We had a family rule where children had to knock on our door for permission to enter and we in turn had to knock on theirs.

Say No to the Phone

The telephone is a major irritation to most of us. If we all made a rule never to buy anything over the telephone, telemarketers would stop their aggressive invasion of our privacy. Having an answering machine where you can screen calls might be the solution, but it seems a shame that our nerves have to be jangled so often by strangers calling, invading our privacy at home. Just taking a stand on this issue alone is liberating. Make this a commitment and don't feel guilty. If all the telephone calls were from loving family and friends, we would be a whole lot calmer and serene and we wouldn't be concerned about our blood pressure. But even these calls can be disruptive if you're trying to concentrate on something important, enjoying your dinner, having a bath, or taking a nap. Turn the ringer off or let the call go on voice mail. What if you were out?

Don't Drop In

No matter how endearing and well-meaning your motives, in these time-compressed, pressured existences, where our privacy is more and more valuable, make it a rule that you will never drop in on anyone. Write a note, hand-deliver it, or mail it, telephone, or send a fax, but don't assume someone you love is in a receiving mode, party ready. It is unfair and disorienting to catch someone off guard, unprepared. While surprise parties are well intended, there are some of us who are such private people we will not enjoy the unannounced celebration as much as we would if we could anticipate it. If someone pounds on your door in an emergency, that is an exception to the rule, but most of our time at home we should feel free from random intruders, no matter how well intentioned.

> *When you reread a classic you do not see more in the book than you did before; you see more in you than there was before.*
>
> CLIFTON FADIMAN

Short and Sweet

If we find ourselves in the bosom of someone else's home, remember we are temporary guests. We do not live the life of those with whom we are visiting. Try not to offer suggestions. Try not to judge. If you enter through the front door of a loved one's home, let all your energy sing out in praise and thanksgiving. No matter how charming our daughter or son-in-law is to us when we visit, we keep in mind that we are not there to settle in, but to have a short visit and leave. We should try never to put ourselves in a position of causing pain to our children if there is any way of avoiding it. The rhythm of daily life is severely altered when parents and guests come to stay. If we have a choice, we keep our visits brief and sweet. We leave before we've overstayed our welcome. Respecting our children's privacy is a high form of showing how deeply we love them. Never, under any circumstances, is it appropriate to criticize your children's home, their choice of colors, their tastes, their use of space, the way they set up their kitchen, or anything else about their lifestyle. How they choose to live is their own choice.

The more we crave our own privacy, the more sensitive we will be to others' needs and feelings. Do everything you can to make privacy at home sacred and undeniable. When we really come down to the truth, how can we have those Jeffersonian qualities of life, liberty, and the pursuit of happiness, without privacy at home?

Fresh Air

Peter had warned me that the hotels in New Haven, Connecticut, were pretty crummy when we booked several rooms for our family for his fiftieth Yale reunion. As much as I loathed the orange-and-brown bedspreads and the brown-, black-, and white-speckled carpeting, I could live with it. I put the bedspreads in the closet and looked up at the sky. As I walked through the room toward the dirty windows, I noticed there was no latch or lever to open them. The room smelled stale and smoky. We were hermetically sealed. Peter called the hotel desk clerk, who got an engineer to come and open the windows.

When we bought our cottage, every one of the thirty-eight windows had been painted shut in the most depressing shades of dead insects. I made it my project to bang away at the cracks, loosen the paint, and slowly hammer the windows open. The contractor told us he didn't have the time. "It's a nasty, time-consuming job," he told me as he shook his head. But we didn't buy a house in an old fishing village to breathe stale air.

Several years ago, a photographer came to our cottage to photograph it for a magazine layout. The photographer loved seeing our white handkerchief-linen curtains dancing in the wind off the water, echoing the sails of a school of boats in a regatta. Starched,

Everything in a house can be improved, repaired, and maintained. Order always gives a sense of more space.

We can control the emotional climate of our home.

The smallest details of this world derive infinite significance from their relation to an unseen divine order.

WILLIAM JAMES

bleached-white, unlined curtains moving freely in an open window have a quiet charm that makes everyone take in deep breaths of air, feeling intoxicated by the freshness. The air gives us vitality, and when it's warm enough we have breakfast outside in our cozy backyard garden. There's something wonderful about beginning our day in a garden surrounded by natural beauty and breathing all the oxygen from the trees, ivy, and plants.

Order always comes before beauty.

Do Your Windows Open?

It is dangerous to our health to be completely sealed against the escape or entry of air. We are not meant to have our windows so tightly sealed that we are impervious to outside interferences and influences. Assess your windows. Do they open with ease? Are there any that don't open at all? Count your windows and doors and evaluate each one separately. Do you enjoy having your windows open? Do you need screened windows? Do you ever keep your doors open, front or back? Do you prefer fresh air to air conditioning? If you have not opened any windows in your apartment because you don't want the soot to come in, how does this affect your health?

Order is the shape upon which beauty depends.

PEARL BUCK

Do you or does a family member suffer from allergies? What is the doctor's recommendation about fresh air versus air conditioning? If I were in an apartment or a house with no access to fresh air, I would become lethargic. Air circulating gives us energy. We should be careful not to treat the fabrics on our furniture and at the windows better than we treat our lungs, and none of them deserves old stale air.

A few years ago, as I was helping clients renovate their apartment, we discovered the windows didn't open in the master bedroom. Apparently there had been a pigeon problem, and not wanting pigeons in the bedroom, the thinking was to keep the windows closed. We immediately worked to get the windows to operate, and we also went to work on the pigeon problem with

I love to lose myself in other men's minds.

CHARLES LAMB

magic solutions. They not only solved the pigeon situation, but they planted a garden on their terrace and now go outside to enjoy breakfast among the pansies and hibiscus. The air in New York is quite clear. All cities are dirty, but we can't shut ourselves inside without the connection to nature. As a child, I lived outside in tents at a camp in Maine and at home in Westport, Connecticut; our whole family slept on a screened sleeping porch for six months of the year. We turned our tiny backyard into our summer living room and spent our days there and lit candles after dark.

Our rooms are boxes with openings, and each window is an opportunity to make a critical connection with nature and fresh air. So many of my clients want to solve their window treatment problems, when the first concern should be the window itself. If the window opens and closes easily and the glass is clean, rather than pouring money into expensive curtains, we should look at each window individually and question whether curtains are needed. I can't force clients to open windows against their will, but I can encourage them to do whatever it takes to have all their windows operative, even if this requires spending money. Windows should set us free, not be another barrier blocking us from nature's air.

There is something so charming about our living room windows when they're wide open, exposing the pink geraniums in their window boxes. Even though these perky blossoms are outside, they appear to be in the room. In my Zen writing room above our tiny garden, I throw open the windows wide before I sit down at my desk to write. I have round dowels painted white to stick in the side to hold the bottom half of the double-hung window up completely. I literally look out into the blue sky. I gulp in the fresh air and seize the moment to work. Fresh air makes us feel wonderful. We should see to it that we have it wherever we are.

Nature

I would live in a garden if I could. I'd never feel at home if we didn't have flowers, plants, and trees indoors. I love arranging flowers and putting little bouquets in all the rooms. Having a rosebud or a hydrangea blossom on a ledge in the bathroom or on the back of the toilet or at the kitchen sink brings cheer. I always have flowers or a flowering plant wherever I write because they are God-created, not man-made, reminding me of the difference, helping me to be myself, not trying to be anything else.

Reading connects us to people throughout time and space. You're able to connect, and be together.

Living with Flowers

Flowers and flowering plants soften the harsh edges and hard angles of rooms. They add sweetness to a space and bring it to life. We always feel good when a flower arrangement is real and ultimately feel disappointed if we were fooled and the pretty arrangement is artificial. There are lots of reasons why we don't grow flowering plants inside or have fresh-cut flowers. Some people have deer problems and can't gather flowers from outdoor gardens. If I had that problem outside, I'd be all the more ambitious to have lots of colorful flowers and plants blooming indoors to counter the deprivation outside. One client had a cat who ate all her flower arrangements and flowering plants. That cat died several years ago and her two new cats don't eat flowers, but she got so used to her silk arrangements that she is out of the habit of having fresh bouquets.

To add a library to a house is to give that house a soul.

CICERO

One client tells me it is too much maintenance to arrange flowers, change the water regularly, and rearrange them in smaller pitchers and vases as some blossoms droop and die. Another client doesn't like the mess and is afraid of bugs. That is why she doesn't have flowers, plants, trees, or a log fire in her house. Another client thinks flowers are an expensive luxury.

You can't eat them and eventually they die, therefore they are unnecessary. One client complained to me that her husband never notices or says a word about the flowers and it hurts her feelings.

Write in your notebook your feelings about living with nature inside your house. Would you be just as happy without fresh flowers at home? Would you miss them if they weren't there? Do you enjoy arranging them? Who else in your family likes to create flower bouquets? Do you have a handy spot where you have your vases, pitchers, and cachepots, a place with a counter space to arrange them? Is this place near a sink? When Peter and I married over twenty-five years ago, I realized how much he loves arranging flowers. As a gift to him I had an additional sink installed near the window in the kitchen, where he can play with flowers undisturbed while I use the other sink for cooking.

Budgeting for Blossoms

Flowers are so important to our family that we all have a flower budget just as we have a food budget. While flowers might be an unnecessary expense to some people, a house or apartment could never be a home to me without the beauty and wonder of nature in all the rooms where we live each day. I want to be continuously reminded of how fragile our lives are. I want to sit and gaze at some colorful flowers and feel inspired and in awe. I want to take time to smell them, care for them, and appreciate their beauty and their blessings to me. Flowers nourish my soul in profound ways. I absorb their powerful hold over me through all my senses and know intuitively they are urging me on in my path, helping me to become more sensitive, more caring. I could exist but not live without flowers because they are as central to my personality and value system as anything can be.

Read, mark, learn, and inwardly digest.

THE BOOK OF
COMMON PRAYER

Being a Co-Creator

I consider myself a gardener of life. I love to be a co-creator, taking a seed or a bulb and tending it until I see the wonder of a bud, and then the magnificence of the colorful blossoms. To make ourselves feel more at home wherever we travel, we always buy some cut flowers for our hotel room and place a bud or two around the bathtub or sink for cheer. If you feel flowers add to your emotional comfort and well-being at home, make a commitment to yourself and your family to live with nature in your home. When your flowers are alive, your rooms will be, too, and you will enjoy your time more when it is spent in spaces where there is something blossoming. Whether you place a copper pot brimming with African violets in the window of your office or on the windowsill in your kitchen, begin your indoor garden today. Just as you may have to hire someone to feed your cats or feed and walk your dog when you are away, you might have to hire someone to tend your plants if you are away for more than a week.

Books encourage us, teach us, educate us, nourish us, stimulate and inspire us.

A Clear Plastic Dropcloth

One easy way to care for flowering plants and ivy when you are away from home for a week or less is to put them all close together in a bathtub. After you water everything well, place a clear plastic dropcloth over the tub to keep the moisture inside the plastic. Try this and see if it works for you. If I have to hire someone to water my plants because of my travel schedule, I always gather them in one place to make it easy on the person hired. When they're all seen together, none is neglected because it wasn't noticed. Most of my house plants can initially be watered well, and then will last without more water for six to seven days.

Learn in order to teach and to practice.

THE TALMUD

Forcing Bulbs

Growing plants from bulbs is inexpensive and fun. I love the scent of paperwhite narcissus and grow them from bulbs in late winter, along with tulips. I've never had good luck with gardenias, but since their scent is so heavenly, I try and sometimes succeed. If I go away, however, I often give my gardenia plant to a gardener friend because they are too tricky to leave in the hands of someone who isn't a garden person. They need mist but not too much water. I remember having one with twelve white blossoms once, and I'd mist it throughout the day as though breast-feeding a hungry baby. I talk to my plants and flowers, and they speak back to me in tender ways. Sometimes I bring flowers and plants on the train between the apartment and house because I can't bear to part with them. Sometimes I put a bouquet at a neighbor's door and the container is returned to me the next time they see me.

Putting Flowers in the Refrigerator

The copy editor who worked at Random House when *Living a Beautiful Life* was published teased me about my suggestion to put fresh flowers in the refrigerator. But one evening she was having friends for dinner and her cat jumped up on the counter and started nibbling on the red tulips she'd just arranged in a vase. Instinctively, she grabbed the container and put the flowers in the refrigerator, safe from the cat. When she later opened the refrigerator to get out a bottle of wine for dinner, she was surprised by joy as she saw how pretty they looked inside. I love to have a few flowers in the refrigerator. I have a few orange roses now, and they're on a clean glass shelf alongside a blue-and-white spatterware bowl filled with oranges, lemons, limes, and green and yellow

apples. It is a feast to the eye and a remarkably pretty still life. I can bring the roses out to place on a table anytime I feel like it. When we travel, I can place cut flowers in the refrigerator, return five or six days later, and they're still fresh. Just be sure the temperature isn't too cold or they will freeze.

Flowers Every Day

We all want to make guests feel happy and at home when they come to visit us. Flowers, along with good food, are one sure way to make people feel welcome. I believe we should not create elaborate flower arrangements when we have a party, and then live without this natural beauty when we are alone or with our family. I'd love to think we can enjoy pretty flowers even if we are alone and no other eyes will feast on them but ours, because whenever we are connected with nature, we are never alone. Flowers have been created for our enjoyment. We should participate in the feast by accepting flowers and flowering plants into our daily lives at home. How lovely to begin our day with a purple gloxinia in a pretty cachepot in the center of our kitchen table.

Flower Designs

All of us who are passionate about flowers can think of our rooms as gardens. To assure you will have blooms year-round, think of all the ways you can decorate with flowers. You may want a flowered chintz in your living room. You can have a hooked rug showing a basket of geraniums or tulips. You may want botanical flower prints on your dining room walls or flowered sheets on your bed. You can have flowered tablecloths, napkins, porcelain dinner and dessert plates, and flowers in the design of your lamp base.

If we love our objects and they bring us emotional comfort, they are no longer inanimate.

I cannot conceive of any room that is to be lived in today without the use of upholstered furniture. The late nineteenth century brought this great luxury to us and we have never ceased enjoying it, and most of us spend much of our lives sitting on it.

BILLY BALDWIN

Walk around your house and see where you can add some nature-inspired designs. Flowers, plants, and trees connect us to the mysteries of our earthly existence. Live with flowers at home and you will indeed be in paradise, right here, right now, every day.

Order

When buying, it is a wise investment to have the best custom-made upholstered furniture because it lasts much longer.

BILLY BALDWIN

How organized are you? How do you handle the necessary, practical aspects of everyday living at home? Do you feel you have a good system for sorting the mail, paying the bills, and filing? Is your house arranged in an organized way, enabling you to function well with as little frustration and disorder and as much efficiency as possible?

Organization is the foundation that grounds us every day at home. Until we have a working system in place where all the parts come together into a whole, we will be spinning around, scattered, wasting time and energy, not feeling the satisfaction of being able to accomplish a simple necessary task in a serene way. If we don't have a functional plan, we won't be able to enjoy accomplishing simple necessary tasks. Take time to evaluate where you are now. Write in your notebook some of your areas of triumph as well as places that need revamping. The way to feel emotionally comfortable at home is to figure out how to bring more order to each category:

—but beauty absolute, separate, simple and everlasting.

PLATO

- sorting mail
- storing newspapers, magazines, and catalogues
- paying bills
- conducting correspondence
- keeping track of telephone messages
- storing household supplies

"It's a Mess"

When I ask clients to show me their organization for the family laundry, recycling, and the storage of cleaning supplies, I'm often given a frown. "You can't see the laundry area, it's a mess." All of us do laundry regularly. Just having a specific basket or hamper for each person's dirty clothes is an obvious first step. Without this, the floor becomes the place for soiled laundry, causing us to feel anxious. I found some great rectangular baskets with cotton liners ideal for stowing clean clothes before putting them back in drawers or closets. I see my accomplishments and feel happy to return fresh, lemon-scented laundry to Peter's or my closet. Colorful laundry bags to sort colors, whites, and fine washables can look cheery even piled high. If some clothes go to the dry cleaners to be cleaned, pressed, or washed, designating a special colored laundry bag for those items can make sorting a snap.

I feel strongly that no room should ever be entirely finished or "done."

BILLY BALDWIN

Our lives are made up of the things we do every day. This is who we are, and what we are doing matters. How we do these necessary things need not be humdrum or tiresome. We should take care to never cheat ourselves of the most important opportunity—to get in the rhythm of everything we do, becoming one with the activity. Whether we're setting a table for dinner, ironing a daughter's dress, sorting the mail, doing the laundry, putting food away after grocery shopping, or cleaning the living room, the thought and care we put into organizing these practical activities will reward us and others each day.

I see beauty that is to be desired.

EMERSON

Setting Up a System to Manage Better

I've had many clients who are perfectionists about avoiding dirt, not wanting dust or to be unclean anywhere, but these same people live with newspapers piled waist-high on the floor of their study. Being organized liberates you from being a perfectionist because there is a place for everything. How wonderful to be able to toss catalogues into a nearby basket when you sort mail, and keep colorful binders labeled *Bills, Banking,* and *Correspondence* for the rest. Even if you don't have time to sit at your desk to deal with the mail, at least you've been able to throw out all the junk mail you never want to touch again.

I've discovered that an accordion A-Z file is handy for paid bills that I file away at the end of a year. For bank statements, insurance statements, and all the documents I need for the accountant, I have wicker file boxes with colored Pendaflex file folders on the floor next to a desk. This seems so simple, but all too often we get behind, and once we start to drown, it's harder to get ourselves back on track. When the mail comes, we need a large wastebasket, a letter opener, some paper clips, and an in-basket—one place for the daily mail. The newspapers can be stored in a rectangular basket, the catalogues and magazines can, too, and when you have time, perhaps in your bedroom in the evening, you can look through magazines and catalogues and finish the newspaper. It's nice to know the newspaper hasn't disappeared into the recycling bin if a spouse finished reading the paper in the morning. Having one place for newspapers saves evening readers from feeling thwarted.

Order Makes Everything Better

Order helps us to rise above the ordinary chores of everyday living, providing an atmosphere that lets us experience little epiphanies throughout our day. Putting our house in order enables and encourages us to accomplish necessary tasks as well as fulfill desires. When clients tell me they dread having to sew on a button, it is usually because they don't have a pair of scissors, buttons, and thread handy. If it seems like a chore to pay a bill, the solution could be as simple as having the checkbook in a desk drawer with envelopes and stamps nearby. Just as we need all the ingredients in place to enjoy cooking, in addition to free counter space and the right-size pots and pans, all our daily tasks need to be set up properly so they can be done as a meaningful ritual.

Figure out what steps you need to take to have things run more smoothly. Even if you don't like to recycle, you might find it more satisfying if you tie the newspapers in wild-colored Day-Glo twine found at the hardware store. I bought a bright-yellow sharp cutter that helps me cut up cartons, thus making this task more tolerable. And, because I love to iron, I bought a new white steam iron that is more fun to use because it is a better quality and design than my old beige one. What are some things you know will improve the rituals you perform each day?

A client who lives alone used to put on her makeup in the hall outside her bathroom. There was a big mirror and good light but, because she'd then rush off to work, the first thing she'd see when she returned was the mess on the table. By installing stronger lightbulbs in her bathroom and adding a makeup mirror, she now enjoys doing her makeup in the bathroom and keeps it all together in a zippered bag that matches her green color scheme. Another client moved into an apartment where there is a small built-in area she uses to put on her makeup. Because the bathroom is small and she shares it with her husband, she's happy to sit down for a few minutes to pamper herself in a space she's made pretty with framed family photographs and even a bud vase with a fresh flower. There can be order inside a drawer, inside a closet or toy box, and in the refrigerator. Look around at your needs and see how you can meet them to put your home in better order.

It was Wordsworth who pointed out that a poor man is just as capable of enjoying beauty, and putting it high on his scale of values, as a rich man.

PAUL JOHNSON

Why beauty? Because there is a kind of harmony that allows the spirit to come forth.

NATALIE DAVENPORT

A Working Kitchen

A kitchen feeds the spirit of the house. Go into your kitchen and look around. How do you feel about what you see? Do things look in order? Do you have enough light? Does it look too crowded? How long have you lived with the kitchen in its current condition? Are there areas you know you want to improve? Who cooks in your family? Is the table in the best place? Do you have enough counter space? Whether you like to cook for recreation or you cook for your family regularly, most of us are kitchen people. This is the heart of our family life and a natural gathering place.

The Kitchen Table

Having a wonderful kitchen makes us feel emotionally comfortable because this is a nurturing place as well as a nourishing one for us, our family, and friends. We create celebrations and ceremonies that involve food and drink. We're able to sit at the kitchen table between meals to read, write a note, or do something for ourselves on the spur of the moment. Whether I use it to sew something that needs mending or I read letters, there is something so special about a kitchen table as a centering place.

Years ago, in the era of household help, kitchens were not designed for comfort, ease, or beauty. Today, we're liberated, and men, women, and children not only cook but know their way around this space. They can recycle, arrange flowers, and putter in an atmosphere that enhances their sense of well-being and enriches their time spent at home. The kitchen today can be an intimate, attractive place for the entire family.

A working kitchen requires having a sufficently high counter for a tall member of the family and a lower area for children. I find the kitchen table is usually a good height for children to work at. The bigger the better when you plan a table, because children love to do artwork as well as homework at the kitchen table. By accommodating everyone's needs and wishes, meal preparation becomes a shared experience.

Convenience

Every household has its own private ways of dividing up the labor. Sometimes you'll cook together, while other times one person does the meal preparation and someone else cleans up. By setting up your kitchen in a practical, convenient way, so there is a logic to where things are located and stored—the filter bags are near the coffee grinder and the coffee maker, for example—you set the stage for ease and harmony as you work. If your kitchen is not well thought out, or if it is crowded or messy or fussy, it will not be as much fun to prepare special banquets or help out with dinner.

Whether you like to cook or not, the kitchen is the center of your house. You may want to spruce it up before you work on other spaces in your home. Maybe you could make this space lighter and brighter by having a skylight installed. Perhaps you'd love a spotlight above where you stand in front of the sink. Open your cabinets. Maybe everything would feel better to you if the insides were painted white rather than that orangy wood color.

Have a table by the window where a child can do homework, artwork, or play games between meals. Have plastic bins for your children's projects to make cleaning up a snap. Set up an area where you can pay bills, equipped with envelopes, stamps, paper clips, and Scotch tape. Have one area for flower arranging, where you store vases and cachepots, clippers and plant food. Plan everything for efficiency as well as beauty. Have a basket full of candles in a cabinet. Light a few candles as you prepare dinner.

Think of your working kitchen as a living, breathing space where you long to be, to enter in the morning and return to at night. Don't limit the kitchen's uses solely to food preparation. Peter and I often sit at a small round table by a window, away from the main part of the room. We go there to talk. In the evening, we often light a candle and sit at this cozy area we call "the café" to have an intimate conversation before retiring to bed. Because we have a good fan over the stove, we're hung a Mühl oil painting of a luncheon feast on an opposite wall. We keep some of our favorite things in our kitchen because it is here where we spend so much time together. When our kitchen welcomes us, day or night, we feel an emotional comfort at home. When we have a working kitchen, our chores become grace notes and we feel blessed and are grateful.

A Home Library

How important are books to your sense of wholeness? How many books do you estimate you have? Where are your books housed? Do you have them categorized, and if so, how? By subject matter or by author? Do you have enough shelf space or bookcases for all your books? Can you easily locate certain books if you want to refer to them, or do you have to hunt in order to find a particular book? Are books among your most treasured objects?

The Author Is the Book

I could never feel at home without my books because so many of them are alive, as important as loved ones. The author is the book. I like having them around me and am grateful they are waiting for me when the spirit moves me to reenter one or to experience a new book by a favorite author. When I was a design student, I roamed around used book stores in hopes of finding a book I could afford to add to my collection. I have some favorite books I continue to buy and give to family and friends. I identify with certain authors, people who have touched me on a profound level, minds who open me up and welcome me into a more soulful, luminous place in my consciousness. Many of these authors have become my teachers, informing me, guiding me, and inspiring me.

For those of us who love books, they are the pulse of our home. You can walk into someone's study and feel the energy. We are greatly influenced by what we read, and having our books in our rooms is far more than decoration. Although libraries are wonderful for research and for borrowing books, one of the greatest privileges is to own your own library of books. Once we identify the priority of having our own collection, we will understand how important it is to us to live with our favorite books every day. One of my most enjoyable pastimes is to wander around glancing at the spines of our books, waiting patiently for one to speak to me. I've even had the right book fall into my hands at just the right time as though by coincidence. A good book, like a favorite hymn, can be reread and resung, and there are times when I feel I am experiencing its wisdom for the first time. My books welcome me home. They are thousands of voices patiently waiting for the right time to be heard.

Every year or two Peter and I sort through our books, weeding out the ones that were disappointments or others we know we'll never take time to reread or use for research. We become so attached to our favorite ones, I often want my own copy, meaning we sometimes have two of the same books, side by side, on a shelf. Peter and I mark our books because we use them for our work. Because our marked copies are so precious to us, we make it a habit never to loan a marked copy. It puts too much of a burden on the borrower to have to remember to return it to us. I'd far prefer to give someone their own copy of a really good book, one they can keep in their own home.

The French writer André Malraux often expressed his passionate belief in the redemptive power of beauty.

Be alert for any sign of beauty or grace. Offer up every joy, be awake at all moments.

SOGYAL RINPOCHE

The Highest Point of View

My best books confirm the virtue of what Emerson and other role models, spiritual guides, and mentors have taught me—trying to contemplate life from the highest point of view. When we feel we need instruction, we can open up a treasured book and receive words that are wise and wonderful. Maybe we're in need of some humor or perhaps we want to look at a picture book of gorgeous photographs from the South of France. We might want to learn more about gardening or low-fat cooking, or we may want to read some really good poetry. Having a working library is the only way to feel you've come home. If reading is important to you, you must recognize how much your books mean to you. I am possessive about my home library. These books are my lifeline. Every few years, weed out the books you no longer want to read and give them to a local library or thrift store. Display stacks of books on tables. In a bookcase, put some on easels so that you can see the covers.

What is beautiful is moral, that is all there is to it.

GUSTAVE FLAUBERT

Favorite Objects

What are some of the things you most adore? Walk around your house and identify some of these treasures. To a stranger, these quirky, seemingly unrelated, objects won't mean anything, but to you they are all part of who you are. Your home should be an autobiography. What do these inanimate objects say to you and about you? What do you see when you look around? Do you see intensely personal objects, things you've found wherever you've traveled over years and years? Touch some of these favorite objects. As you fondle them, recall when this particular treasure came into your life. Where were you? Who were you with? Do you still love having these objects around? Do they open you up to good emotions?

Objects from Your Past

Are there some things around your home that tend to make you feel sad? If you've moved through certain periods in your life and something that was once very meaningful is now less so, even bittersweet, consider whether you still want to have this reminder. No one can answer these questions for you. When you have an engraved silver cigarette box with the signatures of your ushers at your wedding, for example, is it wrong to have this polished and out on your coffee table after your wife has died and you have remarried? Do some of our favorite objects cause our spouse to feel jealous? I don't think our past life should cause any pain to those in our present life, because our past is an important part of who we are now. The good memories should be kept alive. Whenever we live one part of our life fully, it should and can weave seamlessly into the next chapter.

Peter has an oval tray that is one of his most treasured possessions because it bears the names of all his friends who attended a bachelor dinner at Yale Law School in June 1948. Most of these friends are dear to me, and I love polishing this tray and using it every day. Our past leads us to where we are today and should be honored in our home. Another of Peter's favorite objects is a small silver frame holding a picture of me hugging a huge teddy bear when I was three years old. He keeps this picture on his dressing table to remind him of me as a child. I no longer am able to play tennis, but I have several photographs of me playing in tournaments when I was in my prime.

Beauty is life when life unveils her holy face.

KAHLIL GIBRAN

Sentimental Gifts

Some of my favorite objects are presents from my children and from Peter. Everywhere I look I see something that holds a special meaning in my heart. Sometimes I remember being with Alexandra or Brooke when we found a scented candle or some paper cocktail napkins, making the object come alive with the experience. Our home houses our memories, memories of special milestones in our life—birthdays, anniversaries, graduations and weddings, celebrations and ceremonies of meaningful times. As you look around your rooms and see the photograph of your grandmother, the seashells gathered on your honeymoon island escape, the first book of poetry you ever read, the crib quilt your best friend gave you when you had your first child, your crystal objects that reflect light, your colorful touches everywhere, you see that these are all significant threads that weave your personal life's story. These treasured objects are not things gathered quickly in a gift store to "accessorize" a tabletop. These personal possessions have an energy, vitality, and spirit that you feel every time you come into their presence. They make you and others feel at home.

Beautiful is greater than Good, for it includes the Good.

GOETHE

Our Objects Speak for Us

The things that define us will be present in our favorite objects. If we love horses, we will have pictures or paintings or statues of horses around our house. If we love color, we will have our favorite colors in the things we select to live with. If we are attracted to leather, we will find ways to use it in our house, whether we frame some pictures in dark-green leather frames, or we have some favorite books leather bound, or we keep our family history in leather scrapbooks, or we cover some benches in our living room in a favorite leather tone. If we love brass, we will have lots of brass objects around—paperweights, boxes, bells, and shiny brass hardware and furniture pulls. If we love silver, we can have silver picture frames, candlesticks, and bud vases, and we can use our baby cup in the bathroom to hold a flower blossom or for a water cup. Even the key chain we carry can be polished silver.

I love glass and colored glass because it is light reflecting and makes me continuously aware of how important light is to me. We should have objects around us that we adore and that also represent things we value that have become symbolic. When I use colorful drinking glasses and glass dishes, I'm constantly reminded that I am happiest when I break free and am not conventional. When something is handmade by an artist, it deepens my appreciation. I'm happy to be the one who enjoys using these colorful objects every day. Whenever we discover something refreshing and colorful that we're drawn to, it is not only fun for us but also for others to enjoy something new that represents our spirit.

Appreciating Our Possessions

Our favorite objects will be a nostalgic mix of things from our past with lots of new finds, new interests we've recently discovered. When you look around your house, identify the meaning of your treasured objects. You may see that a favorite leather box needs to be waxed and the brass handle has to be polished. As you do so, reminisce. A nice idea for making these "chores" more like little prayers is to remember where you found each object and dwell on how much it means to you. A picture of your wedding day might need the glass cleaned and the brass frame polished. It's a good time to remember how much you love your spouse and how fortunate you are to be happily married. You might want to sit in a favorite chair and silently flood your mind and heart with all the memories of why this particular chair is so meaningful to you. You remember rocking a child to sleep, sitting up late reading favorite books, or being curled up beside a cozy fire with your spouse, talking for hours with no interruptions, or going to your favorite chair to meditate each morning with a cup of tea. Most of us can identify one favorite piece of furniture, one that is as alive as a friend. Walk around your house on an appreciation tour and touch those favorite objects, giving them a little love pat.

The good is the beautiful.

PLATO

When we identify and care for the inanimate objects in our home, we give thanks for them and our consciousness has been raised. These favorite objects become filled with the breath of life, imbued with our spirit. These bits and pieces of our autobiography should be spirited but quirky, each having an interesting story behind it. When we live with these favorite objects, their energy is felt. What are the things you've grown to love that make you feel most at home?

Comfortable Furniture

All high beauty has a moral element in it.

EMERSON

Most houses that feel stiff and uncomfortably formal don't have enough well-made upholstered furniture. Looking at a room and feeling enveloped in it are two different experiences. We don't like to sit down and feel let down. Our home should make us and others physically and emotionally comfortable. When I offer my clients aesthetically pleasing designs for chairs and sofas that are also extraordinarily comfortable, they are most appreciative, but they often complain about the prices. Sitting down, lying down and putting your feet up in your living room should be divinely comfortable. The successful room is always one we want to spend the most time in, yet, ironically, living rooms are usually the most uncomfortable in the house.

Physical Ease

If a piece of furniture looks good but is not enjoyable to use, it is not appropriate for your home. Comfort should never be secondary. If you have one favorite piece of upholstered furniture, where is it located? Why do you find it comfortable? Does it soothe you, giving you a pleasurable sense of ease and well-being? Well-made upholstered furniture has the capacity to give physical ease.

Comfort comes from the Latin *conforto*, "strengthen." Clients who invest in comfortable upholstered furniture tell me they use their spaces in whole new ways. They gravitate to a high-back swivel chair near a window to read. They love to put their feet up on an ottoman. Having a nap on a long sofa with loose pillows that you can move to an ideal place, curling up under a comforter, can be a heavenly experience on a Sunday afternoon.

Too few people understand the therapeutic benefits of furniture that provides individual comfort and puts you at ease. A favorite desk or table can give us a great deal of emotional comfort, flooding our mind with good feelings and nostalgic memories. A good mattress provides support for our back for the one third of our life spent sleeping, and therefore is more important than the design of the bed itself. If you have a reading chair that is the right proportion for you—the seat is high enough and has the right pitch, the arms are in scale with the height of the back and seat—chances are you will enjoy longer, more frequent moments to read in this ideal chair.

How Do You Feel?

While it is true that an uncomfortable piece of furniture can look graceful and inviting, the test is when you use it. Try walking around your house and sitting on all the sofas and chairs. Lie down on the beds. Evaluate how comfortable each piece is for you. Where did these pieces of furniture come from? Were you there at the store trying each piece out to see if you fit well in the chair or sofa, feeling secure that you'd feel comfortable once you brought it home?

Comfort is an art. When I diagnose clients' upholstered furniture, I seek the help of a master upholsterer. It amazes me, as well as my clients, what a profound difference this comfort factor is to the quality of their living at home. We come home from a hectic day with some aches and pains. To be able to sit down, to feel the luxury of ease, the sense of contentment, the sweet sense of sinking into another world, one that is intimate, warm, soft, and safe, is the ultimate pleasure. Think of softening the hard edges of your life at home.

Re-covering the fabric on your upholstered furniture, replacing it with another, is strictly cosmetic. To reconstruct your upholstered furniture requires major surgery. Reconstruction requires going down to the frame in some cases and rebuilding the piece completely. Clients complain that a sofa or pair of chairs was recently re-covered, but as expensive as this was, they are not comfortable. If the sofa seat is not deep enough, there is no real way to correct this. If you make deeper cushions, they will look sloppy. If the arms of a sofa are too thin, they can be padded to soften the look and feeling, but this will require making new seat cushions because they will have to be made smaller. All things are linked in the making of good furniture.

Handmade Comfort

Good upholstered furniture, when it is made by human hands and not machines, lasts forever. It can be repeatedly slipcovered, re-covered, and occasionally reupholstered and can be passed on to children and grandchildren. We should buy the best we can because physical comfort is translated into our emotional and spiritual state of consciousness. Just as important as having your bad knee operated on (if that is the doctor's recommendation), is investing in upholstered furniture that will be comforting in the long run.

The ingredients used to build a chair or sofa are the keys to its comfort. Our workroom has shown me the most appalling stuff they have had to take out of the belly of a sofa or chair owned by clients. If you buy a sofa with a foam rubber cushion, in time the rubber dries up and becomes hard before it disintegrates. Goose feathers and down are ideal, but Dacron is less expensive and a good substitute for foam rubber. Furniture that once felt all right could now be hard; we should pay attention to how it cur-

Art is a microscope which the artist fixes on the secrets of his soul, and shows to people these secrets which are common to all.

LEO TOLSTOY

rently feels. Everything deteriorates gradually, but we must be sensitive and not turn our back to reality.

Comfort Is the Health of Our Home

We want our furniture to be comfortable because this is the health of our home. When we are comfortable, when we can anticipate sinking into a reading chair with ease, we are at peace, we feel serene, and we become more appreciative, more open. There are ways to make people who have back problems more comfortable. Chairs can support the lower back. Look around and feel around to evaluate how comfortable your furniture is. You might want to add some pillows to a sofa or one small one to the back of a chair to support your back. You might want to put an ottoman or a footstool in front of a chair. If you have the money, you might decide to have a chair cushion made to order for your physiological needs. Perhaps you'll add some cushions to the kitchen chairs or to those on the patio. Comfort is appreciated every day, hour by hour. Just as you deserve good food and fresh air, you deserve to feel divinely comfortable at home.

Beauty

A house is not merely a well-run machine for living. In order to elevate your daily life above the mundane, there has to be a strong aesthetic element that threads through every detail. There are many houses that run efficiently and are as clean and practical as a hospital room, but they don't elevate us to our highest creative or spiritual powers. A home that values beauty as the underpinning of all our daily rituals elevates our lives to an art form. When beauty is central to everything we think and do, our ordinary domestic chores and routines can continuously be transformed into loving grace notes.

To the best of our ability, we should see to it that there is nothing ugly in our home. Go on another tour around your house. Evaluate whether you feel uncomfortable seeing something unsightly. What is it you see? You could shudder at the mess on your spouse's desk or dread looking at the beige plastic wastepaper basket with the black plastic cinch-top bag. You may look at an arrangement of dried flowers that has no energy or color and is depressingly dusty. There might be some cutesy gift store items you never liked but tolerated.

Look in a kitchen cabinet. Examine your pots and pans. When you are cooking, these decorate your kitchen. They can be handsome, if not beautiful. In our cottage we have cobalt-blue pots and pans. Examine the knives you cut with and the tools you use. Are they efficient for you? Sharp enough? Colorful whenever possible? Look at the objects you use and see every day. There are thousands of different details at home. We should be cheered up by what we see and touch.

When we see with the consciousness of beauty, we add finishing touches that create more grace in our immediate surroundings.

Art is the communication of a state of mind.

IMMANUEL KANT

If we have an ant problem, we can hide the gray trap behind the coffee maker in order not to be confronted by it unnecessarily. Medication can be stored in attractive pill boxes, not in prescription bottles lined up on the kitchen window ledge. We can work out a solution to our garbage containers in order not to offend ourselves and our neighbors. We can repot our pansies or blue hydrangea in terracotta pots or colorful cachepots to hide the green plastic of the florist's pot. Looking in the linen closet, examining our supplies of towels, sheets, tablecloths, and napkins, we can weed out what we no longer find attractive. By reviewing our possessions, we can upgrade our home with some of our favorite things.

Beauty Day by Day

Many of my clients have set themselves free by using their best china, crystal, and silverware every day at home. Beauty makes every moment memorable. Whenever something is mediocre, we tend not to remember it at all. But our good memories of being at home nourish the present moment and give us hope for the future. I have a client who loves to set the table. She takes pictures of her everyday table settings and keeps the images in colorful storage boxes. The mentality of saving the best for company is wrong. We work hard, and whenever we nourish our souls with beauty, we are lifted up on angels' wings. We are meant to celebrate each moment with as much thought and care and beauty as we're capable of. If we put a little extra thought and care into creating something pretty, we set the stage for intimacy and contemplation of life's beauty and mysteries that go beyond the four walls of our house. The reason beauty is so important is that it opens us up to love. Beauty and love can't be reserved for rare occasions any more than breathing can. They are a way of living at home.

Light.

HENRI MATISSE
(In answer to a journalist's question on the meaning of modern art)

We can soak in beauty in every corner of our home, in every ritual we create, in every tea celebration, in every contemplative moment when beauty rises us to a higher, lighter, more ethereal place. Looking around, feast your eyes on some beautiful objects and identify how they make you feel. I always get an instant uplift when I look at our paperweights, hand-colored marbles, marbleized boxes, cups full of colored pencils, hand-blown colored glasses, botanical watercolors, porcelain fruits and vegetables, and Mühl paintings. Beauty can be our teacher, helping us to live on a level held up by a power greater than our own. Beauty comforts us in our sadness at our losses and makes us euphoric when we celebrate a marriage or a christening or an anniversary. To try to make our modest, even private, moments more beautiful is one sure way to assure we will live a beautiful life. Living at home is a dynamic process of self-attunement and self-expression that increases our faith and enlarges our hope. We need inspiration to want to live beautifully. The beauty in our midst sustains us as well as inspires us. If we believe the beauty we feel inside us can be expressed outwardly, we will be free to have our surroundings be an expression of our true selves.

Each of us has to choose beauty as our daily bread. We can't put our lives on hold waiting for more time after the children are older. As parents, one of the greatest gifts we can give our children beyond food, clothing, shelter, love, and an education is a sense of humor and a sense of beauty. To go anywhere in the world and feel comfortable is a rare and liberating gift, one we can pass on to future generations once we feel comfortable ourselves. When we sit down as a family to a pretty table, we will be nourished. It is this grace that prepares us to give of our own gifts to others.

Beauty is a quality that both pleases and delights the senses, the mind, and the spirit. When we are sensually pleased, our mind can think in clarity. We must not feel beauty is a luxury. Beauty is God's way of our living more divinely on earth. Let the hand of beauty touch everything you do at home. Regardless of what you do, do it beautifully. Challenge yourself to strive for beauty in every act. Have a beautiful bath by lighting a candle, using an herb bubble bath, drying yourself in an iris-blue oversize towel. Have a beautiful evening. Listen to favorite music, dine under the stars by candlelight. With beauty there is no end, only your beautiful precious moments at home.

Art

Whether we paint, write poetry, garden, or cook, we are happiest when we do creative and imaginative activities at home. Even if we aren't professional artists, we are appreciators of others' works and benefit from having meaningful art in our home.

Most of the art Peter and I collect for our apartment and cottage is by living artists. We know each one of these artists, ranging from our grandchildren and our daughters to master watercolorists and painters. Selecting favorite paintings and hanging them on the walls of our rooms gives us and our family and friends a great deal of daily happiness. We move our paintings around regularly so that our vision of them will stay alert and fresh. Two of my favorite Mühl paintings are now in my Zen writing room, where no one sees them but me. One is of a rooftop with sky and water merging in the background, and the other is of a cottage by the sea. The art we live with should be there for us, every day, in the places where we spend our time.

I've never asked anyone's advice about art. I just buy what I am passionate about. In 1961, I bought a tiny watercolor, the size of a postcard, of Lake Como, in Italy, from an artist on the street for $1.50, and I consider this one of our greatest treasures. I have it on my desk in my Zen room because it is so delicate and refined, and I like being able to observe it without interruption.

I've found that the paintings I was drawn to when I was younger, I still adore. In fact, I discovered an artist whose work I loved when I was twenty years old and I've gone on to collect his work ever since, for more than thirty-eight years. Just as with the creation of music or a poem or prose, we are attracted to certain works of art because they enter into a chamber inside our soul where we feel a connection, exhilarating and rare. All too often people buy art to decorate a wall. While this isn't a terrible thing to do, the problem lies in the lack of passion. Selecting a painting because of its size or color scheme might mean you will pick one that you like, but don't love. The wall space and color scheme you have today could be very different tomorrow. And if you move your collection from wall to wall or room to room or even house to house, you realize that so much more goes into the placement of a painting than the size or colors. The subject matter of a picture has more significance than where you locate it. I've seen a six-inch-square oil painting, beautifully framed, placed in a hallway on the stairwell that looks spectacular because the flowering apple tree in the sunlight gives you the experience of being in an orchard. Whenever you make this spiritual connection with a painting, it is no longer a picture in a frame hung on a wall, but a window opening you up to experience light, color, and beauty. You are there, one with the painting, experiencing something beautiful.

When you fall in love with a painting, and your hair stands up on end and you have goosebumps everywhere,

> *I don't think anyone has a right to possess anything he doesn't love—art or anything else.*
>
> BILLY BALDWIN

pay attention. Don't regret, years later, that you didn't purchase it because it wasn't a "perfect" size. I've removed frames from pictures in order to add a "window with a great view" to a room. In the living room of our cottage, we have a painting resting on the mantel because it is too high to hang. It looks fine and I would feel deprived if there were a smaller picture there.

If you buy what you love, and then find a place to hang it, chances are the painting will always be an important part of your permanent collection, moving with you wherever you call home. If you buy with size or other factors in mind, you may grow tired of these pictures in the years ahead.

Art is not handicraft, but rather the offspring of a touch of genius.

PETER MEGARGEE BROWN

As we mature and our tastes and aesthetics evolve, as we become more discerning, we will undoubtedly outgrow some of our art and objects. Knowing when it's time to "retire" an object (maybe put it away, sell it, or donate it to a charity) because we no longer resonate to it is healthy and a concrete sign of our individual growth. I have four flower paintings I no longer love because I now realize I don't like pictures with dark backgrounds. Peter has some nineteenth-century pictures of cows in bucolic settings I don't like because they are too dark.

While most living artists' work is priced according to the size of the canvas or paper, no artists' creations are equally good. If you buy what you love, you will probably be buying the artist's best work. You have to trust your feelings. An art dealer wants to sell the good with the less inspired. You will always know how you feel, and your sense of connection to a work of art is central to making a selection.

Art gives our daily lives significance.

The investment you are making is one that will bring you joy for years and years, influencing you, cheering you, keeping you company. What is beautiful and fine and uplifting to you is what matters. Now that Peter and I select paintings together, we both have to love something in order to buy it, but we've found over all these years how similar our tastes have become.

If you feel strongly about a work of art, make whatever sacrifices you can to buy something that speaks to you in powerful ways. Set up an art fund. Go to art shows, auctions, and galleries to educate your eye and discover your tastes. Check out the local school's art classes. Age has little to do with talent. Consider commissioning a young artist whose work you like to paint a picture of your garden or your house.

Purchasing favorite posters or prints from museum collections is inexpensive and will bring you great pleasure. While there is nothing as good as the original, reproductions on paper are fine, especially if you are familiar with the original in a museum. The oil reproductions that are popular I think are wrong. They're too expensive for what they are; they're fakes and have no soul. Far better to buy a poster, put it under glass, and save up for an original you can afford.

Art points the way to how beautiful our daily lives can be.

Lithographs are a wonderful way to have original art that is duplicated but in limited editions and numbered. A lithograph maintains its value and is a fraction of the cost of an oil painting or a watercolor by the same artist. There are some lithographs that are so beautiful, they look like watercolors.

Artists who try to point us to the light and beauty in our everyday existence are grace bearers to us. When it is storming outside, we can look at the beautiful botanical prints of all our favorite flowers and know that spring is around the corner and that our garden, once again, will begin to bloom. Knowing as many artists as we do adds a big dimension to our happiness at home. If you like certain living artists' work at galleries where you look at art, inquire when the next show of their work will be and whether the artists will be there.

Just as an autographed book connects you to the author, a signature on a painting or a lithograph makes a more important connection between you and the work of art and the creator, and being able to meet the person who opened up your heart is an added pleasure.

Let the artist's spirit be your way to greater harmony and comfort at home. Let favorite artists paint the way for you to rise up above the day-to-day frustrations, anxieties, and stresses that urge us to compress time rather than live beautifully. Let these men, women, and children whose art we adore be constant reminders to us that we are surrounded by a spiritual ambience. The atmosphere at home should be full of artistic grace. Whether you collect ceramics, quilts, or hand-blown glass objects—glasses, paperweights, and bottles—they will collectively add to your happiness at home.

Change

Every new day at home should have some surprises, some newness that stimulates us and awakens us to be fully alive. Change can be refreshing to our eye and our spirit. One of the saddest ways to limit our live's possibilities is to be rigid at home. The atmosphere that increases my ch'i is one that arouses my senses, awakens me, stirs me up, and excites me. How much stimulation each of us desires is decidedly personal, but I would be frustrated and bored in an inflexible environment, regardless of my inner resources. Changing my surroundings encourages me to improve things around me and invariably increases my energy as well as making me more optimistic and hopeful.

Keep Your House Current

While it is extremely important to have certain elements of our home be predictable, such as clocks, newspaper delivery, the stove, and the kitchen table, we should never close our minds and have our houses locked in a state of status quo. Every new day we are a different person. We see the world with fresh eyes and we have new needs and desires, new possessions, new goals. At home, our house must keep pace with our changing lives as they unfold, staying current with our interests and life passages.

Change Is Good

Why are so many people afraid of change? I've helped clients decorate their houses, and when I go back ten years later everything is
the same but tired-looking. Chances are, the way we're living at
home can be improved. Change gives us the opportunity to be different, to alter our current way. I believe we can improve
our lives every day at home and change is the instrument for
doing so. Perhaps one reason I love to garden and tend living plants is that nothing ever stays the same. After a heavy
rainstorm, we have to prune and remove the dead blossoms
to make way for the buds to bloom. There is always some
fresh color appearing that wasn't there yesterday. We can
observe changes in nature, and we can be inspired to create
changes in our immediate surroundings. By accepting nature's
changes, including the weather, we learn about our strengths as well
as our shortcomings and can make constructive change.

> *No pleasure endures
> unseasoned by variety.*
>
> PUBLILIUS SYRUS

Seasons Change, So Must We

When the seasons change we can make some adjustments in order
to celebrate the shift of weather. What feels cozy in December
could feel confining in July. In the summer, we can take up all the
rugs and put slipcovers on our furniture to give a clean, pared-
down feeling that cools the spirit. In the winter, we can add a
wool throw to our sofa and cozy up to the fireplace. Your desk
can be placed against a wall in your study in the winter, but come
springtime, you want to feel free. You can place it in the middle of
the space with your chair facing the window and view.

We all set up ways to live, but when we strictly adhere to
them, turning ways into rules, we are living in the past rather
than looking at our needs right now, finding fresh ways to adapt
to change. Because there's not one right way to live at home, we
should question everything, looking for ways to modify, replace,

or even transform not only our spaces but the way we live out our rituals.

How Receptive to Change Are You?

How receptive are you to change? One of my clients has a cleaning helper who always places the umbrella stand kitty-corner in their elevator hall. Rather than placing it on one wall or another, it is displayed in order to hide the harsh corner. This change seems to make sense and is endearing. Why shouldn't someone who helps us clean our house also be able to leave an imprint? We had a cleaning woman from South America who always folded the quilt at the end of our bed in a triangle, rather than the rectangular way I always folded it. Long after she left to live with her sister in Peru, Theresa's way of folding our various quilts at the foot of the bed still gave us a lift. Sometimes when I go to a friend's house for dinner, I see the tongs of the fork facing down. To my accustomed way of setting the table, the fork is upside down. But when I set my own table and experiment, I find the change refreshing.

We can make a deliberate decision to use different rooms at different times for different uses. For example, if we only think of our living room as a formal place where we entertain our guests, we will be robbing ourselves of the pleasure of going there in the afternoon to have tea, read, or have a conversation with a spouse, a child, or a neighbor who dropped by. Some of the most glorious times in our living rooms are during the daylight. Whether it's breakfast by the windows, soup and salad seated by the fire, afternoon tea, or Peter enjoying working at his desk, we use our living room throughout the day. If we limited this room to being used in the evenings, we would be depriving ourselves of some of our most memorable moments at home. It is extremely limiting to name rooms, because the tendency is to put them to their literal use. When we call a room a living room, we wrongly think of it as only for entertaining, not for every day. When we have a guest room, we forget to turn on the fan and have a nap in the cool side of the house in July and August when we're not having house guests.

What are some changes you've made at home in the past year? Do you tend to make seasonal changes, where you have breakfast on your terrace or patio or balcony during the summer months? Do you follow the light and use your living room in the afternoon in order to enjoy the setting sun in the west? Moving around to different parts of various rooms to read and work is stimulating. How often do you change the way your bed looks when you change the sheets? Do you have different quilts or comforters to coordinate with other sets of sheets? Duvet covers are great for instant new looks. Always alternate patterns with solids and color changes. When you wash the bathroom towels, do you put back a different color just for variety? When you reach for a plate for cut-up fruit for breakfast, do you select one you haven't seen for a few days?

By continuously trying to bring more variety into our daily lives at home, we remain stimulated and find that the routine things we do take on a spice that perks up our appetite for life. For a start, look to the four seasons for stimulation. Become more aware where you like to be at home during the winter, spring, fall, and summer, and what times of day, during different weather, you like to sit by the fire or by a favorite window with a view of the garden.

All things change, but nothing dies.

OVID

Nothing is static. Human nature either goes up or goes down.

MOHANDAS K. GANDHI

My Dopey, Inspirational Day

Recently, I woke up and felt awful. I had a dopey day, flopping on every chair, lounging on every sofa, trying to get comfortable in order to feel better. While resting on a love seat in our study, looking up at the ceiling, I realized it should be painted pale blue.

I saw a lithograph in the back hall that would look perfect in the kitchen. I saw a mirror I wanted to place on a wall opposite a window to bring in more light. I had to get sick in order to have a new perspective. All the changes improve the way the cottage looks and feels. There is now a flower watercolor in the back hall that looks so attractive with the flower chintz on the love seat in the study. I realized I'd never stretched out on the love seat. I'm glad I did.

Nothing ever is, but all things are becoming . . . All things are the offspring of flux and motion.

SOCRATES

Experimenting

Open yourself up to the fun of using different-colored candles, colored napkins, different plates for salad and dessert. Recently, I ran out of terra-cotta pots for several flats of white geraniums. I looked around for containers and ended up using a series of blue mixing bowls. They couldn't look more charming. The fact that they have etched on their sides *Salt, Pepper, Flour,* and *Sugar* adds to the charm. Enjoy using your things in fresh new ways. A little etched-crystal wineglass can be a flower holder for some miniature rosebuds or some pansies. A quilt you usually have at the foot of your bed can be hung on a wall in your family room. A hand-painted porcelain food platter with handles can be used as a tray for tea for two in the garden. Dessert plates you rarely use can be hung on the dining room wall for decoration until you want to change them and use them for fruit in the morning or for salads at dinner. Your colorful plastic-handled stainless steel flatware is so good looking, you don't use it only for picnics, but enjoy it for festive breakfasts in the garden or for hearty winter soup, salad, and homemade bread by a crackling fire in early December. A friend received a fine china jam jar for a wedding gift that she used on her dressing table to hold her jewelry. I was given an ashtray in which I put my rings on my mother's dressing table that I inherited. If you inherit two jade-green egg cups, why not let them hold your loose change on your dresser?

Everything is connected . . . no one thing can change by itself.

PAUL HAWKEN

Whatever takes place inside us should have expression in our immediate surroundings. By making significant little changes, we're improving the quality of our experiences. This should be an ongoing process that never ends. Embrace change as your teacher. Let your environment always be receptive to your growing needs, anticipating them in creative, useful ways. Once we accept change and greet novelty and newness with an open mind and heart, we're free to live the way that brings us the most emotional comfort. When we act on our instincts, we're constantly on our path to set ourselves free.

As Samuel Johnson said: "To be happy at home is the ultimate result of all ambition, the end to which every enterprise tends."

There is nothing in this world constant, but consistency.

JONATHAN SWIFT

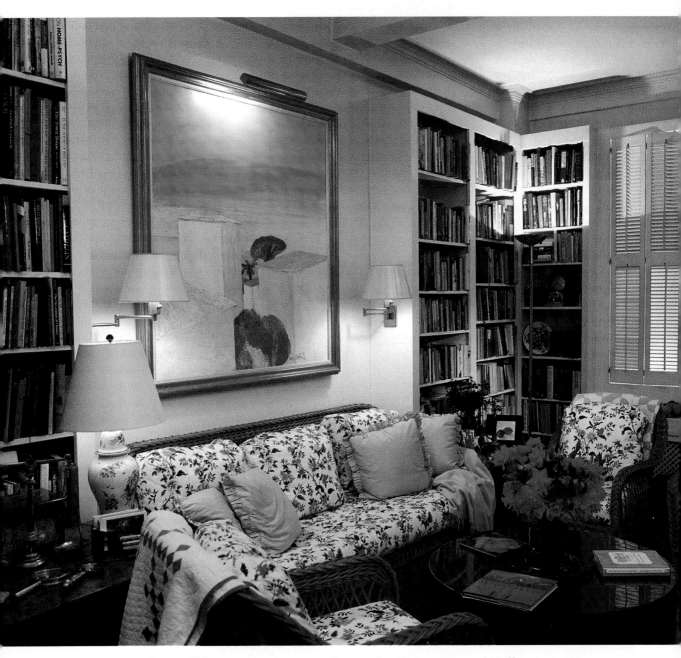

In this well-lit room we can read, rest, listen to music, or talk,
surrounded by our home library, under the "sky blue" ceiling.

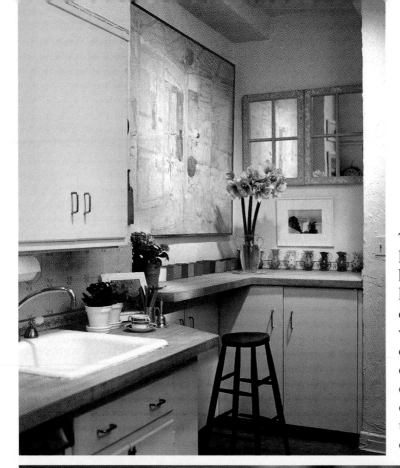

The far end of the kitchen has windowpane mirrors that bring in more light. We don't hesitate to hang fine art in our kitchen because this is where we spend time and can appreciate the art. I designed a group of spiral colored glasses we keep on display and put to constant use for drinks or as flower containers.

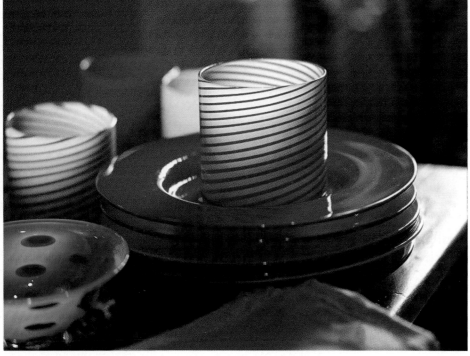

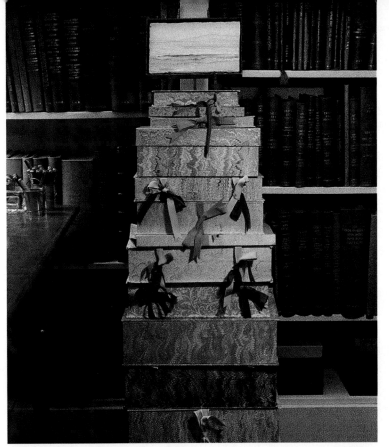

Storage can be beautiful and accessible. These boxes, next to the desk where Peter and I work, contain everything from family photos to important documents. Quilts bring us emotional comfort.

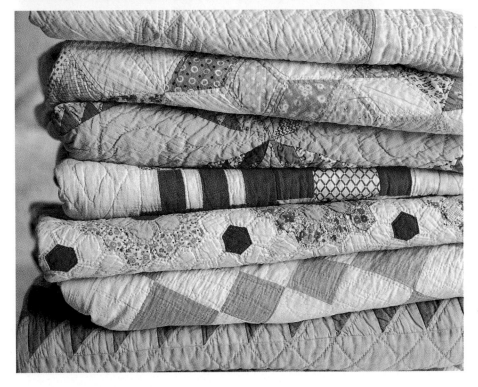

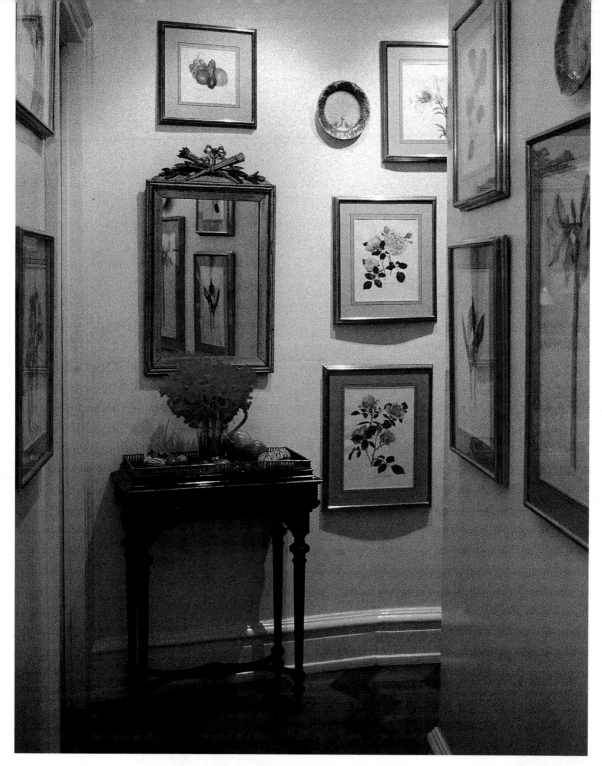

A hallway can be an experience. Here, because of our botanical water-colors, we feel we're strolling in a garden in full bloom.

CHAPTER 4

Balancing Your Time at Home

May you live all the days of your life.
—JONATHAN SWIFT

Where You Spend Your Time

How do you spend a typical day at home? First, think of a workday, say Monday or Tuesday, and then think of a weekend, Saturday or Sunday. Assuming you feel "time bankrupt" along with most of us, these questions will help you to clarify what you do so that you may better plan your time. Seeing where you are wasting your energy helps you to balance your time at home. In addition to your notebook, buy an inexpensive digital stopwatch, or use your kitchen timer. If you have one of those old-fashioned, three-minute hourglass timers, the kind we used to use to time eggs and keep our telephone calls to three minutes, that will also come in handy. Now, let's examine, under a magnifying glass, what you do at home each day, Monday through Sunday.

No time like the present.
MARY DE LA
RIVIÈRE MANLEY

*Lost, yesterday somewhere
between sunrise and sunset,
two golden hours, each set
with sixty diamond minutes.
No reward is offered, for
they are gone forever.*

HORACE MANN

First, let's look at the pattern of your day. What time do you usually get up on a weekday? Do you feel rested, or would you prefer to sleep some more? Do you get up at this prescribed time because you have to? Is it because you have to go to work, or you have to get your children up for school, or is it simply a habit?

Who else in your household gets up at the same time you do? Do you make your own breakfast? How long does it take? Do you read the paper while you eat your breakfast? How long do you usually spend eating and reading, where you're relaxed enjoying some uninterrupted time? Do you feel pressed for time or have you built in enough time to make this morning ritual a pleasant one? Where do you eat breakfast? Always the same place? What do you eat, usually? Do you eat the same thing every weekday morning? Do you ever change the way you cook your egg, or eat a different kind of fruit? Do you have any other daily activities you do every morning? Do you take a run before you eat? Do you walk your dog? On average, from the time you wake up, get up, do your bathing ritual, exercise, prepare breakfast, read, dress, and leave the house, how much time have you spent? In the bathroom? In the kitchen? Exercising? How long have you been in this breakfast routine?

*Each day we should give
ourselves time to grow into a
more loving, generous,
spirited, content individual.*

If you had more time, would you develop more variety in what you eat for breakfast? Would you ever have breakfast in the dining room or at the table in the sunroom? Is it possible to take a later train to work? Who expects you at your desk so early? What time do you return home after work? Five days a week? You're home after dark except around the summer solstice. You leave home in the dark. Do you wish you could spend more time at home?

More Time at Home

It takes time to save time.

JOE TAYLOR

Often we get into patterns and do the same things year after year, forgetting we are older now, and there are different ways of accomplishing our work goals. A busy executive who has to lead others and who spends a great deal of time in long meetings, might be wealthy monetarily, but is clearly not spending enough quality time at home to balance his professional or business life. A client explained to me how he longed to have a more flexible schedule at the office. By evaluating how time deprived he was at home, confessing he spent an average of only ten minutes a day with his children during the week, he was able to work out a schedule where he went to the office four days a week. On Fridays, he worked from home, wore jeans and a T-shirt, had lunch with his wife, did some gardening, had a late afternoon tennis game with regular partners, and had time to play with his children. The company didn't suffer from this change of work patterns. Meetings were shorter and better organized. Now he is free to enjoy his home three out of seven days.

A mother of three young children confessed to me that she felt as though she was drowning in housework. When I asked her the following questions about how she spent her time, her answers were most revealing: What time do you get up in the morning? Do you have any quiet time alone before the family awakens? What do you do in that time? Where do you like to sit? If you are interrupted during this time, how do you feel? Who helps you prepare breakfast? Why don't the children help you? Does your husband pitch in? Why not? How long do you actually sit at the breakfast table with the family? That doesn't seem enough time for you to enjoy your breakfast. Do you eat standing up? Why? What's the rush?

The woman was physically at home, yet she was not at home emotionally. I learned that this client is a perfectionist who likes to control everything. She begins her day alone when she sips coffee, meditates, and reads the Bible and inspirational affirmations. Then she goes flat out for the rest of the day in some kind of turbo work mode as though she were a hired hand. She does the breakfast dishes, the laundry, irons, waters the plants, changes the cat litter, and vacuums the pet hair off the furniture and rugs. Between going to the market, shopping, putting the supplies away, dusting, polishing, and preparing dinner, this woman, who does not have a paying

If you are fundamentally on your path to your true home, channeling your energy upward toward more beauty and more light, your struggle will be lifted up to be part of a more universal perspective.

One must learn to husband time carefully, in order to enjoy life in the here and now.

MIHALY
CSIKSZENTMIHALYI

Time ran like immortal
water; I felt my head sailing
above time.

NIKOS KAZANTZAKIS

job, has turned into a machine at home. No wonder she isn't feeling wonderful on a daily basis at home. She wasn't aware that from 7:30 A.M. to 11 P.M. she never stopped to sit down except in her car, whirling around doing errands and shuttling the children to choir practice and soccer games. She ate a snack on the fly. This lifestyle is insane.

Why?

We all want very much the same thing. We all want to be happy on a day-to-day basis. When that isn't happening, we have to stop and ask ourselves: Why are we doing what we're doing? When the children are off at school and our spouse is at work, why can't we do whatever we darn well want to in these hours of free time? Let the cat play in the fenced-in yard and not on the living room furniture. There are always unfinished chores that can be done at another time. People who can't sit down and be still until everything around them is in perfect order may end up having a nervous breakdown. The house is for everyone's plea-sure. Just because we are born female doesn't mean we have to assume all the domestic responsibilities. I would never sit down if I had to have everything clean and in order beforehand. Our identity shouldn't be in how the house looks as much as how we feel as we live our lives each day at home.

My client lacks self-esteem and tries to please others at the expense of enjoying her own life and at the tragic waste of her energies. Rather than proving herself to the world through housework, she could spend more time developing her ambition to be a writer of fiction. She never has time to read or write after her day begins at breakfast.

Being there.

SOCRATES

What Do You Want to Do More Of?

Do you feel you are spending too much time on routine mainte-nance? Federal Reserve economists recently concluded that "the real cost of living isn't measured in dollars and cents, but in hours and minutes we must work to live." If you feel time squeezed, what would be some ways you would like to free up some time? What are some things you love to do that relax you and give you pleasure? Take time now to identify some interests you'd love to spend more time pursuing. Some of mine are:

Reading
Writing
Gardening
Interior house painting
Photography
Correspondence
Polishing brass and silver
Organizing family memorabilia
Editing my slides

Being at home is better than an ideal vacation because we have all the comforts we love under one roof.

Write down as many things as you can think of, being sure not to write down projects you feel you *should* do. If you don't feel like cooking more, don't list cooking because you feel you might learn to like it. If you want a break from entertaining, admit you want some time off. If your garden is too big, either get a teenager to come help you pull weeds and prune, or redesign your space so it is manageable.

Our Own Terms

We all have to design our own life on our own terms. We do this by defining what we want to give to our life and what we want to get out of it. Both the high-powered executive and the client with three children (who wouldn't have help in the house because she assumed the role of housekeeper) needed to reevaluate how they were spending their time. The president and CEO worked so doggedly to climb the corporate ladder that he forgot he was on the

When no one asks me what time is, I know, but when I would give an explanation of it in answer to a man's question, I do not know.

SAINT AUGUSTINE

top rung. He could now take a deep breath and contemplate a more balanced life and be more available to his family. My female client had to learn to ease up on her role-playing of wife, mother, and housewife. By writing her habits in her notebook, she was able to analyze why she wasn't progressing with her desire to write. With discipline she was able to spend two hours a day at the computer, sitting down!

The stimulation comes from within when we're relaxing at home.

Setting Yourself Free

How much time he gains who does not look to see what his neighbor says or does or thinks, but only at what he does himself, to make it just and holy.

MARCUS AURELIUS

I remember *Working Woman* magazine photographing my green office at the apartment; the journalist quoted me as saying, "If I'm not having fun, I don't do it." I was slightly embarrassed at the time, feeling selfish, but all these years later I believe that what I said is pretty accurate. Doing what seems like fun at the time is an excellent way to set yourself free. None of us achieves the satisfaction and fulfillment of personal accomplishments without balancing our time and reclaiming more for ourselves to use as we choose to spend it.

Why do so many of us have such unrealistically high standards for the way we live? We have limited resources of time, energy, and money, yet we often make foolish choices. Not only do they cost us too much money, but in order to pay for them, we work too hard, which causes us to feel tired, anxious and stressed out. For many of us, the scale of our lives is too grand for our limited resources. We might have to make some adjustments to free up more time for doing some of the fun things we want to do, not all the chores we feel we should do. There aren't many things I do that I dread doing because I do them in the swing of the day when the spirit moves me and not because I'm driven by someone else's expectations. I do things in a comfortable rhythm. I spell out my needs and make it clear what my intentions are. If there are too many conflicting demands on my time and things are not as much fun as they should be, I simply cut back, even if I have to cancel dates and reschedule. I refuse to

raise my blood pressure because of other people's agendas. I try to
live by my own design and on my own terms.

Letting Go

Although I am fairly organized and usually know where
things are, there is a lot going on in my mind and in my life,
and keeping up with everything sometimes seems impossible.
No matter how well I try to plan things, there are often too
many demands on my time, and deadlines come at busy
times, often in confluence, making me have to overstretch
myself. This happens to all of us, and we have to cope and
even thrive when we're too busy. To relieve this dilemma,
I've learned to let go. I refuse to lose sight of the fact that I love what
I'm doing. I just need the freedom to spend the necessary time to
accomplish my goals. I do one thing at a time and focus on it to the
best of my ability and don't try to clean the house and have
friends over at the same time. There are periods in our lives
when things are not normal, and we should feel free to get
through them as pleasantly as possible. I've learned how to
say no in order to free up the space for me to say yes to my
own dreams and work.

Chits of time
so few remain
treat them with care
treat them with love.

SAYING

   As much as we love our house, housework can and should take
a backseat during times when we have set goals to accomplish something specific, and all our energies need to be focused on that project
if we intend to succeed. Look at your list of things you want
to spend more time doing. Do at least two of these things
today. Sit down in a favorite chair and spend one hour reading the book that you've had on your bedside table but have
been too tired to read. Set the kitchen timer for sixty minutes
and don't get up until it rings. If you have to do your reading when your children are having their nap, do. Discipline
yourself not to answer the telephone or be distracted in any way. If
you really value spending more time reading, only you can put the
book in your lap. You have to read it. Choose something else on

We all need time and quiet
just to be at home.

There is a budding
morrow in midnight.

JOHN KEATS

your list, say correspondence, and write three letters today. Sit at your desk, get a favorite pen, open a box of stationery, address the envelopes, put on some stamps, and write away. Tomorrow, select two more things you wish to do. Don't tell anyone what you're doing. No one really cares as much as you'd hope they would. Just do it. Within a few days your family will feel you're happier, lighter, and softer. Try this for a week and then continue it as a way of living at home. You'll see that nothing breaks and you learn to bend. Life has a sweeter, gentler rhythm.

Some clients confide in me that they're too nervous to sit still, to read, or to write letters. Their minds are racing in a thousand directions. No matter how hard it is at first, force yourself to concentrate. It is impossible to ever be content if we can't amuse ourselves sitting still, focused on our own desires, our needs, and feelings. How did you feel after spending one uninterrupted hour? What did you choose to read? Did you learn something useful for your life from the hour you invested in yourself? How did you feel when you sat at your desk and took the time to write three letters? Who did you write? Did you enjoy yourself in the process? Did it feel good to have an intimate conversation on paper with several people you love and want to let know you are thinking of them? How did you decide whom to write to? Was it intuitive, or were there unanswered letters on your desk you felt obligated to answer?

Living Well Takes Time

I used to pride myself on answering every letter I received until I received a flood of letters and the joy turned into an obligation, and rather than loving the process, I lost my Zen and timed myself to see how quickly I could write a note. Whenever we try to speed things up in order to be more efficient, we deprive ourselves of the sensuous satisfaction of the process: savoring the color of the stationery, enjoying seeing a series of pretty flowered stamps, appreciating the squeak of the fountain pen as it marches from left to right on the page. When we crack open a book, we like to examine the jacket design as well as the text, we look at the copyright page to see if it is a first edition, we browse the table of contents and begin our journey of discovery. All of this takes time. To dart into a chapter, speed reading, without this preamble is a mild form of deprivation. Every time we don't give ourselves time, we are in danger of becoming imbalanced. Reading slowly, savoring the way the words paint pictures, losing ourself in a writer's story, daydreaming, musing about our lives, is a most relaxing way to achieve more balance in how we spend our time.

Living well, we all know, takes time. Whenever we are lost in enjoyment, time disappears. Only when we lose ourselves in the swing do we find our true selves in a moment of ecstasy and delight. Modern-day irritations seem almost to conspire to keep us from losing ourselves in our higher awareness. A fax comes in, the telephone rings, the clothes dryer buzzes to alert us that the clothes are dry. Do we jump up with jangled nerves and automatically fold them? Yes, if we do this when they're hot, there are fewer wrinkles. But what about the wrinkles in our soul that only we can smooth out? Time is our greatest healer.

Value your individual needs separate from the collective needs of your family.

Balance Means Equal

One important discovery in our brief lifetime is to take our *self* as seriously as we take others. There are interests and hobbies and things we enjoy doing that have nothing to do with the home or our family but can be accomplished in the home. We should not get distracted by fixing up and maintaining our physical environment at the expense of nurturing what is inside us. The house can run smoothly. A good balance for me is fifty/fifty: spending half my time filling my own well and half my time maintaining and sustaining my life as a wife, mother, friend, worker, and volunteer. If we are not personally fulfilled in ways other than our relationship to our work, our house,

Time is the distinctive dimension of human personality.

O. HOBART MOWRER

our spouse, and our children, life at home will become drudgery rather than a blessing. If I didn't have my own time, I'd give to others with a less loving heart because I had not nourished the giver. We should always give from a feeling of fullness and pleasure.

Today, women are liberated in many ways, but many haven't freed themselves of the guilt of not having a perfectly kept house and garden on display twenty-four hours a day. I refuse to let my household responsibilities and maintenance ever get me down, because my house should hold and cradle me. I love our house with such devotion; it is a hymn, a symphony of all I've ever hoped or dreamed of. I respect its energy and sacred atmosphere too much to ever feel put upon when I know that our home is our greatest blessing. If I can't do something around the home in a gracious, loving, appreciative consciousness, I don't do it. Feeling at home is too precious. I do soul work before I do housework, so that when I putter around the house, it is a meditation.

Yellow Pages

Write down what you spend a lot of time doing that you wish you could and would delegate. Some men know how to mist a shirt, fold it with the collar tucked in, and then spray-starch it so there are no wrinkles. I'm not married to one of those guys. If something in our household has to be ironed, I am the laundress. Peter helps out in other ways, but he doesn't do laundry or ironing. And even though I love to iron, when I am in the stream of my writing, I don't like to feel obligated to iron Peter's shirts. They are sent to the dry cleaner when we're in New York, but our village cleaner went out of business and Peter's dirty shirts piled up. By looking in the Yellow Pages we found a dry cleaner who picks up on Fridays and delivers on Tuesdays. This frees me to iron tablecloths or pillow shams or press my slacks when I feel like it, without having to worry about Peter not having a clean, ironed shirt to wear to dinner. I iron when the spirit moves me, and when this happens, I am happy. I let it happen and it is effortless.

Debbie Folds Our Clothes

To free up my time to read and write more hours a day, we use a local laundry when we're at the cottage. Debbie picks up our colorful laundry bags on her way to the bank to deposit checks and delivers them back to us the next day, clean, folded, and ready to wear. I love to do laundry and never find it an effort in New York because the laundry room is off the kitchen with a window looking east, and I use this time to think and ponder. While the morning coffee is being made, I can fold a load of wash and start another batch. But in our old cottage there is no place for a washer and dryer except in the basement, and it would be a chore to go down there to do the wash. Someday we'll have a washer and dryer downstairs, when we have more grandchildren, but for now it is easier this way. Even if I'd like to do a few loads of wash, not having the equipment frees my time. This is one less thing to think about and one less thing to do.

Each of us has projects we don't want to delegate, regardless of how much time these tasks take or how much money we save. If we enjoy baking, for example, why would we buy an expensive strawberry tart if it would actually give us pleasure to bake one ourselves? If we're spending too much time doing household chores we dread, we're not free to do some of the time-consuming things that bring us great satisfaction.

Ah! the clock is always slow;
It is later than you think.

ROBERT W. SERVICE

"Hurry Never"

What are some of the things you most love to do around your house? Write down the things you do when you are in the best of moods. The way to enjoy what we're doing is not to be in a hurry.

The Buddha instructs us to "Hurry never." Whenever I am in the swing of the present moment, not concerned about the future, not worried about what might or might not happen, I usually have a good time. Any task done well in a glad frame of mind is satisfying. When I'm not watching the clock, I'm perfectly content to polish some silver and brass. The same task would be a strain if it were executed under duress. Timing is propitious, the kindly gracious moment. Let your spirit guide you when you do dishes or pay bills or do some hand-washing or scrub the bathroom floor.

My favorite time to do the dishes at the cottage is when the sun hits the white porcelain sink and I can see the rainbow in the bubbles of the Joy detergent. When we are at home, we should be guided by our spirit, letting our will, mind, and feelings inform us as often as possible. The key is to stay alert to how we want to live and how we are currently living. No matter what adjustments we have to make, we should do whatever it takes to never feel coerced in our own house.

Our emotions change quickly depending on how much we're enjoying what we're doing.

Resources: Ours and Others

Traditionally, the running of the house was left in the hands of the woman. Today we're working, helping with the finances, and we have less household help than ever. But husbands are also helping out more. They cook, do laundry, garden, shop, and help care for the children. We have amazing services now: people who clean our house with their own equipment, people who mow the lawn with their own mower. Services pick up and deliver. We're more health and weight conscious and are serving simpler meals using fresher ingredients. For those who enjoy cooking, it is a creative time, and you can get in the swing of orchestrating a wonderful meal, making the process a relaxing, happy experience. The same meal you prepare lovingly could be done begrudgingly. Rather than feeling the weight of all those meals, write in your notebook all the easy ways to simplify your efforts.

No one can enjoy cooking from scratch every day. There are

Transcend the boundaries of the present moment in time.

ROLLO MAY

places where we can pick up a roasted chicken, and Chinese and Japanese restaurants that deliver. Food is not love. Love is love. We should cook when the spirit moves us and gather food other times. Keep a healthy balance so you won't become stale. Can the fish store poach your salmon? Can some young students bartend and serve at your Saturday night dinner party? Can your spouse use the grill to prepare salmon, swordfish, shrimp, and chicken as well as corn on the cob, roasted vegetables, and glazed fruit? Feel the ease of slicing open some vine-ripened tomatoes with a sharp knife, spreading them out on a pretty platter and putting some fresh basil on top. This is not an effort, this is a joy. A child can shuck some ears of corn. Throwing them in a pot of boiling water is not an effort; this too is a pleasure.

Most deliberate changes are vast improvements to your daily rhythms.

What things do you do that give you pride and joy? When is the last time you baked a pie from scratch? By not doing something you don't wish to do, you free yourself up to do something that will nourish you. And as you are nourishing yourself, you can nourish others. We give our energy in different ways. We may love to eat, and food is very important to us, but it is perfectly all right to admit we're not in the mood to cook. We enjoy it most when we have lots of free time and can enjoy the relaxation of cooking without feeling pressured. My mother got tired of cooking, and once we were old enough, she had each child cook dinner one night a week. None of us starved.

Our identity should not be in doing everything ourselves. Peter doesn't love me any less because Debbie folds his clothes at the laundry. He doesn't love me less when we go out for supper at a bistro. I'm a reasonably good cook and when I do cook, I do it with enthusiasm. When we were raising the children, I cooked our family meals and always tried to make the food taste good and look appetizing. Because I enjoyed it, this wasn't a chore but a balancing of my energy and a way to feel at home. Now that we live alone I cook less. I'm delighted when a friend wants to cook an elaborate meal for us but don't feel guilty when we serve lobster, corn on the cob, and tomato and basil salad. No cooking is involved, only boiling water and slicing.

Modern man thinks he loses something—time—when he does not do things quickly; yet he does not know what to do with the time he gains—except kill it.

ERICH FROMM

Write in your notebook the truth. On a scale of one to ten, do you enjoy cooking? Ten means you love to cook, that you're in your element, and you find it calming and happy; one means that you think it is a lot of work and a waste of your time. What is your score? Guess what your spouse's score would be. Now ask your spouse his score. How accurate was your guess? Of course, each of your scores will change with your energy level, your mood, and your time constraints. If you are under a great deal of pressure and deadlines, cooking is just one more chore. You'd probably rather take a walk and then sit by the fire and have champagne and smoked salmon, hardly a time-consuming effort to prepare. But on Saturday night when you're home alone, and you've had plenty of physical exercise and freedom, I'm sure it is most pleasant for you and your spouse to prepare a favorite meal together.

Timing is key to balance. Remember: "Hurry never." Any form of rushing causes us to feel anxious, and even things we normally would enjoy doing lose their luster. Evaluate when you tend to enjoy certain necessary tasks and when they become burdensome. Sunday night might be the time not to cook at all because you've probably cooked a lot all week; as you prepare for the new week with all your obligations, it's a nice feeling to have some free time that night. Whether you go out to a local family restaurant or have take-out food, if this is a time you want free, take it. No one *has* time, we have to *take* time.

One luxury of a home is being able to catch up on sleep. I notice people in airplanes and trains so often sleep, trying to catch up. How wonderful it is, however, to be in the security of our own home, and lie down on a bed or a sofa and have an uninterrupted nap. I love to take a nap. The best naps I've ever had have been when we're alone in the house, with no dinner dates, no houseguests, and no immediate plans to preclude me from total freedom. A house is not a home unless we can come and go freely, doing and being, as we see fit.

Even if we don't sleep during a rest period, it is probably good for our health and balance for us to build in this time, at least on

weekends when we're home more, to lie down and rest. How often do you take a nap at home? When do you tend to like to take a nap? Try taking a nap in a different place for the next few weeks. How long are your naps usually? How do you feel when you awaken from your nap? Do you feel guilty for having had a short rest during the day? Do you wish you took more naps?

An artist has to be true to his muse.

The dishes will still be in the kitchen sink. The laundry will be left undone. There will be small messes on tables and counters and even the floor, but until we have a rest, we won't even have the energy to go about our puttering, tidying up our house. I enjoy reading before I take a short nap. I sit in a favorite chair, put my feet up, rest my head on the back of the chair, and read several pages. When I feel the overwhelming urge to take my glasses off and close my eyes, I smile in utter delight as I feel a sweetness in the atmosphere when my body sinks into nirvana. When you are able to let your hair down and do exactly what you wish to do at the moment, that is freedom and joy at home. If you have young children, you will have schedules to keep, but there should be times off from responsibilities when you treat your home like a fantasy spa or ideal inn. The little, less obvious things in a home are the most pleasant and interesting. Where else can we do what we want?

The trouble is that you think you have time.

THE BUDDHA

The Nightshirt as a Morning Uniform

Now that I don't have to get up and rush off to an office, I find it a great luxury to stay in my nightshirt all morning until I've finished my writing. Getting dressed is a transition. I can sometimes garden surreptitiously in the backyard in my nightshirt, clean under the bed, and putter around the house before I bathe and dress. I've claimed mornings at home as mine and, because we travel so much, they have become sacrosanct to me. What is ideal is a stretch of time when I can concentrate and relax into the moment. We all

The eternity of every moment.

HERMANN HESSE

A little gleam of time
between two eternities;
no second chance to us
forever more!

THOMAS CARLYLE

have defining elements in our life that are here to hug us and spiritually feed us. What are some of yours?

My editor uses the first ten minutes at home after work to change clothes—often into beloved pajamas—but maybe someone else loves satin lounging pants! Toni never starts cooking until she's in her nightshirt and the "work uniform" is off. She has a glass of red wine, turns on classical music, and cooks dinner, often after lighting a candle. A husband and wife who are business partners take their shoes off the second they open the door to their house. It's hard to feel at home with aching feet. Whether you take a bath and change clothes, shed your tie and jacket, or put on comfortable slippers and an apron, it is always important to personalize the way we settle into our feeling of being glad to be home. Whenever I return home, I like to putter around, change the water in a flower vase or water a plant, fold some laundry, do some hand washing or pay a bill. Before I settle down to read or cook, I like to tidy up because this is a concrete way to love up our home. It's usually after I have been away for several hours or a day or more that I can see with fresh eyes something that needs my attention. The more physically comfortable we are at home, the more sensitive we are to our environment and how we can improve it. This is perhaps the greatest luxury of our home, having these private experiences that transport us into higher realness.

A writer friend told me she isn't entertaining anyone, all summer, except family, at their weekend house in Connecticut. Sally is a food and travel writer. She and her husband had gotten into the habit of slaving away cooking and serving elaborate meals to their weekend house guests, feeling exhausted when they'd leave Sunday night to go back to New York. To her friends who invite themselves she simply says, "I'm sorry. Our house is booked for the summer." In our own home, who is in charge? Who sets the rules and the schedule? When I wrote the first draft of *Creating a Beautiful Home*, I had a chapter called "The Guest Room." Then I called my literary agent and confessed, "I don't feel comfortable with house guests. We're not set up to provide enough privacy for them or us." Carl listened, and then suggested the chapter be revised and retitled "The Question of Guests." I rewrote the chapter but in the end took it out completely.

There are times and places to see friends. Home is mainly for your family. Most people live hectic lives and the added burden of having to be host and hostess for several days can cause a strain in the fabric of the home. We don't live the way Edith Wharton did: She had a house full of guests who were taken care of by a willing staff of twenty or so, and she'd stay in bed and write until noon. Most of us simply aren't set up for house guests. Find a lovely inn nearby.

Take care of the minutes, for the hours will take care of themselves.

LORD CHESTERFIELD

What I Don't Do

I'm often asked by my clients how I am able to do all I do. I don't *do* any more than anyone else does. It's what I *don't do* that frees up my time to do what I choose to do. In order to live beautifully, we have to have a strict understanding of our limits and be careful not to test them too hard. I don't need to own a car, for example. I take taxis, trains, and airplanes, or I walk or ride a bike. I can read or write, do correspondence, or pay bills in the time that others spend sitting behind a steering wheel. I don't know of another family that doesn't own or lease a car, but being without a car works for us.

Have you and your spouse or partner figured out a good plan and schedule for balancing your time at home? Do you feel one of you does more of the housework than the other? How many hours do you spend per week doing something helpful around the house? How many hours does your spouse or partner spend? Do you feel there is sufficient income to hire a cleaning service or have them come more often? What are the areas that seem to bog you down? What times of the year do you feel impose the lightest work loads around the house? Do you like to cook on the grill? How often? In an ideal world, what are some things you wish you didn't have to do around the house? Write them in your notebook. Tell the

All my possessions for a moment of time.

ELIZABETH I

truth. Several clients confide that they no longer enjoy cooking. What are some of the things that need to be done that you enjoy doing? I enjoy:

- Changing the bed linens
- Setting a pretty table
- Arranging flowers
- Painting anything
- Rearranging furniture and objects
- Straightening out closets and drawers
- Waxing and polishing our antiques

Ch'i

How do you evaluate the ch'i, or energy, of your home? How do you evaluate your ch'i? If there's a screen door that needs replacing, or the washing machine needs to be repaired, we know we have to take care of these things, and sooner is usually best, so we don't have to waste our energy brooding about it. But we must balance this get-it-done energy with maintenance or taking it easy. We have a friend who lives alone and stays undressed until he takes his dog for a walk after lunch. Soon he'll be ninety years old, and I am certain he knows what makes him feel comfortable. Frankie has a twinkle in his eye and a smile on his face and still loves to go out dancing at night. He's figured out how to maintain his vigorous energy.

When we're sick, everything shuts down. Why wait to be sick to flop around, sleep late, have breakfast in bed, read magazines, and have some Zen time? Why wait to go on an expensive vacation to have time off? One of the reasons we love to escape from home is that we know we won't have to do housework. We can read and relax, care-free. When we're home we should feel the same freedom we do when we're on a vacation, not all the time certainly, but half the time.

First Things First

The happier we are with ourselves, the more tenderness and care we express in our surroundings. There is a happy swing and natural rhythm. When I work I have to sit still. Suddenly, I'm full of energy and want to do something physical. Exercise trainers claim that housework doesn't count as a proper physical fitness regime, but I disagree. We can stay quite fit scrubbing the bathtub and the kitchen cabinets. I wait until I have an excess of this wonderful psychic energy when I feel I can do anything. This is the time you should use your timer. You'd be amazed how few minutes it actually takes you to scrub the bathroom floor. How long does it take you when you're full of excess energy you want to expend? Because I've soaked the breakfast dishes in boiling hot water in the sink until I'm in the mood to wash them, they're ready to be rinsed. They've practically washed themselves. When balancing your time, always do what you want to do, first.

Home should never be taken for granted.

After you've taken care of your immediate responsibilities, such as caring for the children's needs, do something you want to do to balance your energy. Whether this means you do what you want to do early in the morning or just upon returning home from the office or doing errands, do what you *want* to do. Most people get this wrong. Tend to your inner needs. First things first. We grow to learn that when we turn things around in our mind and take care of our own needs, when we care for the house, it is an added way to stay fit, get some exercise, and make ourselves happier. With this shift of consciousness, our housework is just another way of taking care of our inner needs, expressed concretely.

Time is both an opportunity and a wasting asset. Seize the moment with vision and courage.
PETER MEGARGEE BROWN

Worry Not

When we fill up our own well, we own the day. We have our private thoughts that keep us in good company. We can protect this inner peace and serenity, knowing we are on our path, living as well as we can under our circumstances at home by not worrying about things beyond our control. When there are situations you have no power over, look at each problem and ask yourself, "What can I do?" As General George Marshall would say to his staff, "Don't fight the problem."

It's amazing how often I realize that so many struggles are not mine to control. Learning how to balance our time and energy at home means accepting things we can't change and not trying to be in control of everything. I had a minister who once told me, "Alexandra, stop trying to be everyone's savior." If we can control our emotions, mood, and spirit, this is a major accomplishment, worthy of all our time and attention. I have learned some things are just not my mission or my business. How I feel is up to me, but I can't control everything that happens.

Rising Above

Do you ever feel resentful that so much of the work and responsibility lands on your shoulders? What can you do about this emotion? Resentment is a piercing wound to the body, the mind, and the spirit, as corrosive as dripping acid. Do you ever feel sorry for yourself? When? Is it fatigue? One evening last winter, I was curled up by a warm fire, feeling cozy and content. Over the holidays, we'd purchased some cinnamon-scented pinecones dipped in wax that turn the flame blue and green. I enjoyed tossing one in and gazing into the colorful flames as I listened to "Chariots of Fire." Suddenly, it occurred to me that it was nine o'clock and I hadn't done one thing about dinner. I was too comfortable to budge. Rather than feeling put upon that I had to get up and concoct a meal for Peter and me, I lit a few extra candles and sweetly asked Peter if he'd do me a favor and heat up some leftover homemade soup and we'd dine by the fire. I admitted I was feeling tired. He said, "Certainly," and we ended up having a lovely, romantic evening talking until quite late. Peter enjoyed help-

Nine-tenths of wisdom is being wise in time.

THEODORE ROOSEVELT

ing out and was glad I asked him to. Peter's mother told him once that sitting by a fire with someone you love, having a meaningful conversation, is more nourishing than going to sleep. I woke up the next morning feeling renewed.

There is never a good reason for feeling sorry for ourselves because this attitude paralyzes us and keeps us from remedying the situation. Not wanting to cook dinner is hardly a problem. As soon as you begin to feel put upon for whatever reason, focus on the big picture. By never giving in to self-pity, you have a clearer mind to rise above the immediate situation and stay focused.

Take time while time is, for time will away.

THOMAS FULLER

The one who suffers is the sufferer. We have role models who give us heart and we persevere. If something is wrong that we have the skill and insight to change, fix it. If something is not in our power to correct, we have to face it without denial. If something *is* in our power to correct, we have to take action.

What Is Your Definition of Work?

Last year we flew to California, where I taped some television shows for the Discovery Channel. The hotel where we was stayed was in lovely Chatsworth, a town northwest of Los Angeles. The hotel is in a canyon surrounded by mountains. After our work was finished, we sat outside around a pool. After a vigorous swim, I stretched out on a lounge chair to soak in the fresh breezes and the awesome view, one I rarely see. As I sat there feasting my eyes, I gazed around at the gardens surrounding the pool area and noticed some fire-red geraniums that needed to be deadheaded. Without being conscious of what I was doing, I got up from the comfortable lounge chair and snapped off the dead blossoms. When I realized what I had done, I laughed out loud. I was homesick and missed our garden and our geraniums; I'd trained a nine-year-old how to water and deadhead, but I never feel anyone loves my geraniums as much as I do. This modest hotel had pretty plantings, and I am sure the person hired to tend the garden is overworked. It was a blessing to me to putter in a pretty garden, reminding me that when we do things out of honest instinct, the definition of work is greatly altered.

Domestic Happiness

While Minister to France, Thomas Jefferson liked to write letters to American women, contrasting their virtue with European decadence by congratulating those "who have the good sense to value domestic happiness above all other." What is your definition of domestic happiness? Mine is to enjoy the process of our lives moment to moment, Monday, Tuesday, Wednesday, Thursday, Friday, Saturday, and Sunday. The New Testament tells us that Jesus told his disciples that

Quietness is indeed a sign of strength.

FRANZ KAFKA

he would prepare a place for them in heaven. By the same token, we have to prepare a place for ourselves on earth that is a spiritual homecoming. In this process we approach domestic bliss. When we create an atmosphere that suits our temperament, taste, and personal style of living, we experience a noticeable enjoyment in the creative process of living vitally at home.

Retreating into Our Home as a Refuge

If we are happy when we are alone, chances are we'll be able to sustain our feeling of well-being more easily than if we feel lively and cheerful only when we are with others. A quiet Monday morning at home alone can be as glorious a time as any other. Make dates with yourself. Have lunch alone. Escape from the hectic noise and confusion all around and turn inward. I've always believed that being happy is an energy as well as a habit. What puts us in the consciousness of happiness? What are some of the activities that sustain us and inspire our higher power? What are the activities that dampen our spirits, leaving us feeling depleted?

Being at home is a platform for joy as well as a refuge from sorrow, strengthening us to "participate with joy in the sorrows of the world" as suggested by a wise Hindu prophet. We're going to have pain, but our home should remind us of our blessings, of our good fortune, not drag us down. When you are sad because of a loss of a loved one or a major disappointment, or are sick and feel awful, how does your home support you and care for you? We should try to spend time nurturing our home, so that when we are in need, our home can nourish us.

Let us be silent—so we may hear the whisper of the gods.

EMERSON

Making Everyone Relaxed

Have you reached the point at home where you and your spouse or partner feel free to enjoy your own activities, doing what you please? Peter and I have, and it is the most liberating feeling possible. We both love our house but never want to be slaves to it. I make what I feel is the best use of my time and energy to maintain a healthy, constructive balance between my personal life and needs and the needs of this home we love so deeply.

Thought works in silence; so does virtue.

THOMAS CARLYLE

When is the last time you put your feet up in your living room? Who were you with? What were you doing? How long were you there? Do you ever feel that your spouse or partner wished you would get up and do something else? Do you ever have arguments over this issue? I don't enjoy someone interrupting me when I'm enjoying a moment's peace and assuming I'll do something on command.

We communicate well when we have a plan. When we're with our family, everyone understands they have free time until we gather in the living room for drinks at seven. Dinner is at eight. It's clear to everyone when there is a group event. Beyond that, people can nap, go for a walk, go for a drive, or wash their hair; everyone in the household is free.

This is a liberating way to live at home. Knowing what time dinner will be served and who is responsible for the preparation is key. I work quickly, so I don't need a lot of time in preparation. Some people need more time. Knowing what others' expectations are makes us feel comfortable. By communicating well, we can help each other not to spend too much time doing things we don't enjoy.

The Telephone and Value Added

Peter protects my private time by answering the telephone and checking our voice mail. I don't like the telephone and, when I receive a call, I often am miles away in a different awareness. I'd far prefer to make telephone dates when I can completely focus on our conversation.

Often I feel caged in when I'm on the telephone. To make me feel freer, I arrange to talk on the telephone when I can iron or polish silver or brass. I tried to exercise, but people heard my deep breathing. (I've scrubbed the kitchen floor while on the telephone; I was able to because of a twenty-five-foot cord.) If I'm seated at a desk, I'll put stamps on envelopes or tidy up papers. I feel happiest when I'm accomplishing something besides the interaction. The telephone requires that we actively listen, but it is not challenging our skills. While I realize it is not Zen to do two things at once, there are ways we all have to economize our time.

Write in your notebook all the activities where you double up. What are some of the tasks you don't like to do, that don't challenge you, and you'd just as soon do in concert with something else? When you exercise on an exercise bike, do you watch the news on television or read *Newsweek* or *House & Garden*, or do you talk on the telephone? What else do you do when you're cooking? Do you ever listen to motivational tapes of some of your gurus, or books on tape? Many of us listen to favorite music when we cook.

Managing the Telephone

Do you enjoy telephoning? Some people are addicted and others have an aversion to it. If you need to use the phone for work, do you prefer not having to use it when you're home except to stay in touch with your children? Try keeping the three-minute timer near the telephone and see how often you have to turn it upside down. Set the timer and write down how long each call takes. Do this for a month, and you'll be surprised at how much time you spend, some of it wasted. How good are you at ending a phone conversation when you feel it's time? Some people are real talkers. Are you one? To analyze how much time you spend on the telephone each day, each week, buy a telephone memo pad at a stationery store. This way you'll have a record of every call that comes in and you can write down every call you make. How many times do telemarketers call you? Do you have an answering machine? I think voice mail is a blessing because we can check for messages at our convenience and answer any calls when we have time or are in the mood. There are only three people other than family who, if they call when I'm writing, wouldn't irritate me, but these people rarely call me, and I prefer the peacefulness of not having the telephone ring in the cottage. Voice mail is hooked up to our New York office number.

There should be times you will not be interrupted, and these boundaries should be understood by your family. Mealtimes, for one. When you gather in the living room for a refreshment and conversation before dinner is another time you should not be available. If you are in the habit of making long telephone calls that take your time and money, remember you are in charge. You can set the rules. By looking at your patterns, you will see you can balance your time on the telephone with a postcard, or a note, or a business letter, and save your resources.

> *Be still and cool in thy mind and spirit.*
>
> GEORGE FOX

> *The time you enjoyed wasting is not wasted time.*
>
> SØREN KIERKEGAARD

Computer Time and Television Time

How much time per day do you spend on the computer at home? What kind of tasks do you accomplish? Do you use it for the household finances? Do you use it for your work? Is it located in a convenient place? Do others in your family use it also? Is this a pleasant time for you? Do you prefer working on the computer to watching television? Do you ever watch television and use the computer at the same time? How much television do you estimate you watch per week? Keep a small spiral pad with a pencil or pen next to the television and each day jot down what you watch and for how long. Are there shows you watch each day? Each week? Are you disciplined to watch only certain programs, or do you channel surf? After one month of accurately recording all the minutes and hours, how close to the truth was your guess? Try this and you'll be amazed how many hours you actually are seated in front of the television when it is on.

Over the years, you must learn to let go.

CLAIRE BLOOM

After you have your accurate accounting, write some notes in your notebook about television. Do you feel you watch too much? How much too much? Would you ever be able to unplug it for a month and use that time for special projects, to spend more time with your spouse, to spend more time with the children? What are some of the activities you'd like to do that you never seem to have time for? List them, in your notebook.

There is more to life than increasing its speed.

MOHANDAS K. GANDHI

Add up the time you spend on the telephone, the time you spend working at the computer, and the time you spend watching television in a given time period. Evaluate how much waking time you spend at home in the same month. Take into consideration business trips away from home, business and social dinners out, activities that take you away from home. Do this as accurately as possible. By assessing how many hours you are at home, retiring to sleep, and how many hours you spend "being connected," you will see that there are precious hours left to stargaze and live sensuously in the serenity of your home.

Time Out at Home

Contemplative persons retreat to a secluded place to listen and be awake. When we do, our senses become more acute and we clear our head and open up our hearts. Would you ever take a week off from using the telephone, the fax, working on the computer, and watching television?

Tell your loved ones you're going to take a quiet week at home on a retreat to refresh your spirits. If you were climbing a mountain, they wouldn't disturb you because they couldn't find you. Why can't we do the same thing at home? Being unavailable, even for good news, for one week, especially in August, is not only civilized, but would do wonders for rethinking our values and considering how we want to step back and see our life from an overview. Could you resist opening the mail, reading the newspaper, looking at catalogues and magazines for one week, cleansing yourself of the immediacy of intrusive details? How often do you wish you could push the world aside for a much-needed break to regain your equilibrium?

> *The question is not whether machines think, but whether men do.*
>
> B. F. SKINNER

Bedroom as Sanctuary

When clients want to have the computer on the bedside table in their master bedroom, next to the fax machine, and a big-screen television opposite their bed, with a telephone and a cell phone near to hand, I see this as a serious danger sign for the marriage.

There is a time and place for everything. We should consider our bedroom a sanctuary, one we retreat to for sensual enjoyment, quiet, and sleep. If one person makes noises that are unrelated to the intimacy of the couple, the disturbance can be extremely irritating. The most romantic bedroom I've ever spent time in was in Bali, where we walked up the stairs of our bungalow to a small square room with the walls and ceiling tented in a heavenly blue-and-white batik print and a window overlooking the pale blue-green ocean. There

The great trouble with the
machine, from the point of
view of the emotions, is its
regularity.

BERTRAND RUSSELL

was one piece of furniture: a high, four-poster bed. I remember this simple bedroom in Bali with grass matting on the floor, the fresh smells of the sea air from an open window, the waves in keeping with the beat of our hearts. We were far away from the fax machine, the telephone, and the hum of technology.

The isolation and primitive setting made us feel calm, content, and happy. Have we complicated our lives by always trying to be available? Can't we reclaim our bedroom as our inner space, where we have peace, have the expectation of feeling composed, opening up to greater understanding and love? The master bedroom should be a place of "I-thou," not, I, thou, and the rest of the world.

So often we complicate our lives in obvious ways and subtle ones. If we spend too much time being informed about what's happening around the globe, we might be robbing ourselves of happiness right where we are. Searching the Internet, talking and being entertained, we might deprive ourselves of soulfully looking out at the moon, the stars, and the cosmos, feeling the power of life's unfolding mystery.

Every minute starts an hour.

PAUL GONDOLA

Simplifying, often deliberately, for periods of time, is an excellent way to balance our time at home. While I can't live in a bungalow in Bali forever and call that island home, I felt at peace there and returned to our cottage with a new vision, a new perspective on how we really wanted to feel without having to go halfway around the world. At the cottage, Peter and I call our master bedroom room number one. We think of it as the best room in some dreamy inn. Its charm is its total simplicity and comfort.

Fresh from the Wash

My mother raised me with high standards of housekeeping. When I was little we lived on an old onion farm with a large garage and household help. There were a cook, a maid, a gardener (who doubled as a chauffeur), and an elderly lady who served our meals, smocked our dresses, and ironed. When I grew up and became a teenager, my father had financial reverses and our lifestyle became much simpler, but my childhood memories are of polished chandeliers, polished floors, polished antiques, and polished silver. I still remember that everything always sparkled. I also remember everyone in the family sleeping in beautifully ironed sheets, even on the sleeping porch. It wasn't until I went to camp in Maine when I was thirteen that I slept in sheets that weren't ironed. Because of the way I was brought up, I assumed I could work hard and strive to live the same way I always had. Until I realized that this romantic hideaway in Bali didn't have ironed sheets, I always thought I had to have ironed sheets in my house. This was so liberating because I realized I could have pretty sheets but didn't have to have them ironed.

Enjoy the present hour,
Be thankful for the past.

ABRAHAM COWLEY

I'd been sending our sheets out to a laundry that used bleach, and although I liked having them ironed, it was expensive and not good for the linens to be machine pressed. I tried making the beds one week with unironed sheets and no one noticed. Once or twice a year when the spirit moves me, I'll iron the fold-over part of the sheet, but this urge doesn't come to me nowadays that often. I have better ways to use my time. If you have nice cotton sheets, they will be just as comfortable if they aren't ironed as if they are. The thread-count is what matters. How different does a bed with unironed sheets look from a crisp, freshly made bed with perfectly ironed bed linen? In many cases it's imperceptible. It's home. Home has wrinkles. When sheets are photographed for the cover of a magazine, they are usually ironed and steamed to perfection. However, when I made up Brooke's bed too perfectly when a magazine came to photograph her bedroom, the editor threw Brooke's blue-and-white nightshirt on the floor and got into the bed and rumpled the sheets. The understanding photographer took the picture with the messy bed because it suggested home and emotional comfort.

No man loses any other life
than this which he now
lives.

MARCUS AURELIUS

Relaxed Style

The object of our technology is to control the world, to have a superelectronic push-button universe, where we can get anything we want, fulfill any desires, simply by pushing a button.

ALAN WATTS

I've learned to live what I call a relaxed lifestyle at home. We were raised to bounce a quarter on our bed. With this training I can make a bed look quite wonderful without ironing. Recently I made our bed with a seafoam-green fitted bottom sheet and some luxurious white linen sheets with hemstitching. Then I put a soft-green seersucker blanket cover over the top sheet and folded a favorite white, lilac, and pale-green patchwork quilt at the end of the bed. It looked so pretty I wanted to crawl under the cool linens. It is not a wrinkle-free bed, but it is still refined, elegantly stylish, has respectability, and is cozy, inviting and real. These wonderful linen sheets will last a lot longer now that I am not sending them out, and they look just fine. I'm simply grateful we have clean, pretty sheets.

What Is Your Standard?

The dangers of technology can lead to a world without a soul.

How we spend our time and money should be based on what we value. I have a client who has a huge walk-in linen closet containing nothing but white, monogrammed, impeccably ironed, perfectly folded sheets and spotless white, monogrammed towels. I've never seen a neater closet. But she lives alone and has Margie, who does her washing and ironing. This luxury is something she can afford and is part of her standard. I'm far more relaxed by nature and temperament, but I enjoy the freshness of the white ironed sheets and crisp white towels when I spend the night in her house.

Some people are too busy to be civilized.

PAUL THEROUX

Each of us has a standard that makes us feel comfortable. What is yours? Are you comfortable with the relaxed look around your home? What areas are you the most fussy about? I love silver but not when it's unpolished. I'd rather put it away in drawers and bring some out for special occa-

sions than have it in view looking tarnished. It looks unloved when it takes on that brownish-gray hue. Brass looks less sad when it is mellow, but to see how it makes us feel when it gleams, all we have to do is take one piece among several and polish it until our rag has no more black on it. I like country furniture that is rustic, showing the dents and nicks, the marks of the years. To me, these add to the charm and patina, but some people would consider it crude, even primitive. Much of our furniture is French Provincial and is so easy to care for. All we have to do is occasionally wax it, rub it vigorously to bring out the shine, and dust it when it needs it.

Being Realistic

I used to keep a high wax on our wooden floors. Maintaining them was time consuming and expensive. Now I wax them or have a service wax them twice a year and occasionally I buff them. They look fine, certainly not the same way they would if they were waxed regularly, but floors are for walking on and we shouldn't have maintenance standards that are too demanding. It may be practical to use paper napkins at mealtimes, but a prettier alternative is to use kitchen hand towels as napkins the way French bistros do. These have the refinement of linen without the maintenance requirements of fine table linens. By turning the air conditioner off during dinnertime, we won't blow candle wax all over our freshly polished dining room table; we'll have silence and we won't have a mess to clean up the next morning.

Let us alone. Time driveth onward fast . . . What is it that will last?

ALFRED, LORD TENNYSON

What are some areas where you feel you can make some changes to save time so that you can make more intelligent use of it? In my next life I'm going to marry a man who has one color and one model of dark socks. I can easily match pink, blue, or yellow socks, but I have to put on my glasses and squint trying to sort Peter's socks into pairs. It is a waste of anyone's time. I'm too frugal to toss them all out and start over, but there are days when I'm tempted. Once I've managed to match most of them into pairs, I roll them up and place them in a cotton-lined wicker basket to feast my eye before putting them away. This is often a task I can do while talking on the telephone with a daughter. I no longer wash and iron my own blouses, but send them and Peter's cotton slacks to be washed and pressed at the dry cleaner. I used to enjoy squeezing orange juice in the morning, but most of the time I buy fresh-squeezed juice from a nearby Korean market. And when I'm at the A & P, I pick up freshly cut fruit and melon to save time.

Look at Your 168 Hours per Week

Just because you love to cook or iron or polish brass and silver doesn't mean you should spend too much of your precious time doing an inordinate amount of it at the expense of having to eliminate other activities you want to do. By evaluating just how much time you're actually home per day, and how much time per day you spend cooking, cleaning, doing errands, and gardening, you're in a better position to set some limits.

There are 168 hours per week. If you sleep eight hours, on average, this adds up to fifty-six hours per week and leaves you 112 waking hours. Some nights you'll sleep seven hours and others nine, but a general average is eight hours. If you have a job away from home and work, on average, Monday through Friday from nine A.M. to five P.M., you will work, on average, forty hours per week. Deduct the forty hours you work from 112 waking hours and you have a net of seventy-two hours each week free from your job.

This amounts to a little over ten hours a day. Many of us are good at budgeting how we will allocate our money, but haven't focused as sharply on how we will spend our time. Take the time to list all the things you need to do to maintain your body and attend to your personal needs. Your list could include:

- Exercise
- Hair care
- Makeup
- Doctors' appointments
- Purchasing prescriptions
- Purchasing food
- Cooking and eating
- Massage, facial, manicure, pedicure
- Making travel arrangements
- Shopping for clothes and personal necessities
- Paying bills
- Banking
- Planning family and social events

How we value the gift of time, how wisely we use it, is the prerequisite to being happy at home.

Now list the things you need to do to maintain your possessions and your home:

- Cleaning
- Doing dishes
- Doing laundry
- Ironing
- Maintaining the car
- Mowing the lawn
- Watering the grass and garden, fertilizing, pruning, planting
- Painting
- Making electrical and plumbing repairs
- Caring for pets
- Recycling
- Cleaning windows
- Shining mirrors
- Vacuuming, waxing, and polishing floors
- Dusting and waxing furniture
- Cleaning fabrics and rugs

The mid-world is best.

EMERSON

To see how much time you really spend, break down each category into more detail. Under cleaning, make a specific list. I have a client who vacuums her seafoam-green carpeting in her bedroom every day. If she added up how many hours she logged per year, she'd be appalled. Fifteen minutes doesn't sound like a lot of time, but when it is spent 330 to 340 days a year, it adds up.

Twenty-five Percent to Maintain Our Lives

Recent studies have concluded that maintenance of our selves and our possessions should not exceed 25 percent of our waking time after we've worked at our job. This is eighteen hours a week for maintaining all the areas of our lives, leaving us now with fifty-four free hours a week, between seven and eight a day, on average.

This doesn't sound too bad. You can seize this time or waste it, depending on many complex factors. Many of us look around and wonder where the time went. Review your patterns of the last three months. How many hours have you been spending at work? I have a good friend who spends over eighty hours at the office a week. If she wonders why she can't stargaze or take a picnic or have friends over for a leisurely dinner, it is because she has to subtract the forty extra hours she works—double the time allotment for the job—from her fifty-four free hours, reducing them to fourteen. Consider that, per day, my friend is free two hours in a twenty-four hour cycle.

When can she practice the piano? If you sleep more than your fifty-six allotted hours per week, each hour, whether taking a nap or sleeping, must be deducted from your fifty-four hours. Clearly, any imbalance will alter the fabric of your daily contentment at home.

If there is an imbalance between the rhythms of work and rest, there will be a risk of health imbalances that will sap your psychic energy and will require you to spend more of your time maintaining your body. We must simplify our needs in order to have these precious fifty-four hours a week free from encumbrances; every day, we must try to hold on to a little over seven hours a day to spend wisely in self-transforming ways. We can and should have freedom, every day, from time-consuming duties or obligations. We should organize our time in thoughtful ways in order to perform all our tasks and projects in a leisurely, unhurried manner. None of us can avoid the rhythms of the twenty-four day where we work, rest, and play. Time is given to each of us in equal proportion. Some people can harness time to use it to their benefit, while others tend to waste their precious moments. If we all are in similar rhythms of giving our energy and replenishing it, what makes the greatest difference in the quality of our lives? I believe it is our attitude about what we are doing. How do we feel as we move freely from one activity to the next? Are we flexible, flowing like a river, proceeding steadily and easily in the direction of our ideal goals? Whenever we hurry, we become scattered, and without concentrating our attention on completing one thing at a time, everything becomes a muddle and a blur.

Don't worry about the past.

F. SCOTT FITZGERALD

Time Spent in Self-fulfilling Ways

How we spend this precious nugget of gold, our leisure time, is key to a life of illumination. The Greek term for leisure is *scholē*, which is also the root of the word school. The Greeks believed the best use of leisure time was to develop themselves to become truly human and wise. This is an ancient ideal but is rare today. Time spent learning, becoming more aesthetic, exploring our own curiosity, is self-fulfilling. We emerge feeling satisfied and content, full rather than empty. What are the four or five major activities you can identify that keep you from using these hours and minutes more wisely? List them. It is not that any one activity is bad in itself. It has to do with the degree of excess. I know people who read several newspapers a day, who keep on top of the news by watching television, but never have time or take the time to read a book, be it a classic or a piece of contemporary literature. It is possible to stay current but still lack a broader perspective on life. Information is not inspiration. Nor is it wisdom. Television, magazines, and conversations are all useful, but need limits so that we may dig deeper into ourselves and stretch our intellectual and spiritual capacities.

I had an editor at *Reader's Digest* who suggested I do my writing before I read the newspaper. In the past week, what time have you taken for your own illumination and self-knowledge? What kinds of things did you do? Do you want even more reflective time? Whether you take time to have a physical checkup or you go to the gym, your body and self-maintenance must always take precedence over the maintenance of your possessions. But checkups and workouts are only a part of our maintaining a healthy body. We need to manage whatever snippets of time we can, to study and think things through, getting in touch with how we feel and how we think to make the most sense of our lives and live to our highest potential at home.

How Do You Waste Time?

This time, like all times, is a very good one, if we but know what to do with it.

EMERSON

How often do you feel you're wasting time? In what ways? What activities do you do that are a waste of your resources? Is it time spent complaining and commiserating with co-workers? Is it thinking dreary thoughts? Do you waste time worrying? I asked a doctor recently what the universal problems are that cause people to get sick. I was startled by his question back to me, "What are the problems that cause *you* to get sick, Alexandra?"

We all have times when there are too many demands on our time. As well as our normal responsibilities to our spouse and children, we may have an ill parent or friend or a tight business deadline. But where do we personally draw the line? I enjoy spending money but not wasting it, and I equally enjoy spending time thoughtfully and not wasting it.

I read that of the average worker's forty-hour week, 25 percent is wasted because of inefficiency. If we are wasting one quarter of our time at the job site, do we tend to also waste our own time? Without clear goals and a plan, we tend to flounder. We all like to feel the satisfactions of accomplishing something we've set out to do. The patterns we establish now will free up our time to meet our set deadlines without allowing extenuating circumstances to interfere. If I waste my precious time, I have only myself to blame. Each day I make the choice to set myself free.

At home, if we are not cautious, our 25 percent maintenance will easily slip into 50 percent because of the waste factor at the workplace being transferred to the home. Rather than having fifty-four hours of discretionary time, we now are reduced to thirty-six hours per week or just above five hours per day. When we are raising children we have so few moments to ourselves, especially if we are working at a job, whether as a volunteer or for money; we have to build in some free spaces in our calendar for reflection, meditation, or just time off.

How We Use Our Discretionary Time at Home

I've always loved the strength I receive from the serenity of solitude because it is my temperament to be alone, enjoying the quiet, to think things through, to plan, to muse, to figure things out. I need this time and space to keep my life in balance. I find it essential to give equal time to the conflicting energies of inner resources and outer stimulation. I need time to *be* as well as *do*.

When I raised Alexandra and Brooke, I was able to escape into play with them in a carefree, timeless way, feeling young and happy. They're now young ladies, living their own lives. As I reflect on our times together when they were young, I now realize how eccentric I was, tumbling down hills with them, playing all the time. I felt that same sense of freedom with them that I felt before I became a mother. When we were together, we were on an adventure, having fun, doing exactly what the spirit moved us to do. No one was looking over our shoulders telling us what to do.

Doing nothing is never dull. I can be perfectly content sitting outside for three hours. If suddenly I see something that needs attention in the garden, I can pull weeds, sweep, water, clip, and rearrange things until I've created a more beautiful outdoor living room. We had a dead space where no one ever sat, and by putting a window-paned mirror on the wall of our house, flanked by two ficus trees in terra-cotta pots, this dull area began to sparkle with energy. We put a low, round, marble-topped pedestal table in the middle and placed four different-colored painted circus chairs around the table. The day I made these few improvements, we had friends over for lunch, and Brooke ended up conducting an art class for little ones in that newly transformed space. I didn't wake up that morning in May feeling I had to rearrange the garden space, but by spending so many peaceful hours there in the morning, I felt inspired to make things even sweeter. We create a home by being at home, giving ourselves time and space to be moved to action. Whenever we do things out of want rather than need, the time we spend is not maintenance but leisure time. We become more self-confident because we become our true selves. Whatever we do to improve our house has an immediate effect on our spirit.

One Third of Our Life Is Spent Alone

In technological societies, we spend 33 percent of our time alone. Is this figure accurate in your experience? Do you value this time for self-reflection and self-development? What are your happiest hours? In your free time, who do you choose to be with? Besides listing your family, write in your notebook some people you admire and like, known or unknown, dead or alive. We can be with these heroes in our leisure time through contemplation, meditation, and reading. Do you feel you have generally achieved a balance between being in public, being home with the family, and being alone, whether at home or out in nature? By saying no to overdoing, we are providing time and space to say yes to our essential nature.

Free Time Is Our Greatest Resource

People in a hurry cannot think, cannot grow.

ERIC HOFFER

Think of this free time as far more valuable than money. It's hard to earn a living but even harder to be in a state of inner peace. Nothing comes easily. If self-attunement were automatic, we would have a healthy, productive, happy society. Just like learning any skill, it takes discipline and practice. How we feel about ourselves, how we value the gift of time, how we use it wisely to develop our skills and talents is the prerequisite to being happy at home. Finding this essential balance, where we learn more about the world, where we can make a contribution, is one way to come home to who we really are, and to live the life we most desire.

Try an exercise where you record everything you do in your notebook. How long does each task takes you? Each day can be a whole page, beginning when you awaken Monday morning until you go to sleep. Rate how you felt about each activity, on a scale of one to ten, with one indicating that you didn't enjoy it and ten indicating that you were fully alive to the experience, with all your attention focused. To save time, write on an index card or a small pad of paper the following:

Stimulating
Fascinating
Challenging
Fun
Difficult
Frustrating
Sensual

Time: That which man is always trying to kill, but which ends in killing him.

HERBERT SPENSER

Delicious
Spirited
Happy
Peaceful
Nervous
Anxious
Sad
Upset

Match these words to your score so you can analyze how you felt during different ranges of experiences. Taking a sick dog to the vet might have made you sad and you didn't like the experience, but you were still paying attention and alert to what the doctor was telling you. You may have given yourself a score of five. Look at all your low scores and note what you were doing. You can see what activities you concentrate well on and others where you really aren't paying attention. Maybe you ate seven cookies from the canister out of frustration because you just heard bad news over the telephone. What would your score be about the cookie binge?

Analyze how self-motivated you are to read or study. How high is your self-esteem when you do something constructive versus counterproductive? If we ate seven cookies nervously on Wednesday afternoon, the body will recover. If, however, we made this a habit, we would see our body enlarge and our clothes would no longer fit. Our bad habits would eventually cause health problems. We have to stay alert to excess in our everyday patterns. Time moves forward whether we're ready to win the race or not.

There is a wonderful reflection pond and fountain in a nearby garden. On the side of the pedestal base, these words are carved in the marble:

Time goes, they say.
Ah, no. Time stays.
We go.

This exercise forces us to look at the shape and quality of our daily life. By looking at our habits, our mood, and our psychic energy every day, we can make subtle changes in the way we approach and balance our time at home. Once we clearly see that we have time, we can then have worthwhile goals, knowing how to put this freedom to the most creative and beneficial use for ourselves and others.

PART TWO

Self-Expression

To be creative, man must
relate to nature with his
senses as much as with his
common sense, with his
heart as much as with
knowledge.

—RENÉ DUBOS

CHAPTER 5

Cultivating Your Gift of Creativity

Why should we use our creative power . . . ? Because there is nothing that
makes people so generous, joyful, lively, bold and compassionate. . . .

—BRENDA UELAND

I can think of no better place to exercise our creativity than within the boundaries of our home and garden. Here we find ourselves, work through what blocks us, dissolve own inhibitions, and learn about our mysterious self through the doing, the living. When we're able to silence our mind for periods of time each day, we are cultivating our intuitive powers.

Who are those geniuses, our guides, mentors, and heroes, who help us to live more intensely and creatively at home each day? Certainly, Swedish painter Carl Larsson, who was born in 1853 and died in 1919, was one of them, a true leader of the home, hearth, and family. He believed an artist's great task was to be "priest of art," preaching and teaching the beautiful and joyful message of art to all people. He believed the mission of art is to create mental and emotional well-being in everyday life. His ideals of brightness, simplicity, and happiness were present in his art as well as in his life.

Larsson poignantly painted the poetry of the daily life he

When one has fire within and a soul one can't keep bottling them up. Better to burn than to bust. What is in will out.

VINCENT VAN GOGH

187

lived at home with his wife, Karin, and his children. In his words, "I'm painting a corner of my yard, with one of my children and a red peony in the foreground, while Karin sits beside me peeling rhubarb."

This visionary artist spoke of his creativity: "My art: it's just like my home. It's modest but harmonious, quiet, simple. Nothing extravagant, nothing for connoisseurs. But good for people and solid work." What gives some the freedom to fearlessly express their truth? What makes his art so compelling is his lack of pretension. Creative energy considers everything as a possibility for adding a personal touch, putting a unique spin on all the details of simple objects and events.

The most important way to cultivate your creative gifts is to have a strong point of view about who you are and what defines you. Carl Larsson's art was a natural extension of his family life. Everything was one because he and Karin were both exceedingly talented, he as a draftsman-artist and she as a textile designer. They were creative partners. Rather than their children interfering with their creative productivity, they were the subjects and inspiration for the blank canvas, the paper, the yarn. The Larssons didn't have to choose between expressing their personal vision and being good parents; they were far better parents because they drew out of themselves all the beauty and joy of this ideal family life they had introduced. When we see the beauty of the intimacy of their home and family, we awaken refreshed to the poetry and beauty of our family life. A child watering the ivy or setting a table reminds us how richly blessed we are to be able to live beautifully ourselves.

I have always tried to hide my efforts and wished my works to have the light joyousness of springtime which never lets anyone suspect the labors it has cost.

HENRI MATISSE

Passionate About Home

Before we take a closer look inward at our own gifts, take a few minutes to think about the free spirits who have had the courage to take what gifts they were given in life and make the very best of

their talent, no matter what the odds. Artist Roger Mühl comes to mind. Roger Mühl may be one of the most prolific artists alive. He is strong, quick, and inspired. His home in the South of France, surrounded by hills, valleys, and the Maritime Alps, is the subject of his luminous paintings as well as the stimulation he lives with in his house and gardens. He paints like the wind, every day. He believes all creative energy comes from passion, that boundless enthusiasm for bringing something tangible into existence. The fire is inside you. When you lose your passion, you lose your creation. Passion is a means to make everything better, a way to ensure that you're always growing. Mühl uses color to intensify the feeling of light in his paintings of scenes from his daily life at home: intimate walks in his garden after luncheon, a table with favorite objects.

When it gets too hot in Provence in July and August, he goes to his other home in Brittany and paints there, refreshed by the change of scenery and the cool breezes of the Atlantic. He's figured out how to balance his time at home. His mornings are for creativity in his studio. He takes a break for several hours midday to create a banquet with his wife, Line, and friends. Everything is effortless and happy because they have found their passion and live it every day.

Finding Your Passion

One of the questions I'm often asked is, How does one find passion? I receive letters from readers who feel something is missing in their lives. They don't know what their passion really is. Wherever there is love, there is passion. Roger Mühl knows this, and builds his life around his passion. If he cooks, it is a creative experience. If he builds a stone wall, he is expressing himself. If he gardens, he is creating a natural canvas. He feels at home with everything he does. He uses his energy to express his love of living. His art is his way of intensifying

People seem to concentrate best when the demands on them are a bit greater than usual, and they are able to give more than usual.

MIHALY
CSIKSZENTMIHALYI

Living well is a courageous act.

In some kind of creative work the creating person unites himself with his material, which represents the world outside of himself.

ERICH FROMM

Creativity springs from our curiosity and our inner resources. All creativity comes from an inner awakening.

his enthusiasm. He looks at life as his blank canvas, with time and space to express himself. Everything looks easy to him because he loves what he does; he loves what he doesn't have to do, and he invests his attention in everything he sets out to do. When he sets a pretty table, it fuels his imagination. When he puts yellow tulips in a blue pitcher and pulls up a chair to the table, it becomes a still life painting. What do you do every day that increases your happiness?

Recent studies have shown that one third of our time we spend doing what we want to do, one third doing what we have to, and one third doing something because there isn't anything better to do. Even if we only spend one third of our time doing what we want to do, we still need to know what we like, what gives meaning to our lives. Mühl works harder than most of us; he's disciplined and works with an energetic enthusiasm. He has a goal to express the spirit of beauty everywhere. If he decides to paint a series of canvases of swimming pools, he makes us aware how splendid it feels to refresh ourselves in the heat of the day and have "a bath," as he calls a dip in his pool. We look at the water and can feel the sense of luxury and freedom. If he decides to paint a series of his chef friends, he reminds us that cooking is an art and that these famous men bring so much pleasure to our senses. If he decides to paint a kitchen table with a pitcher of flowers and a bowl of fruit, we see the beauty of the simple white tablecloth and feel refreshed.

Creativity is work that goes some place: it is sustained effort toward an ideal.

MICHAEL DRURY

Because he has found his passion, he helps us to find ours. Unless we use our minds to the fullest potential, unless we dream big dreams, take lots of risks, and pursue activities that give our lives meaning, we won't have a steady stream of good feelings, and will deprive ourselves of keeping our enthusiasm and passion for life alive and intensely exciting. Life's challenges are what fuel our psychic energy. Everyday events to an artist are not mundane, because they see life as an opportunity to cultivate their gifts.

Constant effort and frequent mistakes are the stepping stones of genius.

ELBERT HUBBARD

The Mysterious Process of Our Creativity

Day-to-day existence can and should be a creative process. The Japanese Zen masters who practice "no mind" are in a mystical state of highly focused yet effortless creative work. If we look at every moment as an opportunity to breathe new life into every little thing we do, we will increase our pleasure in the process. As we know, everything is a process, a series of actions that bring about results. We are always expressing something, but for many of us, discovering our originality is not easy. Perhaps that is the challenge.

Out of the common everyday experiences we see a way to improve our lives.

I wrote a book called *Daring to Be Yourself* because I have always believed that until we can express what is inside us that is our own, we will never be at peace, or at home. Each one of us can find life a creative challenge and not a burden. All we have to do is to put our personal spin on everything.

Turning Chores into Grace Notes

I've never liked the word chore. I remember with great poignancy going into the kitchen of a client in Greenwich, Connecticut, where I saw a notepad next to the kitchen telephone with one word printed on the top: CHORES. Some stationery store is making a profit from this numbing idea that the things we all do routinely are unpleasant tasks. Everything we choose to do or not to do is an opportunity for self-fulfillment. We can focus either on our achievements or on our drudgery, our problems or our solutions.

Leisure is time for doing something useful.

BENJAMIN FRANKLIN

I had some notepads printed up with the words GRACE NOTES on the tops of the pages, with several typographical ornaments, in an effort to counter the notion that the things we all do (rich or poor, healthy or ill, creative or dull) are a burden.

Whenever we feel anxious, overworked, and overwhelmed, maybe we are not living as creatively as we know we can. The writer Tom Wolfe's editor for *A Man in Full*, editor in chief of Farrar Straus & Giroux, wrote in the margin of one of his writers' manuscript, "Is this as good as it can be?" The art of living well is in taking the circumstances of our lives and making them as good as they can be. I believe we need Zen time to recognize the sheer glory of each new day. By flinging our energy into projects that interest us, by persistent recognition that now is the only time to dare and try and lose our fear, we can use the hours of our lifetime to express our unique gifts and talents. Our skills increase and meet more challenging obstacles. How can we live in this new creative awakening without retreating to the lower, more common, conventional ways of our past?

If we can't change reality, why shouldn't we change our attitude about each new day? A Sanskrit text comes to mind:

> Look to this day
> For it is life,
> The very life of life.
> In its brief course lie all
> The realities and verities of existence,
> The bliss of growth.

What Do You Love to Do?

You always should ask your own questions. What are my unique talents? What can I do that no one else can do in the same way? Roger Mühl has no competition in his genre of expression because all the imitators create fussy pictures, not being capable of the bold simplification of the original creator. They should be finding their own creative thrust, not imitating his. The first step toward cultivating your unique gift of creativity is to look within your soul, yourself. Ask yourself, "What do I want?" "What do I seek?" What are the moments when you've felt free and light and whole? Where were you and what were you doing? You may remember sensual moments of extraordinary beauty. You may also remember times when you were at the height of your creative powers, in tune, in touch, and in ecstasy. When have you loved being astonished by some simple revelation that made you feel rapture?

Most people don't believe they are creative. In reality, we all are creative, in our own way. We are original human beings.

In your notebook, list the activities you most enjoy doing. Go back to your early childhood and remember what you most loved. By the age of three, I realized I was far more enchanted being in my mother's garden than being inside playing with dolls. At camp, when an instructor put a tennis racquet in my hand and showed me how to hold it, I became one with the racquet, the ball, and the game. No one ever had to urge me to practice. If I couldn't find someone good to play with, I'd work out on a backboard. If I couldn't find a backboard, I'd practice my serve.

What are some of the interests you would like to spend more time pursuing? How would you ideally wish to engage your creative energy? What activities cause you to concentrate so completely on what you are doing that you lose your self-consciousness and all sense of time?

Do you enjoy sailing, hiking, biking, playing tennis, loving, gardening, flower arranging, painting, swimming, building, dancing, communicating, sewing, writing, inventing? What are some of the most absorbing activities you've enjoyed in the past year? What are some of the ways you've been able to become one with an activity? When was the last time you let yourself be free, where you felt all the weight of the world lifted from you, and you were in a rhythm where you experienced a momentary joyful ecstasy? What were the circumstances that fostered this experience? When were you last able to throw all caution to the wind and follow your impulses? The more you know yourself, the more often you'll have a sense of delight and joy in the process of whatever you choose to do. Studies show that when you enjoy what you're doing, your focus is so spe-

Creativity is our tool to adapt well to life and express ourselves in every undertaking.

To be able to fill leisure intelligently is the last product of civilization, and at present very few people have reached this level.

BERTRAND RUSSELL

cific that your brain uses less energy than when you're thinking a lot of random thoughts and about problems. We obtain for ourselves in this experience the exhilaration of "swing," a rhythm of heightened spirit.

Childhood Exposure

Self-knowledge deepens throughout our life. Do you feel you were raised in a creative family? Were there lots of rich materials to use to create things? Were you allowed to make a mess? Were you given ample freedom and time to fantasize and play? Most children have natural talents, a flair for particular activities. Is there a common thread between what you were good at as a child and what you do now? What are the resources you draw on? What are your greatest strengths?

My parents wanted to expose their children to a wide range of aesthetic activities. We were given piano lessons. I played the clarinet and my sister played the flute. We took ballet lessons and were sent to dancing class. At camp I practiced riflery and archery. (I sometimes hit the mark.) We took singing lessons and acting classes. We learned how to figureskate and ride horses. What were some of the skills you acquired in your childhood that you still enjoy doing? Are there some hobbies or activities you did as a child that you've given up and would like to take up again?

Pleasing Yourself

One of the great thoughts of Dr. Samuel Johnson that encourages me to continuously pursue activities that bring me personal fulfillment and give my life meaning, satisfaction, and a purpose is: "Men seldom give pleasure where they are not pleased themselves."

One of the killers of creative energy is a persnickety perfectionism. The most creative people are obviously the ones who make the most mistakes because they experiment until they figure things out. Rather than doing what has always been done, creative spirits juxtapose unusual and unlikely elements in such a way that something new emerges.

Rather than just stack wood in rows, you may be amused to alternate the rows with logs that are vertical, and then horizontal. At the top of the stack of logs you might want some ivy. By turning a fat round log on end, you have an ideal place to put a pot of ivy. By placing some of these fat round logs on end in the garden, you can arrange flowering plants at different heights to create more variety and interest. Sometimes I group together several different-colored candles rather than limit myself to one color. I also use different-colored napkins and plates as well as colored glasses. I have a hand-painted basket filled with rolled-up sheets of marbleized paper that I like to display in the bedroom because I like looking at the swirls of pastel colors. Rather than hide pretty colorful quilts in the linen closet, I stack them in the bedroom. Try putting some African violets in a gleaming copper saucepan or some daffodils in a cobalt-blue water glass. Recently I painted a delicious shade of blue inside the medicine cabinet, and I lined the drawers of a blanket chest with sheets of wrapping paper printed with Claude Monet's water lilies.

> *The spirit of a person and the spirit of the place where one lives is actually felt.*

> *God has created Man to be God's free partner in the works of creation.*
>
> ARNOLD J. TOYNBEE

Intuition and Mystery

What have we ever created that didn't involve mystery? When is the last time you had a powerful feeling that you felt a sublime presence? When we bought our cottage twelve years ago, we saw through all the depressing colors and the tar paper on the floor and actually felt the ugly house was speaking to us, encouraging us to take whatever risks were necessary because we both intuitively felt this was our house. We felt at home. The house had been on the market for four and a half years. It was unbearably unattractive, but underneath all

> *I'm more than ever disgusted at things that come easily, at first attempt.*
>
> CLAUDE MONET

the horror was an old sweet house that cried out to be loved. What gave us the confidence to take this utter wreck and commit ourselves to it completely? We relied on our intuition and trusted the mystery of our bond with this house.

When is the last time you took a great risk because something spoke to you? This cottage has challenged our creative energy every day. It is alive and has mysteriously nourished us, bringing us joy and comfort and great contentment. Every time I strip old peeling paint off one of the eighteenth-century doors, I feel I am revealing the honesty of our house. When we do something in this consciousness of love, we are not only being creative but we are doing the work for our creator. We do not run the universe. But we can learn to cultivate our divine intuitive spirit by exposing ourselves to activities and environments that foster these sublime feelings. When I see the entire sky become bubblegum pink at sunset and the water turn lavender, I stand before this scene in great humility; as a result, I have more trust and more faith in a wisdom superior to mine. At home, every day, we can live with the direct experience of being in an encounter with mystery.

This exercise forces us to look at the shape and quality of our daily life. By looking at our habits, our mood, and our psychic energy every day, we can make subtle changes in the way we approach and balance our time at home. Once we clearly see that we have time, we can then have worthwhile goals, knowing how to put this freedom to the most creative and beneficial use for ourselves and others.

Intuition, Time, and Stick-to-itiveness

For creativity to happen, something within us must be brought to life in something outside of us.

PAUL KAUFMAN

Although I believe all ways of knowledge are important, I favor intuition because it is pure, direct, and true. This is the most penetrating way to examine our own mind. In order to cultivate our gifts of creativity, we have to spend more time doing what we're talented and skilled at, so that we have knowledge about the subject and competence to do a satisfying job. We then enjoy solving problems because each problem becomes a situation, a challenge we can figure out. Our solution stretches us, turning a seemingly intractable problem into a creative opportunity. When one of our maple trees was rotting the roofs of our cottage and our neighbors', it became necessary to cut the tree down, something we were reluctant to do. But we now have a larger-looking backyard with more sun, and my Zen writing room now has brilliant light all day. The small strips of lawn on the south side of our house received too much shade to have healthy grass, so we eventually turned the loss of the tree into an opportunity to plant myrtle that has wonderful periwinkle-blue flowers and curvaceous green leaves. Our creative energy makes us more persistent in finding ways to turn problems into opportunities. We don't procrastinate or give up. My parents called this "stick-to-itive-ness."

I almost think that these canvases will tell you what I cannot say in words.

VINCENT VAN GOGH

When we live with this creative spirit, our life becomes ever so much more diverse. We try different ways, we learn from experience; we also learn to trust ourselves. We are no longer paralyzed by fear of failure. If we don't make mistakes we will fail to learn and to grow. The attempts we make are what counts. We have to keep on trying and not hold back.

Bathtub Art

The creative drive can be increased, just as our self-knowledge can improve over time. The first step toward improving our creativity is to give up all preconceptions—our own and others. We should cultivate a childlike innocence about everything we do. I have an artist friend who finger paints with Mr. Clean as she scrubs the bathtub. In this new way of living, the only prerequisite to any task is that we put our personal spin on it. Creative moments can't be forced and come naturally when the circumstances are right.

Everyone knows what it means to clean the grime from the bathtub after a bath. This is a necessary task, but with an illuminated attitude in which we put our creative spin on everything, the chartreuse color of the cleaning liquid contrasting with the white tub can be an inspiration to an artist to dream up a theme for future work. Who is to know if the finger painting in the bathtub doesn't provide a Eureka!—a creative moment.

A Matisse Moment

I bought some square Post-it Notes in Day-Glo colors at an airport recently and began to play with them. In order to see all the colors, I separated them and began to fiddle. Before I knew what I was doing, I was cutting up different shapes, playing as though I were Matisse. Certainly he encourages us to see the potential shape in a piece of colored paper. I played with the different-colored forms until I'd created my own abstract collage without having to use glue. I amused myself as a diversion from my work.

This simple activity brought me a giggle, some joy, a private moment of revelry. We can learn to do more things for enjoyment and private pleasure. I have no idea why I bought these brilliantly colored pads. I thought I'd write notes on them when I bought them, but ended up using them for a different sort of self-expression. My little Day-Glo collage wasn't perfection, but the happiness it brought me was complete.

Seizing Time and Space

So often we are cut off by time constraints where we are in the middle of a "swing experience" and have to stop because it's time to pick up a child at school or it's dinnertime or it's time for bed. How many times a week can we stay with an activity as long as it captivates our imagination? How often do you have open-ended time? Is it rare?

Few of us have uninterrupted time for more than short moments snatched here and there—when we're walking to work or waiting for an airplane, or in the morning when we get up before the rest of the household. One father of four would park his car in a parking lot a mile away from his house in order to spend twenty minutes reading before driving home to his demanding wife, who puts him to work the moment he walks in the door. The telephone rings, there is a knock on the door, and no matter how creatively we want to spend our time, there will be demands on us because of all the chaos around us.

But only he can give, who has; he only can create who is.

EMERSON

Early morning or late at night, there is time to put to creative use. Whenever you are alone in the house, you should feel free to spend your time doing something for yourself. We should choose our time and seize it. Before I knew how to claim my creative time, I had to leave home and go to a library. To avoid distractions I went to the reading room at a New York City library and logged in several uninterrupted hours. But home is the best studio for creativity. What I've learned is that if I respect and honor my will to create, others do, too.

If we set aside specific times at home to practice certain skills and improve our abilities, honing our craft—whatever it may be—we will have a fresh new way of thinking about our home. Once we establish this time and create a sacred place to work, we will discover all the other tasks and domestic activities are accomplished with greater flair. Our creative forces spill over and we feel more freedom in all we do.

I want to get to the point where people say of my work: that man feels deeply.

VINCENT VAN GOGH

When are you the most creative? Is it in the morning? Do you like to work at night after the family goes to sleep? No one else gives us time; they take our time. We have to set up times when we will not be disturbed. Whether you use this uninterrupted time to garden, ride a bike, paint, or write music, you need to be free to melt into the moment with a patch of time on a regular basis. Interruptions slow us down, interfere with our swing, and cut us off from our intuition. Einstein evidently did a great deal of thinking. He thought for hours on end. Ninety-nine percent of his hunches did not pan out but his one-hundredth guess was right. If our lives are so hectic and scheduled that we can't dig deeper into that power surge of intuition, we'll be living only on the surface of life. We need time and space to draw on a wiser resource that is already inside us, waiting to be activated.

If your spouse doesn't understand, communicate with compassion and empathy until your needs are met. If your children are screamers, tell them you need quiet. Let them go play in the yard, quietly, while you work, or get a sitter so that you can go into a room and shut the door. Claim a specific space in your house that is yours alone, where no one is allowed to move your papers or supplies around. Any house that doesn't accommodate some degree of mess is a cold, hard house. You have the space and it is ready to be discovered. A room of your own, even if it is small, is essential. Just as an artist needs his own studio, so do you. Where will you create your sacred space? If the room you claim doesn't have a good view or a lot of natural light, paint it brilliant white to make it appear twice as big and bright. All creative living is somewhat messy. If we don't spread out our materials we're mere dabblers. Make a commitment to live with this creative spirit at home.

The most important first creative step is to find your spot. A botanical watercolor artist climbs up attic steps to go to a room with rafters where he can draw and paint uninterruptedly. His wife turned their one-car garage into her ceramic studio. She earns her living from her work and now has a rent-free studio that connects to the kitchen. She had three windows installed to flood her studio with light. Anne's work is a higher priority than a garage for their old Jeep. Our daughter Alexandra and her husband, Peter Scott, park their car on the street in order to use their separate garage as a work space for Peter. Look in the basement or the attic or the room of a child who has left home. Reevaluate a mudroom, a pantry, or a bathroom. In a client's apartment, a guest room had a private bathroom and access to a second bathroom that was used by a child. We turned the private bathroom into a sacred space because the occasional guests can share the child's bathroom. We removed the toilet and kept the sink and the tub as an ideal darkroom for a photographer. Tom locks the door to his room, making it off limits to everyone else.

We must be flexible to put our spaces to better use as our needs and circumstances change. If your guest room isn't used that often, consider turning it into your sacred space. If most of your life is spent with your immediate family, at home, claim and reclaim the best spaces for yourself and those you live with every day.

A client let me help her create a sacred space in her large New York apartment. There was an ample area in a former butler's pantry with a window that faced east. By removing the glass cabinet doors, we could put bookcases on two walls. We built a glass door for privacy and also to admit light from the west window in the dining room. We built a forty-two-inch-high ledge on the eight-foot width under the window. Karen sits on a high stool because the window of the apartment building is high, designed for people who are standing, not sitting, and we raised the floor on a platform so she can easily see outside.

If you are really in a pinch, don't give up on the laundry room. One client has a frontload washing machine next to a frontload dryer that is hidden from view by cabinet doors when not in use. The counter ledge is two-inch butcher-block maple. We installed a counter opposite the washer and dryer, wall to wall, with ample space to work on the computer, with hanging bookcases above. Sharon does the laundry at night in order to have a sacred space by day, where she retreats as soon as the children leave for school in the morning.

The electronic calculator compresses creativity. It can only verify results, not anticipate them.

DANTE GIACOSA

Living More Intensely

I believe we should live every day as though we're going to die in our sleep and also live forever. This attitude helps us to live intensely, using our creative powers constructively and feeling the ecstasy of being alive. When we put our stamp on everything we do, from writing a poem to keeping a journal to preparing a dinner for friends, we can use our creative potential to bring us and others more pleasure, greater hope, and serenity.

I think of Helen Keller often because she became one of our greatest teachers about living creatively. She believed we should use our senses as if tomorrow we would lose them. In her words:

Hear the music of voices, the song of a bird, the mighty strains of an orchestra as if you would be stricken deaf tomorrow. Touch each object as if tomorrow your tactile sense would fail. Smell the perfume of flowers, taste with relish each morsel, as if tomorrow you could never taste or smell again. Make the most of every sense. Glory in all the facets and pleasures and beauty which the world reveals to you.

Variety and Your Improvisation

Every day, set some small challenges for yourself. Stretch yourself to go beyond the routine or conventional way. If you usually have breakfast in the breakfast room, try having breakfast out in the garden on a warm spring morning. Throw open the French doors and pull up some chairs to the garden table. Rather than cook dinner, buy some wonderfully fresh, prepared salads at the delicatessen, select some cheese, bread, and fresh fruit, and have a picnic at the beach. When you plant your garden, do it in a different way. Around our small patio, each year we select a different flowering plant to pot in terra-cotta to circle around the ivy. One year white geraniums, another red hibiscus, another purple and yellow pansies. Each new day, try something you've never done before that gives you a kind of pleasure you've never had before.

Take up modern dance or try your hand at ceramics. What have you tried recently that you had never done before and that you found out you enjoyed? Maybe you went sailing solo or went out on a canoe at sunset on a small lake in New Hampshire, and you felt rapture inside and out.

Try giving a lecture if you've always been afraid to stand up in a room full of people, and tell them something you are

passionate about. If you don't think of yourself as a creative person, change your energy by going to the art supply store and purchasing some small canvases and brushes and tubes of acrylic paint in your favorite colors. Go to a beautiful place, either inside your house or in your garden or some place you love, and absorb the feelings. Sit patiently. Don't paint until you feel you are one with this place, until there is no separation. Breathe in the spirit of the place, then meditate about this experience with a brush in your hand. Never wonder whether you are painting something that is good or bad. Paint what you feel, not what you literally see. You are painting your picture. You'll see some quiet beauty emerge because you overcame your fear and just tried it.

The moment of truth, the sudden emergence of a new insight, is an act of intuition.

ARTHUR KOESTLER

If you don't feel you are particularly talented at arranging flowers, take a bunch of some of your favorites and let each stem speak to you. Watch and see how they will arrange themselves if you don't rush or force them in any way. The flowers will inform you. You just have to show up with a vase of water and some clippers. If you've never baked chocolate chip cookies, go to the market, buy a box of mix, come home, mix the ingredients, put them on a cookie sheet, and turn on the oven. If you haven't written a poem since you were forced to in school, sit under a tree with a pad of paper in your hand and feel the lines forming into harmonious rhythms.

As knowledge increases, wonder deepens.

CHARLES MORGAN

When we make a salad, why do we need a cookbook? We can decide what items we want to toss together in a bowl that taste luscious and look pretty. If you are someone who likes to rely on recipes when you cook, try experimenting without a cookbook for a week. Try not to make a favorite sauce or salad dressing the same way. There are infinite combinations and ways to put ingredients together that taste wonderful. Trust your taste buds and play until you feel satisfied.

When we put our personal touch on every action we take, we are more open to being in the awareness of being guided by a divine presence. How often do you feel aided in what you are creating by a force more powerful than your own? When you are doing carpentry work, do you ever feel the ecstasy of effortlessly having the

> *The genius is especially inspired with the good spirit of recognizing quickly what is useful to him.*
>
> GOETHE

nails go into the wood so straight that your hammer, the nail, and you feel in unison? When we're good at something, we can elevate ourselves into a contemplative trance or state of "no mind" as the Zen Buddhists taught us, in which we completely become one with what we're doing.

Just Do It

Even though I'd worked hard and had a lot of fun playing tennis when I was young, I was always concerned about how I looked on the court, especially if a boyfriend was watching the match. As I matured, I discovered it was far more fun to pay complete attention to where the ball was on the court and how I would move to be in a position to hit it well than to be distracted by spectators. As soon as I focused on how wonderful it felt to hit the ball well, not concerning myself with my appearance as I played, it liberated me to just play the game, just hit the ball. Often, after a good match, I'd feel such tremendous satisfaction because I felt I had almost become the tennis ball. It was far more exciting than when I was also trying to model as I moved about the court. Sweaty, I just played the game. I just tried to hit the ball. Whenever anyone enjoys what they are doing, this is most compelling. You are in the swing with the swing.

> *All great art is the work of the whole living creature, body and soul, and chiefly of the soul.*
>
> JOHN RUSKIN

Not only do we have to be willing to take risks, we have to set ourselves free from the confines of routine and the anxiety of how we appear to others. We make this choice minute by minute, now, this evening, tomorrow morning, and forever; always, we choose to suck the marrow of the bone of life and live as interestingly as is humanly possible.

Be an Inventor

I have been in thousands of houses in the course of my fifty-eight years, and I've never wanted to live in any one of them because they were designed for other people's lives. Our home should be a place where we can live with unrestricted creativity. We just have to release this powerful driving force from within, expressing ourselves as truthfully as we know how. The twenty-four-hour cycle is the divine order, the basic pattern of our lives. Within this form we have limitless power to carve our lives into something inspired. We should wake up every day and think of ourselves as inventors. If we paint our picket fence a brilliant white, we are adding to the beauty, energy, and spirit of our yard. If we create a brick patio, we are adding to our pleasure in sitting outside in our garden to eat our meals, dance under the stars, or have a place to read and contemplate. I have an ancient stone Zen meditation bench where I sit and ponder life's mysteries. If you can't have a Zen meditation garden, what kind of a space do you want where you can go, curl up in a cozy chair, and read? What are some unusual ways you can arrange and decorate a room so it better suits your needs? What are some tasks you set up to do and where is the space to do them inventively? Tasks such as:

- Wrapping presents
- Sewing and quilting
- Working on scrapbooks
- Indoor gardening
- Exercising
- Letter writing

When we see more clearly what we want, what's missing after our basic needs are met—food, clothing, and shelter—what can we create that will nourish us and our home? We see this seamless connection between creating something out of passion because we've learned necessary skills and honed our talent—playing the piano, painting, or creating ceramics, and doing creative things around our house that express us and comfort us.

I have a predilection for painting that lends joyousness to a wall.

PIERRE-AUGUSTE RENOIR

The truly artistic response is an expressive and creative behavior for self-actualization.

RENÉ DUBOS

At home we can use all our gifts to create a warmer, more welcoming, more open, spirited environment. Some portion of our leisure time will be spent working on our house, although we'll also spend regular hours creating something for ourselves that seems unrelated, such as writing poetry. But the poet and the poem are one and so are the poem and the poet's home one. Read Emily Dickinson's poetry to have this thought ring true. Our home has a powerful hold on us. As we make personally meaningful improvements, doing things that don't just look nice but are practical and make our lives run more smoothly, this home atmosphere is the greatest source for our inspiration. Artists feel like fish out of water when they are not able to work in their studio or garden or a place they find profoundly meaningful.

> One of the first obligations of art is to make all useful things beautiful.
>
> EDITH WHARTON

Home as Inspiration

Ultimately, our home is where we cultivate our creative gifts. By improving our home and garden, we are elevating our mind as well as our natural abilities and aptitudes. When we feel this intimate connection between our own uniqueness and our home's unique spirit, we understand that we are inimitable as our home is inimitable.

When we look at a decorating magazine, we are meant to get ideas that we can adapt to our house. We should never think that one way of doing something is the correct way or the only way. When a reader sent me a thoughtful letter telling me she enjoyed reading *Creating a Beautiful Home*, she ended by saying she wanted her living room to look just like ours. This idea of copying, hailed as the greatest form of flattery, doesn't help the imitator to cultivate her own gifts. We can pluck certain elements out of what we like, but the essential benefit is to make everything into something personal. You may, for example, like the chintz I used in our living room for the upholstered furniture, but you may decide it would be perfect for curtains and bed hangings in your bedroom.

Ask yourself again, what do you want to do more of? What passions and interests do you have that you want to pursue at home? What are some aspects of your family life you now feel you have the time and interest to improve? What do you wish you could do to express yourself? Do you want to do more entertaining, when you can cook for your friends and use your pretty china and linens? If you do, you can create a wonderful shallow closet for your tablecloths, napkins, and dishes near your dining table. If you can't build a closet area, perhaps you can find an old high cabinet that will be a focal point in your dining area. I have a passionate interest in collecting postcards. This interest led me to write *The Postcard as Art*. I have several thousand postcards and enjoy sorting them into different categories—artists, gardens, seascapes, designs, and travel. I've now bought dozens of colorful boxes that have a place for a label so I can easily add to my collection and keep it in order. Boxes of the same size are great for VCR tapes.

In order to create there must be a dynamic force, and what force is more potent than love?

IGOR STRAVINSKY

Maybe you want to do more gardening and you need a potting shed or an area for your tools and flowerpots. In our New York apartment, I claimed the cabinet under a bar sink in our kitchen as a flower-arranging area for terra-cotta pots and plant fertilizer and tools. When I buy inexpensive flowering plants from the grocery store, we can repot them easily, clean up the mess, and wash our hands. The whole process is effortless because there's a place for our practical needs.

By painting the sky, van Gogh was really able to see it and adore it better than if he had just looked at it.

BRENDA UELAND

A client asked me to help her create a flower-arranging room out of her apartment powder room. Because the bathroom was rarely used and her kitchen was too small for her to spread out all her flower vases and containers, this solution provided her with counter space, running water, and shelves for her attractive necessities. How wonderful to walk into this small space and not feel you're on the sixth floor of a modern apartment house in a city. By placing a thick, rectangular, bull-nosed slab of weathered maple on top of the toilet, she is able to pot and arrange regularly. When guests come, the bouquets and flowering pots are dispersed throughout the apartment and the low counter is raised and hooked to the wall with a heavy brass piece of attractive nautical hardware.

Finding Creative Spaces for Two

If you decide you want to spend more time at home with your spouse, are there favorite spaces where each of you likes to spend time? Peter and I have created several places in the cottage where we have lots of different light sources to make our work and play more enjoyable. One is the round kitchen table, another is the round table in the center of the living room, and our favorite winter space is at a French Provincial table in the dining room. This is an ample table where we can do projects together between meals. There's plenty of space for Peter to read the newspaper and for me to spread out my notebooks and papers. How many places do you have where you and your partner can spend time together without getting in each other's way? Identify the people you love with whom you want to spend more good times. How can you create settings that will be most conducive to having fun together?

A Place to Write a Personal Note

Perhaps you want to spend more time writing letters, staying in touch with family and friends. There is a grace about a letter you write with a fountain pen on stationery. Letter writing is the beginning of writing. I owe being a writer to writing thank-you letters and sympathy letters as a little girl. If a friend's dog was sick, I'd write a long chatty letter to my friend. Recently I went through several boxes of my mother's memorabilia and came across letters I'd sent from camp.

A client who loves to write letters asked me to help her set up a small desk in her bedroom where she could store all her pretty note cards and boxes of stationery and also have attractive storage boxes where she can save the letters she receives. It fills her with joy to sit there in the sunny corner of her bedroom, where she can look out onto her backyard and garden and send her loving thoughts and news to family and friends. I am the recipient of some of her wonderful letters, and I'm reminded what a huge difference her writing desk has made to her time at home. Often when her twins are in the yard playing, she'll go to her desk to muse, feeling grateful, and effortlessly write several letters from her heart.

We have two desks facing the water in our tiny cottage study. The large French farm desk is where we usually sit to work. The smaller drop-leaf desk ended up being a place to put things. One day I took everything off the surface, cleaned out all the cubbies and drawers, polished it, and created a letter-writing place.

The Journal Writing Ritual

A client who keeps a daily journal wanted a place in her house where she could go every morning to write. She also wanted a chest where she could store her journals. We chose a favorite chair in the living room near a window overlooking a pond, discovered an old wooden mahogany box that locks, and placed it next to the chair to rest her coffee and a book on, and she can store her private notebooks inside this large attractive antique box. Kathy loves to keep this box highly waxed because she believes her truth is on the pages of these books. Inside, she also keeps a tin of lemon wax and a soft rag in a Ziploc bag to make it effortless to give her special box a vigorous rubbing after she's emptied herself in her journal. Having this special place ready and waiting makes it a welcome and easy morning ritual to go there to write.

Spending More Time Outside

Maybe you've decided you want to spend more time out of doors in fresh air. When we escape to our cottage, Peter and I want to be outside every minute we can when the weather is good. We both want more uninterrupted time and privacy in order to read and write more. In a wonderful book entitled *The Garden Room* by Timothy Manson, we read about a beautiful concept: "Occasionally, summerhouses, sometimes called, evocatively, shadow houses, were open on all sides, with delicate columns supporting the roof." In our Zen garden, we have a sixty-foot-tall maple tree that is too close to our wood frame house, causing tremendous damage, clogging the gutters and blocking the sun, never allowing the wood to become completely dry. Mr. Reardon, a local tree doctor, told us he recommends not just pruning this giant tree, but removing it. At first when anyone suggests cutting a tree down, we are hesitant, especially while still mourning the loss of our other maple tree, removed not long ago. But what dawned on me was to turn the Zen garden into another outdoor sitting area. I can't be anywhere for long without books and notebooks. If we laid a stone floor and erected an umbrella overhead, we could have a table and chairs there as well as our potted plants. Until now this space was one we looked at but didn't use for any practical purpose, other than sitting on the stone bench, because it was too dark.

Living Spaces

Now, I often go out on our round patio and sit at our round table under an umbrella and pay bills. We can eat meals in the garden and also read and write there. Why sit at a desk inside on a sunny day if it is more fun to be outside?

We have so little land that we need to put it all to the best possible use. Having a different private place to work while enjoying our tiny walled garden fulfills dreams as well as needs.

Taking a Siesta

Another of our wishes for us is to have a light siesta on a summer day. Our cottage bedroom has a western exposure and is hot in the afternoon sun. The downstairs bedroom off the living room gets no direct sun. It is decorated in blues and white, making it a lovely spot for little naps. What makes this room ideal is the white paddle fan overhead. We can read ourselves into a sweet rest, feeling we're being caressed by gentle sea air, a peaceful, heavenly illusion. Maybe you'll want to hang a hammock from two trees in your garden for a siesta. If you live in an apartment and don't have a garden, you might toss a colorful patchwork guilt over the back of a sofa for a spontaneous nap in the living room.

The Fresh Fruit Salad

My editor identified her desire to eat more fresh fruit. Toni ate lots of vegetables bought every day from the Korean market, but she needed to find a way to add more fruit to her diet. The solution was something as simple as using a large crystal bowl with a blue band around the edge as the vessel for the fruit. She loves to select each piece, realizing that handling the kiwis, grapefruits, oranges, bananas, and pears is pleasant. She's reminded of the miracle of nature, enjoying ripening the fuzzy peaches and kiwis on the southern windowsill. People who live in small spaces can have sun-ripened fruit that connects them more to the creative process of nature. This bowl with fruit sits on her kitchen counter, giving her visual pleasure. Not only can she and her husband have some fresh fruit after dinner, enjoying the sweetness, but also she feels she's doing something nice for herself, nourishing her soul as well as her body. Just before she goes to bed she puts a pink grapefruit in the refrigerator to enjoy cold with her breakfast. The fruit ritual is so simple and costs no more than it

The man or woman who makes no mistakes does not usually make anything.

E. J. PHELPS

would if her fruit were selected ripe and put right into the refrigerator, but it makes a big difference to her enjoyment of her time spent in their New York apartment.

Pursuing Your Own Creativity

What are some of the passionate pursuits you want to enjoy more of at home? Now that you've opened up some time and space, look inward to examine what you want to spend more time creating and doing both for yourself and for your home. Spend some time in contemplation and write some notes in your notebook. No one should expect us to be anyone but our true selves, and no one has the right to control our creative energy.

What are some of your unfulfilled desires? By identifying some latent gifts, we can dream up ways to express them. All creative energy is a divine gift, and only we can use this life force to bring something into existence. Whenever we do anything out of passion, it will have a spirit that is felt by everyone. Matisse claimed throughout his life to be able to control the mood of the people who saw his pictures.

Our creativity is our own torch. Let it light the way toward self-expression as your way to know and understand yourself as well as to uplift others by your creative example. Let's use the tools handy to us at home to express our appreciation for superior spiritual gifts.

CHAPTER 6

Creating Your Ideal Home

Without hearts there is no home.
— BYRON

What Chapter Are You Currently Living?

Look back on the past five years of your life, at all the changes that have taken place. Are you living in the same house or apartment? Are the people you're living with the same? Think back to your age and the ages of your family members five years ago. My spiritual guide, John Bowen Coburn, former episcopal bishop of Massachusetts, who married Peter and me at Saint James Church in New York City, May 18, 1974, believes we live in chapters, one after another. When we live at home alone, that is a beginning chapter. When we live with a roommate, that is another chapter. Marriage, raising children, children growing up and leaving home is another chapter. It is exceedingly important to look reality in the face and be up to date on just what chapter we're living in. John Coburn believes we must live

*The word which credits
what is done,
Is cold to all that might
have been.*

ALFRED, LORD TENNYSON

each one fully, before beginning another. We can't skip over any life passage chapters without being out of harmony with ourselves.

What chapter are you living in your home right now? In your notebook, write the date on the top right-hand corner of a fresh page and identify your profile. How old are you? Who are you living with? What are their ages? How healthy are you? What is the status of their health? How do you feel about your life at home right now? Do you feel you have found a way to fulfill your own needs and passions and still balance your time between working around the house and enjoying time with your family? Think about what you want to be doing five years from now. Do you want to live in the same house or apartment? Who do you think will be living with you? How old will you be? What differences in your daily living patterns do you foresee? Do you feel you will be more free in the next five years or less free? Are there some improvements you want to make to your house? Write them down in your notebook. Are there some changes you want to make in your living patterns?

On a scale of one to ten, rate the quality of your life at home, ten being ideal. I've never been in a room I couldn't make better, more harmonious, more inviting. Do your rooms smile at you? Identify what is missing in this chapter of your life at home that you want to bring into existence. Do you feel your house is too much work for you to keep up? Do you feel you spend too much time, energy, and money on your house and family needs and have too little time to do things for yourself?

As a woman, I fiercely defend my need to have free time to create, to muse, to ponder, to putter, to love, and live without pressure or unrealistic expectations. I love my home and family too much to ever feel either is a burden. I've seen "successful" business people who felt out of place in their own houses because there was an assumption that they would perform certain useful tasks, on call, losing their freedom to enjoy free time and space in the privacy and sanctity of their own home. Many of my clients confide in me how

To build a life as if it were a work of art.

ABRAHAM JOSHUA
HESCHEL

Take in fully the bounty of life.

Beauty is an accumulation of details, the kind of layering that takes a long time.

HÉLÈNE DAVID

uncomfortable they feel when they're lounging around spending leisure time in their house because their spouse can't relax.

Time at Home Can Be Sacred

Why is it that many of us want to do more things at home that express our uniqueness, but we don't let ourselves do them? Do you want to participate more fully in decorating projects? What are some of the reasons (or excuses) you don't enjoy expressing yourself more at home? Does your spouse want to make all the decisions? Do you feel you spend enough time with the children? Do you spend enough free time with your spouse? Do you have friends over as often as you'd like? Look reality in the eye and live this "today chapter" with as much pleasure and vitality and as wisely as you can. Four of the saddest words in any language certainly must be "it might have been." Being at home can be sacred time. How we feel when we are home is of the utmost importance. If we aren't pleased, no one else will be, either.

If you wish you had more unstructured time at home, who is keeping you from this freedom? What can you do to free yourself up more? If you want more intimacy, whether between you and your partner or more cuddling time with your children or grandchildren, what kinds of changes can you make to invite this sweet atmosphere? You might want to add a wicker toy basket to the living room for easy play access and cleanup. Maybe you want to do more artistic projects and you need a space where you can go and make a mess, get paint on yourself and on the floor, and not have this be a problem. We have a friend who is a ceramic artist living in a small house with her husband and two children. Her solution was to claim the garage as her studio. The car stays in the driveway. As relaxed as Peter and I tend to be about our home, we found that turning our basement into an artist's studio, and calling it "the studio," helped everyone to have a place to release their creativity without spattering paint on living room antiques. We installed a wet sink so that everyone of all ages could be self-contained in their preparation, creation, and cleanup. Rain or shine, this space is ready for any form of creative project. Maybe you and your spouse want a workbench and a handy place to store all your tools.

Finding a Way

"Good" is what helps me and others along on this journey of liberation.

E. F. SCHUMACHER

Many of the things we want to do more of don't require a quiet atmosphere, but some do. We should find a way to take charge of these times to satisfy our needs. There will probably be misunderstandings at times when someone thinks there should be an exception to the rule, but each of us has to find ways to protect ourselves in order to function and feel we're maintaining a balance between being with others, working around the house, and having free solo time. I am always looking for more time to write. Ever since I began my first book, *Style for Living*, in 1966 when I was pregnant with Alexandra, I realized how difficult it is to find this freedom to create when we're at home. At first I went to coffee shops and libraries and park benches, but then I changed my timing and I got up early or stayed up late.

After I gave birth to Alexandra, and then to Brooke two and a half years later, life got more hectic and I was tired, but I carried on and got up early, figuring I could do some writing before anyone in the family woke up. All these years later, I still begin early and still write in my nightshirt. Whenever the telephone rings, I ask Peter to "protect" me. We have to make a commitment at home to this time that is free, where we can surround ourselves with creative play. Creating is just plain fun. We have to just claim the time and have the fun. Emily Dickinson retreated to her bedroom to write a trunkful of poems. If we have a door to shut, shut it. If we need to tell a white lie and pretend we're resting, we will be forgiven. But the secret is to always

By doing good we become good.

ROUSSEAU

fight the urge to do the dishes or water the plants or do more laundry. If there is an activity you need to do alone, make your needs known and be firm. In time, the rhythms of the day will accommodate your private time. The worst defeat would be for you to give up and leave home to accomplish your goals. Ideally, you'll be able to do more and more things at home because you grow to find the atmosphere so nourishing and rewarding.

Where could one settle more pleasantly than in one's house?

CICERO

What are some of your interests you want to have the option to pursue in an uninterrupted atmosphere? Maybe you are an executive and you'd rather bring work home than stay late at your office and miss the sunset over the water at your seaside home. If your family would rather have you home than away at the office, certainly there can be ways to allow you to do paperwork on your deck without being disturbed. One way to avoid random distractions is to have friends and neighbors who want to come by for a visit write you or call you in advance. The same courtesy people pay you in a business situation should apply in a household. I think it is sad to have to hide yourself out of sight to meet your need for uninterrupted concentration. I read recently that women find the bathroom to be the only place in the house where they're not expected to be doing some domestic activity. I love the bathroom, but I'd hate to write my books there.

The Zen of the Laundry Room

Even parents of young children can find ways to write or invent or think. Several of my clients use their laundry rooms to do the wash and to iron while they listen to inspirational tapes, take notes, or even tape-record their thoughts to be transcribed later. Since washing and ironing are usually done alone—because no one volunteers to help out—having a notebook and some motivational, spiritual tapes could be a good creative solution, providing you with some quality, productive time alone to think and study. Hang up a few colorful plastic clipboards with pads of paper on them so you can write down thoughts and ideas. We think we will remember a flash of insight, but soon it fades unless we write it down. I think on paper, so I always have a clipboard or a pocket-size pad with me wherever I am. Some of my best ideas come to me when I'm ironing, so I keep a small spiral pad and pen at the end of the ironing board next to where I rest the iron.

An Awkward Room Is Transformed into a Treasure

Once when I was ironing, I had an idea how I could turn the upstairs sitting room into a laundry, ironing, and dressing area for myself. I realized I didn't have to ask permission; I simply claimed this space for myself. My clothes closet is in this room, so this idea seemed practical as well as making me feel good. There is a television in this room but I don't encourage people to watch it. I have an old blue folding rack I put my ironed linen on, and it hides the blank screen. The magic of this multipurpose room is that there is a door I can open to see the boats in the harbor through our bedroom windows. The back of our four-poster bed is in front of this door. All I have to do is open the door and slide the bed hangings to each side. The pretty white flowered chintz of the bed curtains frames the view nicely.

You are a king by your own fireside, as much as any monarch on his throne.

CERVANTES

Living in our house over the years made me realize we rarely used this room because it doesn't have a nice view. It also has five doors, an old-house phenomenon that makes it difficult to use the space efficiently. But now, with the ironing board in front of a door, I have the benefit of the bedroom view for only one reason—I'm standing up when I iron, seeing over the headboard of our bed. When we're sitting on the sofa or in one of the two wing chairs, we can't see anything pretty. Other than for occasional television viewing and watching films, this room was rarely used.

This is the room where I sort clean laundry. On cold winter days, I can light a fire, and as I iron in a cozy warm atmosphere, I can look out the windows at the snow and enjoy the sparkle of the icicles. I'm drawn to this room because of its intimacy. One day several years ago, Peter and I were antique shopping in the village, and I saw the most heavenly blue hutch. It looked Shaker in its simple honesty and usefulness. The entire top half is open and the bottom half has doors. To rationalize the expense of an antique we didn't need but both loved, I thought we could use it in the living room for books. Peter smiled and told me I should put it in my dressing room for bed linens. This room could never feel wonderfully inviting as a sitting room because of its awkwardness, having five doors and two windows overlooking another house, but we have found a perfect use for this room. It is large and works ideally in its present incarnation. The blue cabinet, to the right of the ironing board, holds spray starch and water, and is filled with our colorful linens. It makes the process of putting linens away and deciding what sheets and blanket covers to use when changing the linens a pure pleasure.

Every materialist will be an idealist; but an idealist can never go backwards to be a materialist.

EMERSON

Off Limits

This space is mine. I use it to the glory of the whole household, but it is off limits to anyone but family. It is hardly for show, but perfect for me. I created a space that makes me feel good as I do necessary tasks. The whole room is devoted to laundry, ironing, and dressing, and if family enjoys using the room for reading by the fire or watching a home movie, they are not offended by the homey scene. I'm the only one in the family who irons. When someone puts a shirt, a dress, or some trousers on the ironing board, they know it will give me pleasure to press out the wrinkles on this piece of clothing to be worn by someone I love. Because the ironing board is always in place behind our bed, I throw a piece of the pretty flowered chintz that matches the bed hangings over it as a grace note when I'm not ironing.

It is not enough to do good; one must do it in a good way.

CONDORCET

Animate Objects

When I am at home, surrounded by so many objects of my affection, I often think that objects are really not inanimate if they were made lovingly and are loved in a home. Most people think a chair or table or bench are passive "things," but I don't agree. Scientists tell us that matter is made up of whirling atoms. There's plenty of action and energy. When something is created by humankind, it has been imbued with the creator's touch of genius. We should recognize this and give reverence to these objects that bring us emotional comfort as well as serve our practical needs. Objects that have been created out of passion and love are alive and breathing.

Adding Touches of Our Spirit in the Spaces

We can improve every area of a house by connecting our dreams and aspirations with the physical space we have at hand. We first take care of ourselves and our practical needs, because in doing so we can then reach out and connect to others.

We do this by preparing personal spaces that will become sacred to us in times of great joy as well as when we're experiencing tremendous pain. Last summer Peter and I drove home from a funeral in Bedford, New York, where Peter had given a eulogy, and we had stayed to have dinner with the family. By the time we opened our front door, it was after one in the morning. Glad to be at home in our sweet cottage, we sat in the living room in comfortable upholstered swivel chairs, put our feet up on a round ottoman, and talked. On our large round table in the middle of our living room, we had a hand-blown glass pitcher brimming with cornflower-blue delphiniums. Several dozen petals had fallen onto the table top. Their delicate blue petals looked lovely lying on the waxed fruitwood table. I remembered that Sid, Peter's good friend who had just died, loved our cottage. That evening,

Peter and I lit several candles. We felt at peace. It had been an emotional day. I looked around at our pretty room lit only by candles and some ceiling lights that illuminate Roger Mühl paintings over each mantel. On one of Sid's visits I had had a huge bunch of delphiniums in a shiny bulbous brass pitcher on our large French Provincial desk in our study. Sid smiled and inquired, "Alexandra, this shower of blue blossoms surrounding the brass pitcher is so beautiful, did you deliberately put them there?" I told him they fell naturally, but because they are so pretty, I never wipe them away. They connect us to the larger rhythms of life. Our homes can help us relax into a higher awareness. We come here in our brokenness and our home heals us. We come here in our wholeness and we feel more expansive, more connected, more awake, alive, aware. I let a few rose petals fall onto a table without removing them. If you buy some small tomatoes that are still on the vine, put them on a favorite plate and let them ripen on a sunny kitchen counter. If you have a dish under a wide candle and the wax drips down onto the plate, leave it there. These little acts of nature add charm to the ambience of home.

Life, like art, should be the celebration of a vision.
MICHAEL LARSEN

At Home with Imperfections

Under all circumstances, whether our cottage is in trouble with a mud-flooded basement, rotted wood, leaks, or peeling paint, we love it and always feel welcomed and at home. When you are at home you live with imperfections. Some of the windowsills of our cottage windows were completely rotted out, and the painters painted brilliant white around them. Our wood frame house needed to be repainted because of the salty sea air. The windows had just been cleaned before the painters came, and now they were covered with plaster dust. Every day we live with the noise of a carpenter's electric saw, the sound of an electric sander scraping the paint down to the bare wood, and the sound of a hammer nailing wood together as the carpenter repairs rotted windows and the bulkhead doors to the

Every state of society is as luxurious as it can be. Men always take the best they can get.
SAMUEL JOHNSON

cellar. When you feel at home, you can sit amid a mess and know it is all part of a larger plan. When the renovation is completed, the windows will be cleaned again and our red cardinal will know it is safe to return to our garden once the shrill noises are behind us.

Loving Up Our Home

When we create our ideal home, more and more we will feel at home with ourselves. I asked Peter recently if our cottage is his ideal home. "Absolutely. If misfortune burned it down, we would want to re-create it exactly as it is now in every detail." When we renovate our old cottage, we feel we are loving it up. Every tap, tap, tap, tap of the hammer is loving it up. Every brush stroke is loving it up. We want everything to be idyllic because this is our strength, our center.

When we bought our cottage, we thought we'd come here as a place to disappear, where we could escape from the stress and problems of life in a city and unwind and write. Our cottage and garden are modest, occupying only one seventh of an acre. Hardly an estate. But it was well built in 1775 by church carpenters and has held up well for us over the years. Removing the giant maple tree that has been dropping its limbs and leaves on our roof will make a big mess, but we will be doing something good for the house, and out of this loss we can create a shadow room in our Zen garden. Without this giant tree this space will be flooded with sunlight. If we need shade, we can buy an umbrella at the Pottery Barn or Crate & Barrel. There are always options, if we keep an open mind and stay flexible. If our house doesn't change and undergo transformation, it is a sign of our limited ability to live as fully as we're capable. Thomas Jefferson continuously renovated Monticello until his death. As our needs change, we change our physical house to aid us on our quest for a more exuberant life. If something isn't working out, you can fix it, change it, remove it, or replace it, even if it is a majestic maple tree. If something feels right, it is right.

The Buttery

One of the things I love to do is arrange flowers. Whenever I am creating bouquets, I experience equanimity and feel calm, composed, and one with what I'm doing. Our buttery is a magical space for me. Not only does it display all our pottery and our bowls, platters, and pitchers but it also has a deep white wood counter space in front of a window with geraniums in an outside window box. What's wonderful is to have all the flower containers right there on open shelves to inspire me to make the ideal connection between flowers and vase or pitcher. Because the teapots are also displayed, often I am drawn to to use one as a container, enjoying the added dimension of the spout and handle. I also love pitchers because of their handles, making it easy for me to carry an arrangement to another room, and how they encourage the flowers to fall into place naturally. They're functional and aesthetically pleasing. There's a deep drawer under the counter for clippers, plant and flower food, and paper towels. I can go into this space with a bunch of flowers, and time stops as I make bouquets for all the rooms in the cottage, including one to leave in this functional, charming walk-in closet.

Each one of us lives in a private world of his own.

RENÉ DUBOS

We should use our own minds and our creative energy to make our inner visions a reality. Whenever you spend time in a space, you make it feel more cozy, more inviting.

Flowers, Food for the Soul

If one of your dreams is to have fresh flowers every day in your home, for the months you can't grow your own (if you're fortunate to have a garden), budget flower money along with your food money and buy the equivalent of one large arrangement a week. This way you can make smaller arrangements as the week goes on, using every bud and blossom throughout its life span. You'll be pleasantly surprised how some tight buds will slowly open and last a week and a half. I spend a great deal of time tending to my geraniums. I do it as a gift I

The strength of a nation is derived from the integrity of its homes.

CONFUCIUS

give myself, never a chore. After sitting on the patio writing for several hours, I'm happy to bounce up and deadhead and water them. They inspire me as I work and I enjoy caring for them, giving them thanks for providing me with so much pleasure and quiet beauty. If you are going to have cut flowers each day, you'll want to create a special place to arrange them where everything is in one place. If you want to maintain flowering plants, you'll want to create a little potting area where you can store your tools, pots, and plant food.

Teatime

Feeling at home is the ultimate achievement of any person, anywhere, at any time. There is no substitute for this pleasure.

PETER MEGARGEE BROWN

And grace will lead us home.

FROM AMAZING GRACE

Do you want to enjoy the tea ritual every afternoon? Whether you have tea alone or with a spouse or a friend, the ceremony is more important than the tea because it is a time you set aside to break free, to listen, to reflect, and to enjoy a simple, inexpensive, gracious act. In the winter you might invite a friend over for afternoon tea after work. By having a cabinet stocked with your teacups and saucers, a variety of teapots, a water pot, plates for cookies, cream and sugar dishes, and a glass holding some silver spoons, you'll be set up for an easy, enjoyable preparation of your afternoon tea. You might be able to store your trays in this same general area and you might choose to store your tea with the teapots so everything is at hand. Even the pretty tins of tea cookies can be right there. The great thing about afternoon tea is there are no interruptions. You have hot water on the tray. No one has to jump up to do anything and, of course, the telephone is off limits to this high art of afternoon tea. This tea ritual could become a very meaningful way for you to to catch up on your child's day at school and stay connected, and there's a good chance this will become a tradition that will continue when your child grows up, marries, and has his or her own children.

Our society is so scheduled; there are few white spaces in our calendars. Years ago, Peter taught me about having more "buffer" spaces in my daily schedule. Whenever we rush and feel pressured, we lose the potential joy of an experience. The tea ritual allows us to slow down, to focus, to open up to a broader view of our lives and feel more grateful for the miracle of our existence. If this is one of your interests, think how easily you can have this wish become a reality. Friends will begin to give you different-flavored teas to try. For a present you might receive a pretty teacup and saucer. It is charming to have each one a different pattern, design, and color. By experimenting with different kinds of tea, you're increasing your pleasure. Try mixing several flavors together—chamomile and apple-cinnamon or lemon blossom and peppermint.

The mysteries always teach us to combine the holy with the profane.

MARTIN BUBER

Hierarchy of Needs

On a fresh page in your notebook, write down your "hierarchy of needs," as psychologist Abraham Maslow called them. We have physical needs, emotional needs, intellectual needs, and spiritual needs. What are some of your specific needs that you can meet right now in your home?

So much depends on where you are on the needs spectrum. If your house is a wreck, and your primary need is to love up your house until it is a more peaceful, serene, orderly place for you and your family, this is where you are now and where you'll want to put your energy. If you've just moved, unpacking the boxes will take precedence over your spiritual longings, but you may decide what you really want is more bookcases, and you might wish to build them yourself. Or maybe your life at home is very settled and your house is in good working order, but you feel some things should be changed to take care of your family's more current needs. What's working and what isn't working? Identify what's wrong, what you want to improve. Walk around room by room and evaluate how you feel in each space. Maybe you'll discover one reason you rarely go into your living room is that it is poorly lit and you can't read there. This can so easily be corrected.

A visible simplicity of life, embracing unpretentious ways.

LAO-TZU

Last winter I realized I wanted more light in the cottage. Although we feel blessed we have so much reflection from the water and the rooms are usually bright, in the dark dreary winter months in New England or on stormy days, all interior spaces become dull and need extra brightness. I love to sit and work at the round table in the center of the room where I can watch the fire and see the sunset at the same time. Even with a halogen standing lamp, I didn't feel there was enough light. Peter enjoys sitting opposite me but he complained about the light on a particularly dreary, stormy afternoon. We had the electrician put in a duplex outlet in the floor near the table, enabling us to place an attractive lamp in the center of the room without an ugly cord that someone could trip over. This was so simple and inexpensive to accomplish. Our lamp was made in Brittany, and being hand painted, added warmth, color, and cheer to a favorite place to work.

Don't Precompromise

Before we say no to any of our needs and wishes, we should look into how we can accomplish what we've come to know we want. If you really want a wooden floor in your kitchen and feel strongly about it, don't precompromise. Estimates are free and you can get expert advice. You may find you can afford to rip up the linoleum and have an organic hardwood floor. I didn't like the orange-tone fir wood of our kitchen floor; it brought the whole kitchen down. Rather than be bothered by it, I hired a man to bleach and pickle the floor, and with five coats of sealer, it is light, cheerful, and practical. I've learned as an interior designer to pay attention to my feelings and not be afraid of the expense until I've done my homework. Maybe you have wall-to-wall carpeting that is an ugly taupe color, and you feel stuck with it because there is so much of it, and you know you can't afford to replace it right away. Even after having it cleaned it still looks dirty and makes you feel sad. I'd rip it up and enjoy the bare wood. If it depresses you, it will probably feel dreary to everyone else who enters your house. Ask yourself, does the carpeting speak for you? What does it say about you? If it is sad, are you sad? Never be afraid to remove something from your house. If you don't feel something is cheerful and harmonious and speaks to you positively, go without. Be patient. Once you identify what you want, you'll probably be able to have it sooner than you think. Maybe you'll leave the stairs bare wood and replace that taupe wall-to-wall carpeting with a green area rug in the living room.

Interest is the ruling motive of mankind.

SAMUEL JOHNSON

Life is short. If something in your house drags you down and is not part of your master plan and color scheme, make a commitment to find an alternative. Why wouldn't it be far more pleasant for you to rip the carpeting up and have wooden floors? There are hundreds and hundreds of objects that make up the atmosphere of our home. Each element either builds toward a harmonious, cohesive whole, a coming together of all the various details into a larger design, a background for our individual lives, or the elements tear down the atmosphere. If having depressing carpeting all over your house can be remedied, and you clearly feel it is wrong for you, wrong for the house, dragging you both down, rip it up. There's really no excuse for putting up with things around your house you find offensive. Keep trusting your feelings. When something doesn't feel right to you, it isn't right for you. You always have the power to change something in your own home.

No object should "wink" at us.

BILLY BALDWIN

Evaluating How Your Rooms Feel

Quietly continue walking around your house with your notebook in hand. Write down anything you see that doesn't feel good to you. Be open and let your intuition inform you. Today you might be in close touch with your feelings. Use this time to become aware of ways you can improve how you spend time in your rooms. How a room looks and how a space works aren't necessarily compatible. There

Home is where we express our passions and our unique creative vision. We should seek and celebrate the poetry of every day at home.

are many rooms that are attractive to look at but awkward to function in. Maybe you'd spend more time in your living room if you had some bookcases, a desk, and better lighting where you can work. Living rooms that aren't lived in regularly obviously don't feel comfortable or they would be used more regularly. Maybe your living room is too formal, not welcoming you on a daily basis. Perhaps the room needs more comfortable, upholstered furniture that you and your friends can sink into. Write down your impressions of how each room makes you feel.

You think me the child of my circumstances: I make my circumstances.

EMERSON

Does a certain space welcome you? Is there a specific area of a room you're drawn to? Why? Do you think you're taking advantage of the view of the lake? Are there certain objects you feel are awkward or the wrong scale or in your way? Are there pieces of furniture you wish weren't there filling up a space? We get so accustomed to the things around us that eventually we don't see them well, and we don't stop to evaluate our feelings about them. All of us have certain areas of our house that need to be reevaluated. A house should never be static, but alive and receptive to accommodate our wishes. After you've assessed how you feel and made notes, ask your spouse and children how they feel about the various rooms in your house.

Future Plans

Home is not where you live but where they understand you.

CHRISTIAN MORGENSTERN

Right now our cottage is ideal, but we will continue to try to have it function well in the future as our needs change. There is a lot we want to do. In the back of the house I'd love to put in a large round window in the attic. In a few years, I'd like to turn the attic into a third-floor living space. That floor is above the surrounding rooftops, and we have an excellent view of the harbor from our seventy-two-inch wide fan window in the front of the house. There is now a separate room in the back of the attic I'd like to fix up as a space to do projects. I envision large counters where we can go as a family and make memory books, putting memorabilia in books and photographs in albums. We could also paint in this room.

We also want to put in a bathroom with a stall shower at the top of the stairs, lit by a skylight. The walls, floor, and ceiling will be tiled and the floor will be pitched so we won't need a shower door; the water will drain naturally. We want to repair and refinish the old wide pine floorboards, Sheetrock the walls, build bookcases, and create a sitting area in the front of the attic (we call it the atelier) in order to enjoy the view. We'll have lots of beds with trundles to accommodate visiting family. But that's down the road. We're content now. Everything is simple for us to maintain and we don't have any unmet needs at the cottage right now. When the time is right, we'll tackle the renovation of the third floor, putting in skylights, air conditioning, and good lighting. I see the whole space in blue and white, clean and simple. We'll know when the time is right.

What are some improvements you'll want to make on your house in the years ahead? Write them in your notebook because you might be able to do them sooner than you think. It's fun to have goals and a plan, even if they are long range.

If a love wants to induce a man or woman to feel at home, the nest must first be prepared.

PETER MEGARGEE BROWN

It's best to follow the Japanese way of not showing everything you own.

STANLEY BARROWS

The Roof Garden

Clients in San Francisco want to turn their roof into a summer living room. Although they have three floors to work on now, the architect is inspired and so is the landscape architect. This roof garden space, when completed, will give my clients and their friends a view of the Bay and the Golden Gate Bridge. I remember with great nostalgia the roof of the building where we'd rented an apartment on East Sixty-fifth Street between Madison and Park avenues in the late sixties; we turned it into a great outdoor space. We whitewashed the brick walls and put down green indoor-outdoor carpeting. We strung up chartreuse Japanese lanterns and set out a grill, picnic table, and some benches. We cooked dinners on the grill, lit the

The smallest part is worthy of the whole.

ELSIE DE WOLFE

lanterns, and dined under the stars. During the day we played with our daughters in the open air and sunshine. Fortunately, there was a sweet lady who ran a flower shop across the street called The Green Thumb. She adored Alexandra and Brooke and loved to give them little potted African violets whenever we'd go in to buy flowers. We ended up having quite a lush roof garden. Our apartment, one flight below, was eventually too small for our family's growing needs, but it was hard to give up this rent-free space we spent so much happy time enjoying.

Plunk Them In

Sacred and happy homes . . . are the surest guarantees for the moral progress of a nation.

H. DRUMMOND

That dear apartment was also the first place where I experimented with indoor window boxes. I learned a great lesson from this attempt at city gardening. The flower shop across the street provided me with pink geraniums for the two living room windows that faced south. I plunked them in and loved the way they looked. But because we were on a busy street and buses and cars added to the pollution of New York City air, the blossoms didn't last long. I'd fertilize and water, but they didn't exactly thrive.

Rather than give up the joy of having geraniums growing inside our living room, I decided to compromise. When all the buds had bloomed and there were only the green stems, I'd remove the geranium, add it to the roof garden, and replace it with a fresh bloom from across the street. New York is not the ideal place to have a garden but it was the only place, because that is where we lived. This resolution was well worth the added cost because of the beauty it added to our lives.

Our apartment was small but cozy and inviting, and the geraniums are what all our friends remember. No one could get over how healthy they were because everyone always saw them in the window box in full bloom. Sometimes, some of the geraniums up on the roof would bloom again, and I'd plunk them back in, but what I learned was not to strive for perfect circumstances or conditions. The geraniums were perfectly beautiful and that is all that mattered.

The Loved-Up, Lived-In Look

A journalist wrote a feature story for *New York* magazine called *Practically Perfect*. She had a photographer take pictures of several interior designers' apartment, including where we live now, in an apartment Peter has lived in since 1959. The article was interesting because all interior designers are paid perfectionists, and many redecorate every five years, giving the press fresh ideas to publicize and clients new things they may want for their own houses. In our apartment, however, the journalist selected rooms that hadn't been redecorated for over ten years. We've had the same chintz in our living room for nineteen years. We love it more than any other we've found, and the screens for printing it have been destroyed, so there is no hope of ever being able to replace it. We have patched the ripped places, we've made new arm covers. One day, when I'm looking for fabrics for a client, I'll happen upon a chintz and fall in love with it, and if everyone in our family likes it, we'll have a new fresh look.

More than anything I must have flowers. Always. Always.

CLAUDE MONET

We actually had enough fabric to re-cover the two chairs Peter and I sit in all the time. It's tricky to re-cover only some of the pieces, because those that have not been freshened up look tired, but this was the best we could do and we're satisfied. Ideally, we would have had enough fabric to do all the upholstery over, but we didn't, and we worked with what we had. My clients often buy double the yardage and stow the bolt of replacement fabric in a closet.

For without the private world of retreat man becomes virtually an unbalanced creature.

ELEANOR MCMILLEN
BROWN

A client who has become a close friend helped me to feel at home with myself. Estelle raised three sons and learned early in life that nothing is ever perfect. She bought her fabric by the bolt, and whenever she'd see a worn-out arm on a sofa or chair, she'd cut a small piece off the bolt and have an arm cover made and pinned into place with special upholstery pins. When she'd buy a new rug

Touch everything.
If something is beautiful to
the touch, it must be truly
beautiful.

she'd leave it outside for a while to fade in the sun because she liked new things to look as though they'd been there a long time. Some people like vintage fabrics that have a mellow look. In the sixties we often dipped chintzes in a tea solution to tint the background so it wouldn't look too new, too fresh, too perfect. I wouldn't take a fresh bright chintz and make it look lived in, but when we spend time in a room and let in the air and light, our fabrics do bleach out and look faded and so does our furniture. I happen to like this look and feel comfortable in a room that is obviously lived in and enjoyed.

No Person or Thing Is Perfect

Everything I have earned
has gone into these gardens.
I do not deny that I am
proud of them.

CLAUDE MONET

One of the greatest mistakes we can make at home is to be obsessed with perfection. It is an illusive goal leading to frustration and unhappiness. To create our ideal at home, we have to work toward comfort, seeing that our emotional needs are met as well as those of our family, but not trying to control everything. There is a danger in striving too hard. It is not healthy and ultimately creates an uncomfortable atmosphere where everything ends up looking stiff and rigid. I've written a book on this subject and have thirty-eight years' experience. Perfectionism doesn't work. It's a quagmire, and if you are a perfectionist, being at home will be like sinking into quicksand. There is no perfect house or garden or family or human being. We can all live a perfectly beautiful life and create our ideal at home if we stop short of perfectionism by being more understanding and, in turn, forgiving.

Do you consider yourself a perfectionist? Take a few minutes to evaluate whether your propensity for being displeased with anything that's not prefect has been helpful in creating your ideal at home. Has it been a stumbling block? On a scale of one to ten, ten indicating a perfectionist and one indicating relaxed, what is your score? If you are not a perfectionist, are you married to one? Do you have a child who is a perfec-

Taste cannot be controlled
by law.

THOMAS JEFFERSON

tionist? Do you ever feel this personality trait is a fault when not kept in balance? Most of my clients are perfectionists. They want things right. We all deserve good workmanship when we pay someone to do something for us, but good doesn't mean perfect. For the best fabric pattern repeat to be beautifully centered on a chair seat, two small seams are required, one on each side, but this is practically perfect, not perfect. If you live in an old house, the floors will not be even or the toilet won't flush when you're running the tub. This isn't perfection, this is reality.

I love beauty and spend my life trying to make everything look more gracious and attractive, but I am not a perfectionist. I will meet my client's highest, most demanding standards, but in my home I only feel at home when the atmosphere is relaxed, casual, and cozy. Living is a messy business. The saddest truth for me is that so many people treat their houses as a place to create a perfect setting for some future event. Eventually, they think everything will be perfect, and *then* they'll start to entertain. In the meantime, no real quality living is going on; there isn't that sense of wonder and appreciation for all the beauty that is available at every moment for themselves and their family. If I cleaned up everything before I sat down, I'd never sit down!

It is wise to overlook certain things, rising above them.

Education, sensibility, and morality . . . these seem to me to be the components of taste.

RUSSELL LYNES

Crash

Somewhere along the way, many of us were encouraged to be perfect rather than creative. Perfectionists are not very creative as a rule because they tend to be too critical, to judge things too harshly. Perfectionists tend to have lost their naive sense of childlike wonder, often looking for the flaw or imperfection rather than appreciating an object for its overall integrity and inherent beauty. One of my favorite columns I wrote for *McCall's* magazine was a hymn to flaws called "The Cracked, Chipped, and Broken." If everything I owned had to be perfect, I'd live in nearly empty rooms. Recently a painting fell off the bathroom wall and knocked down two of my favorite hand-blown bottles from Venice. A plumber was fixing a clogged sink and was startled by the noise. He threw out all the pieces. I picked them out of the wastebasket and was able to tape the bottles together. They have missing pieces and are far from being perfect.

If something breaks, I mend it if possible. If it is shattered, I throw away the pieces of glass or porcelain and I move on. I can't waste precious time grieving over material objects I can't bring back to wholeness. The Buddha believed all our suffering comes from attachments. If we get upset when something becomes scratched or chipped or broken, we could be upset a lot. The more richly we live, the more wear and tear we'll put on our possessions. This is a normal reality of life. All we can do is appreciate what we have when we're blessed to be surrounded by things we love. I become very attached to our favorite objects and try to maintain them reasonably well, but when an accident happens, I try not to let it break my heart. More important, I try not to dwell on something I can't change.

Someone broke one of my favorite porcelain dishes. I have no idea who did this or when it happened, but one day I saw this graceful dish with a piece missing. It was similar to looking at someone with a front tooth missing. What could I do with this pretty dish without always wishing it were whole and perfect? I walked around the cottage holding this sweet dish I'd found in an antiques shop in London over twenty years earlier. I was drawn to a hanging rack in our living room filled with our collection of porcelain fruit and vegetables. On one of the shelves is a porcelain object of three tulips, and the colors of the dish were identical to the colors of this decorative piece. By placing my dish behind the base that holds the tulips, the missing piece is not seen. There's almost always a way to place your objects in a harmonious way so the repaired or missing pieces don't show.

Peter and I have been able to buy a great many of our eighteenth-century antiques at affordable prices because they had been repaired over time. We aren't antiques dealers and have no intention of reselling them; they're all an important part of our family history.

We're not purists, we just like to have attractive things we care deeply about around us to inspire our best thoughts and actions.

From Generation to Generation

We are the caretakers of our objects. Rather than find fault with a mended dish or a worn-out rung of a chair, with the dents in the silver baby cup or the ink stain on the desk, we should rejoice that they have been used and enjoyed. These signs of life add to the charm of our possessions. We care for the things we love and hope our children and grandchildren will enjoy living with some of our furniture and objects they've grown up with and also loved. I have several antique tables that belonged to my mentor, Eleanor McMillen Brown; I purchased them at two different auctions, and they are extremely meaningful to me. The fact that they were purchased originally in France and Italy when Mrs. Brown was on a buying trip with the famous interior designer William Odom gives them an interesting provenance. I remember exactly where each table was located in her house in Southampton, Long Island, and in her Sutton Place duplex in New York. One table is a late eighteenth-century Italian Directoire piece that is a lovely addition to our New York City living room. When I purchased it, however, it was in bad condition, and that's why I was able to afford it. The marquetry inlay on the top was all loose and crumbled, with several pieces missing.

I paid $750 for this antique in 1980, and a few years later I could afford to have it put into mint condition for the same amount I had paid for it. Now I have a treasured eighteenth-century antique, lived with and enjoyed by my mentor and former boss, that shines brightly, as though Mrs. Brown is smiling at me. I like the idea of being able to repair, care for, and live with a favorite table of hers. I also appreciate seeing her ivory checkers every time I open the drawer. I feel the table's energy, I feel her energy, and I know that table is alive.

Decoration is not the end, but the means toward the end. The home should be complete—and that means good housekeeping and good food as well.

BILLY BALDWIN

True simplicity consists not in the use of particular forms, but in foregoing overindulgence.

BOOK OF DISCIPLINE
OF THE SOCIETY
OF FRIENDS

If I hadn't seen beyond the condition of the table to its essential spirit, I wouldn't own such a treasure. If it had been in perfect condition, I would have been outbid at the auction because it could easily have sold for five or six thousand dollars.

Change It, Fix It

When you see the charm and spirit of an object, it's fun to love up the table or chair you found at a reasonable price because it needed work. If something is dark, it can be lightened or bleached. If a table has cracks in the wood, they can be filled in; wax does wonders to bring a wooden table or chair to life. If you're not a perfectionist and are willing to sand, stain, paint, and wax, there could be a great chair waiting for you at the village fair or even in a thrift store. Look at something you're intrinsically drawn to and visualize it transformed. I bought some painted Louis XVI chairs for a client at one of Mrs. Brown's auctions, and we had them stripped down to the most lovely honey color. If you find a mahogany table you like that you buy for a bargain, you own it and can paint it French blue if you wish.

The Hidden Dimensions

When we can see the potential of how something could look and feel, whatever we do to love up our home will be rewarded. Last summer we spent an exceptionally pleasant week loving up our cottage. We did a lot of gardening and little things around the house to improve the way things worked for us. We rearranged the two deep drawers in the desk in the study, putting checkbooks and financial folders in one drawer along with a calculator; in the other drawer we organized stationery, envelopes, notepads, clipboards, labels, stamps,

and the address book. We didn't improve the way the desk looks on the outside, but we greatly improved how we function seated at the desk.

At Home Depot we bought a wonderful fan that moves the air in different directions. This was a great addition to our enjoyment of our time spent in the living room. I bought two-gallon aluminum watering cans to make it easy to nourish my plants with Miracle-Gro. I organized my ribbon drawer as well as my candle drawer, and rearranged the shelves of napkins, tablecloths, and place mats in the dining room closet. By having our scissors and knives sharpened, we made all our cutting tasks more enjoyable. Slicing open a cantaloupe or an apple or a tomato can and should be a joyful act when you have the right sharp knife. The clippers I use when I arrange flowers were worn out, so I bought a new pair. I also stocked up on my writing tablets and little spiral notebooks, making me feel organized and inspired to write.

I discovered a magical place to add more geraniums on the roof outside my Zen writing room. I now can look at white geraniums as I work, feeling the garden is reaching up to the heavenly blue sky above. I love white flowers in my Zen room. I often have white lilies because they're spiritual flowers to me. For someone who loves color as much as I do, white flowers are a refreshing contrast to all the Matisse colors of my many boxes and folders.

The entire week we spent so blissfully in the cottage was a celebration of the pure pleasure of being at home. We listened to classical music and to the birds singing their hearts out. We ate fresh fruit, vegetables, and fish. There was nothing that interrupted this extraordinary peace and feeling of contentment. We realized after we left that this had been the happiest week's vacation. We had all our physical, spiritual, emotional, and aesthetic needs met. The house became our amusement, our entertainment, our constant companion, and our faithful friend.

There's nothing quite like one's own electricity and hot water to put one in a good mood, is there?

STANLEY BARROWS

Decoration in good taste is savored by people of good taste.

JEAN-FRANÇOIS
DE BASTIDE

Creating More Ease

Once during that magical week I caught myself thinking how marvelous it is to have sharp pencils, paper clips handy on the desk, ink flowing freely from a fountain pen, a notepad next to the telephone, stamps handy to envelopes, Scotch tape in every drawer, the address book always in the same location, and good reading light wherever there's a chair. How simple it is to accomplish these little grace notes at home, and yet so often we don't, and doing the most humble task can become a burden. Walk around your house again and evaluate how well you've organized your space in each room. Ideally, we should all try to make everything as logically arranged as possible. I love to enjoy the entire process of doing anything. If my pen runs out of ink I want to be able to reach into a drawer and select a color ink cartridge without having to move an inch. Because I also write at the kitchen table, in the cottage I have ink cartridges in a box on the table. In the apartment we have a small pine set of drawers on the square table against the wall in our kitchen, and I keep ink in those drawers. In fact, I have ink cartridges in every room where I live, and even carry a box with me in my tote bag. If I had to get up and hunt around for ink, it would interfere with my concentration as well as my serenity. Ink cartridges to me are as important as car keys to someone else. I like to have my ink at hand. What do you like to have at hand?

Do you have enough scissors in your house? There is something so wonderful about having scissors in every room. You never know when you have to cut a ribbon or an article out of the newspaper or a picture out of a magazine. When we have scissors handy, just like pen and paper, we're more likely to be encouraged to clip an article to send to a child or friend, just as we're encouraged to write a thought down if we have the pen and paper next to where we're seated.

The Zen of Drawers

When we're physically comfortable, we're more emotionally content. Unlike an office setting where you work in one space you can call your own, at home we can use all the spaces for different activities at different times of day. When I looked around at how we have arranged our various spaces, I realized that most of our tables have drawers. Drawers make living more graceful. You can keep coasters, cocktail napkins, candles, notepads, Scotch tape, and pencils in a drawer. How nice to have matches in a drawer on a table where you have a candle.

Open the drawers of your tables and chests and have a look. What would you like to put in each drawer? Peter clips articles out of newspapers and magazines to save. We keep a file folder in the drawer of a table next to a living room chair where he enjoys reading. He puts his clippings in the drawer, knowing they're safe until he files them or sends them to family and friends. Everyone loves the "Brown Clip Service" he set up in 1984. Peter had small tags of shiny, folded paper printed with his family crest and there's room to write a note on the front and back. He can fold these tags over documents to hold the pages together and send them with a note. We keep these tags and paper clips in the same drawer.

We also have Post-it Notes in the drawer. If Peter is reading a book and comes across a passage he wants to duplicate for someone, he sticks a Post-it Note with the person's name on the page. When he's in his writing room he makes a copy and sends it in the mail. Peter keeps his favorite pens in the drawer, too. He can't think without a pen in his hand but doesn't like fountain pens because he likes to be able to press down on copies without having to switch pens. Also, unlike my pens that explode with great regularity on airplanes, ruining my favorite skirts and blouses, Peter's Pilot "precise" rolling ball extra fine pens are there for him as friends and constant companions. We buy his pens by the dozen and spread them around.

It is a feeling of love and enthusiasm for something, and in a direct, simple, passionate and true way, you try to show this beauty in things to others.

BRENDA UELAND

Mrs. Brown's Gold Compact

Fantasize what you would want in the drawers of your desk, your tables, your bedside table. Mrs. Brown kept a gold compact and a lipstick case in the drawer of the end table on the left side of her living room sofa where she usually sat while waiting for her guests to arrive. When the doorbell rang, someone would answer the door, and she would open the drawer of her Louis XVI end table, reach in for her compact, powder her nose, and check her lipstick before her friends entered her drawing room. (Mrs. Brown told me the reason she called her living room her drawing room was that in the court of Versailles, the private, intimate room of the palace was called a withdrawing room, but over time this has been shortened to drawing room.) This great lady knew how to live. In her eighties she entertained beautifully and enjoyed a few sips of a martini before dinner. On a half-round console table against the far wall of this classically elegant room, she had a small tray with a gleaming silver martini shaker and some wide V-shaped glasses, thin to the lip. "Martinis, anyone?"

Fashion fades. Only style remains.

COCO CHANEL

Mrs. Brown's home was perfectly attuned to her needs, freeing her to fully live a civilized, cultivated life. I always think of her martini shaker when I see photographs of her drawing room, and I also visualize her gold compact as she checked her face before greeting guests.

Out of perfection nothing can be made.

JOSEPH CAMPBELL

Sun-Dried Clothes

I have a client who loves her garden. One of the most satisfying things for her is to have an outdoor clothesline where she can hang up the family clothes with wooden clothespins so that they will be kissed by the sun. Harriette likes the hinged pins, as they do not make a mark on the clothes (as she experienced with the old-fashioned kind we all made into stick figures and decorated as children).

I have a similar urge to wash things by hand and hang them up on a line to dry in the fresh air and sunshine. I often use a ribbon as a line and am amazed how quickly the linens dry. While we wouldn't want to have our laundry billowing in the sea air when we have a garden party, think about how much pleasure this outdoor line could bring you from day to day.

Memories of Places with a Spirit

Think back on all the places and environments you experienced in your childhood. What are some of the scenes that touched your soul? In your notebook write about these places where you've felt an awakening of spirit, and jot down why you were so attracted to these specific places. Because our childhood houses and apartments have a great influence on our attitude and feelings, we spend much of our adult life searching for the place where we can awaken these positive emotions in our soul. For me, the most powerful memory is of my mother's garden when I was very young. All gardens ever since have become sanctuaries for me. My imagination also takes flight when I'm at a beach. There's a continuity in the rhythms of the waves, but everything is always subtly different every time I go to the water's edge and sit in the sand. I love to walk barefoot on bleached floors because I feel I'm walking on warm coral sand on a heavenly secluded beach in Bermuda with the turquoise translucent water rhythmically pounding onto the beach, day and night.

Write it down.

All of us have memories of places where we felt as one with the setting, internally expansive, and in awe of its beauty, charm, and authenticity. What are some of the most compelling places where you've spent time in the past that have a profound effect on your consciousness? I have memories of gardens, woods, mountains, beautiful houses, beaches, meadows, horse barns, and tennis courts. I also am affected by memories of rivers, lakes, ponds, waterfalls, and fountains. There are places to which we might have an emotional attachment—a cathedral, an island, or a particular area of a country. By identifying our feelings about the places where we feel most in tune and in touch, we can make our house more of a place that nurtures us with symbols from these places and former chapters in our lives. By using a silver tray won in a tennis tournament, I am reminded of my love of tennis. I have many silver trophies and use them regularly. A silver cup is ideal for cut flowers and little bowls are good for chilled gazpacho soup or cold borsch. You might frame a drawing of a favorite building or church. We have lots of photographs around the cottage and apartment taken in favorite places—Greece, Italy, Bermuda, and France. Use your baby cups in the bathroom. A grandchild's odd-shaped, handmade ceramic bowl can hold paper clips or hair pins. If you love churches, cluster some votive candles where you dine, meditate, or bathe. The rough, plastered walls with hand-painted yellow, white, and blue French tiles in a ribbon design in our kitchen keep the memories of Provence alive each day. To keep alive our memories of trips to visit our friends in Acapulco, we have brightly colored ceramic tiles from Mexico on the floor of our front hall closet. To always remember the lilac tree of my early childhood in Massachusetts, we have a watercolor painting of lilacs in a pitcher that was painted by a friend.

Memories are a great source of enrichment that help us continue to stay connected to our roots. I'm a New England child. All my early memories are of Massachusetts, Connecticut, Maine, New Hampshire, and Vermont as well as Rhode Island, where we spent a month in Newport every summer. Whether it was camp and tennis tournaments in Maine or later teaching tennis and theater at a camp in New Hampshire, I feel spiritually connected to the trees, flowers, mountains, lakes, and beaches, as well as to the village greens with their white churches and towering steeples and brilliant white clapboard houses with dark green shutters, all old and full of history. Needless to say, finding our eighteenth-century New England cottage on the southeastern tip of Connecticut near Rhode Island was a dream come true.

Alexandra and Brooke spent a great deal of time in Connecticut

For beautiful art, therefore, imagination, understanding, spirit, and taste are requisite.

IMMANUEL KANT

For nothing is pleasing to God except the invention of beautiful and exalted things.

WILLIAM BLAKE

when they were young and Alexandra went to Connecticut College. On weekends she would go to scenic Stonington Village, near her school, and that's how we found the spirit of a place where we wanted to find an old house and to plant our roots.

How far away do you live from where you were raised? What do you miss about your childhood environments? Because I was born in Massachusetts and went away to boarding school in Northampton, I have close ties to that beautiful state, but Connecticut is the most powerful place that ties my whole life together. My parents moved there when I was five. My father, older brother, and nephew went to Wesleyan University in Connecticut. I became captain of the New England tennis team and we played all over these beautiful states I love so well. Whether playing tennis, riding horses, climbing mountains, canoeing on a lake, or teaching one of my daughters how to swim, I have my roots deep in New England, and finding our old house was a true homecoming.

It is very beautiful here, if one only has an open and simple eye, without any beams in it. But if one has that, it is beautiful everywhere.

VINCENT VAN GOGH

Everything Matters

Creating our ideal home is a process of getting in touch with our interior world, opening up to that kind of environment that makes us feel the most peaceful and whole. If you love to go to the beach but can't call a beachhouse home, even in a small apartment you can bleach the floors to look like sand, paint the ceiling sky blue, and surround yourself in seafoam greens, cool blues, and turquoise colors to remind you of your Bermuda vacation.

Make every effort to have meaningful objects around you, possessions that you find attractive, that you are personally drawn to. Arrange and rearrange your spaces as practically as you know how so that you can live as abundantly as possible. Every day you will be closer and closer to your ideal at home. Keep in mind that everything matters. Just because something is practical and functional doesn't mean it has to

He who loves the beautiful is called a lover because he partakes of it.

PLATO

look dreary and make you feel life is mundane. The more beauty we surround ourselves with—the quiet, subtle beauty of the shadows of leaves against the living room wall, the sunshine's dappling light causing the garden's colors to smile at you, the beauty of the grain of the mahogany on the dining room tabletop, or the beauty of having your own library of books by favorite authors, where all your passions commingle—the more you will feel your energy all around you and will long to be at home.

Our Own Reality

Ideally, home is a place we create, where we liberate ourselves from the fear and anguish of insecurity. Home is a place where we can break free of convention. The way others live should not be our goal or our ideal. We have to realize our own reality, our own truth, and open the doors wide to whatever will give our life significance.

Continue to daydream and fantasize about what you can do to your physical environment that will expand your spirit and awaken you to your fullness and creative powers. As you love up your house you will feel loved and lovable. Each day that you wake up and feel at home, be grateful and give thanks for this blessing because this is your greatest success in life.

CHAPTER 7

Enhancing the Quality of Each Day

Home—it's a constant renewal, a constant need for care and love.
—PETER MEGARGEE BROWN

A Shift of Consciousness

Now that we've identified our creative passions and have arranged the various spaces to accommodate them, we still have prosaic aspects of everyday life at home to deal with. No one spends their entire day doing creative work, pursuing their passions. But with a shift in our consciousness, we can look for creative solutions to our most serious problems; we can lift our lives above the commonplace, and all our domestic tasks can be a loving meditation. We can elevate ourselves out of routines where all the homespun tasks and activities can be lovingly done with our own flair, personal style, and sense of beauty.

My soul hath content so absolute.

SHAKESPEARE

Attitude Is Key

When we feel at home there is an openness that we embrace the world with that must be shared. Loving ourselves, and loving the atmosphere we create out of this love, is our life's work.

Liberty consists in doing what one desires.

JOHN STUART MILL

There is no joy but calm!

ALFRED, LORD TENNYSON

Simple-minded does not necessarily mean stupid.

BENJAMIN HOFF

There is nothing common and ordinary about anything unless we have the wrong attitude. Even cleaning a toilet bowl can be satisfying if you have the right brush and Lysol blue toilet cleaner. Everyone loves a fresh toilet, and we all need to maintain our house as well as ourselves. What are some of the chores you do repeatedly around the house that you really do not enjoy doing? List them in your notebook. Look at each one and ask yourself, what can I do to enjoy the process more? What can I do to make a routine task a more creative, alive activity? What can I do to transform what I've identified as a dull, mundane chore into a meaningful grace note? How can you add some element of spontaneity and surprise to what you know you have to do? Why wouldn't you want to make it as enjoyable as possible? What is holding you back? What is your attitude, your way of thinking about the necessary daily tasks, the rituals we perform each day? What can you do to add an expression of love?

If you don't like cleaning the toilet, examine your brush and cleaner. I like the blue liquid color of the cleaner because it reminds me of the ocean and clear, fresh water. If you wrote that you don't enjoy scrubbing the toilet, do it tomorrow with the commitment to make it a pleasant task. As a treat at the end, you might want to put a flower in a water glass to rest on the back of the toilet or on the sink. If you previously haven't enjoyed making school lunches, you might ask your child what she wants in her lunch box, and there will be so much more pleasure making a sandwich you know will be enjoyed. You can throw in a love note that will touch your heart as well as your daughter's. What we do at home, for our home, and for ourself, our family, and friends need not drain us, but can fill us up. It all depends on our mind-set.

Having Everything Handy

If the reality of your daily life is washing lots and lots of dishes, by setting up your area around the sink and dishwasher so you can be in the swing, emptying everything from the dishwasher, being able to put everything away without wasted motions, the task can be a meditation. It's satisfying to have an empty dishwasher, ready to be filled with your pretty plates, glasses, and flatware. The next time you unload the dishwasher, put everything away in the immediate zone. If you have some sharp knives, stemmed glasses, or good silver you can't put away without walking around the kitchen or pantry, consider rearranging your cabinets and drawers to put the items you use every day near the sink and dishwasher. I found I had put my sharp knives on the far side of the stove, making it inconvenient to put them away. Now I reserve a portion of a drawer opposite the dishwasher for sharp knives. If in your case this means having duplicates of several items in various locations, the convenience of being able to do your tasks with ease and grace is worth the added expense. Take some time to rearrange your spaces to accommodate your needs.

A day is a sound and solid good.

EMERSON

Look to the source of all light and life with newness and love.

Identifying What Is a Waste of Time

Go through your list of all the chores that you have not enjoyed performing in the past and evaluate whether any are a waste of time. If you dread cleaning the dog mess from the white carpeting, eventually you might decide to rip up the carpeting and have hardwood floors. If you don't enjoy vacuum cleaning, you can have less carpeting and more hard surfaces which you can sweep and dry mop. If you don't like to iron or feel it is a waste of your time, don't iron. We have some yellow-and-white-striped sheets we often use to make up Brooke's bed in

Whoever is in a hurry shows that the thing he is about is too big for him.

LORD CHESTERFIELD

our cottage. Because they are unironed, they look like seersucker, and their puckered surface reminds me of summer, the seaside, and carefree living. If these sheets were crisply ironed, they wouldn't have the same nostalgic charm. My mother always used seersucker blanket covers on our beds in the summer and, in turn, so do I, because they are pastel and humble and evoke earlier days when I was young; they connect me to my childhood environments, the three houses of my youth.

Is ironing a waste of time or a way of using our time? For me it is an important meditation and something I don't want to ever give up. Ideally I'd like to wash my dishes by hand and dry them with a colorful cotton dish cloth and put them away. But that's the romantic spirit in me. I love to examine all our pretty dishes. I'm not fond of the time-saving devices that are ugly, noisy, sterile, and cold. That's probably why I don't love vacuuming because the noise keeps me from having an uninterrupted dialogue with my heart.

Tom Sawyer

Last summer when we painted our picket fence, unlike Tom Sawyer, we did not feel this was a waste of time. And just as in *Tom Sawyer*, everyone stopped to chat and to watch. Charlie, our next-door neighbor, saw the contrast between the gleaming white on our side and his side, gray from mildew and neglect. Charlie inquired what kind of paint we used so he could buy the same brand and color. We didn't paint the fence so it merely looks good. We painted it so it feels good to us and our neighbors. It's personally satisfying and fulfilling to have the picket fence bandbox crisp, clean and gleefully bright white, sparkling in the sunlight. That's the real reason we love up our house, because whenever we do things to our house to improve it, to bring out its inherent appearance, we are rewarded by a powerful feeling of contentment. When we're loving up our fence, we're loving ourselves, our neighbors, and life. We're having fun, using our energy positively, turning something dull into something dazzling, bright, and cheerful. For the cost of some primer and a few gallons of paint, we were indeed richly rewarded.

I love to paint and brilliant white paint is magic to me. I enjoy going around the cottage touching up a baseboard or a door trim. I'd rather paint than clean. To me it's intensely pleasing, similar to hanging a bleached, starched pair of white cotton curtains in the window to dance to the rhythm of the wind. Whenever I have a paintbrush in my hand, I am never wasting my time.

Our lives at home will have more substance when we love our true selves. By honoring our higher selves, knowing and trusting that what we do matters, we're able to value ourselves more.

Cutting Back, Cutting Less

Recently, Peter and I drove by a favorite Greek revival house on North Main Street in Stonington and noticed that the four acres of grass lawn had been altered. Because four acres became too much of a burden, this couple gracefully turned two acres into a field, and sprinkled colorful wildflower seeds all over this lovely area with an ancient stone wall and tall trees behind. It is just as pretty and reduced their lawn maintenance by half.

Where the good things are, there is home.

EURIPIDES

We met a couple from Maryland who live on a 360-acre farm. When I told them we lived in a village on only one seventh of an acre, they asked if we would be willing to swap houses. The husband told us they used to have fourteen acres of grass, but because it cost so much to have people come and mow it, they cut back to six acres. When they saw that the weekly bills, while considerably less than before, were still high, he bought a tractor and mowed the lawn himself. "How much time does it take you to mow six acres?" I inquired. "Too long. Eight hours, a full day. We have the farm on the market. After what we just told you, I'm sure you won't want to buy it."

Anything for a quiet life.

CHARLES DICKENS

What are some of the areas of your house you want to cut back on, in terms of both expense and time? I've heard of people who can't be bothered having the maintenance of grass to tend and mow and who replace the lawn with brick or put down stones. That seems hard and cold. I'd rather have a tiny blanket of grass than none. If you're fortunate to live on the water, while you risk storms, you also see that incredible water with its sense of timeless continuity; yet it is alive with subtle changes, keeping you company without ceasing. You don't have to get on a tractor to mow the ocean. The tide rolls in, the waves wash ashore, making the beach all new again with no footprints from yesterday's visitors. Whenever we accept the gifts from the sea, we awaken to utter simplicity. When we simplify, we clarify, making our lives easier and less tangled up in activities that bog us down. What are some areas of your house you feel you want to streamline?

We're Not Getting Any Younger

When we aim at enhancing the quality of our lives each day, we should bear in mind how important balance is as we grow older. What we did twenty years ago in the yard and in the garden may not be appropriate now. We live through each life chapter as richly and fully as possible, and then let go of certain things to free us up to engage in other activities with our time, energy, and money. Our goal should be to make all the daily stuff of domestic life more efficient and better organized so that the rhythms of living at home flow more harmoniously. When our house is well run, all our movements can be more graceful and pleasant.

What Do You Complain About?

Write in your notebook what you tend to complain about. Who do you usually complain to? Who in your family and among your friends complains to you? How does it make you feel? Be as truthful as possible, because this exercise will bring to light an important bit of self-knowledge. If you complain about your house and how hard you work, pay attention. There are house hypochondriacs, people who have an unhealthy relationship to their environment.

If our house is too large and becomes too difficult to keep up, we can always downsize and move. We're either in synchronization, in the swing, where we're rolling with whatever comes our way, harmonizing well; or we're feeling bad.

We are not defined by the work we do around our house to maintain our lifestyle. We are defined by the thoughts we have and the emotions we feel as we do it. If we polish a silver pitcher before we fill it with daisies, it will smile back at us. If we listen to Chopin, Handel, or Mozart as we clean the kitchen floor, we will literally be on our hands and knees in gratitude to be alive, to have a home, to be in reasonably good health. Our hands are our tools in action to express ourselves. Nothing we do is unimportant or insignificant. Everything is part of the symphony at home. All the senses can be stimulated to enhance our instinctive feeling of love of home. It's normal to want to improve, upgrade, and enrich our physical dwelling each day.

The longer the grass grows, the sweeter is its flower, and the more it nourishes.

T. H. HUXLEY

I had a dream which was not all a dream.

LORD BYRON

The Art of Puttering

The way to transform our energy at home and re-create our everyday life, eliminating frustrations and misunderstandings, is to understand the joy of puttering. None of us knows our fate; all we know for certain is our aliveness and how we feel now. There is a little of Thomas Jefferson's spirit in all of us. He wanted Monticello to mirror his soul and spent his entire life creating his mountaintop home as the center point of his happiest days. Here he would farm, invent functional furniture and devices, and when not out riding Old Eagle, he would tinker around the house. He was basically a domestic genius.

Write in your notebook some of your house puttering rules. One of ours is that people's comfort always comes first. We try never to interrupt someone who is enjoying what they're doing to insist on working on the house. Timing is everything. Whenever someone is dragged into a project against their will, the task will not be done with love and vital energy will suffer.

Puttering is a way of freeing your spirit so you take pleasure in every experience. When we putter, we do things in a desultory way, shifting from one thing to another. We amble, moving at an easy pace. The house gets straightened out and cleaned without effort because we roll along, move slowly but in a pleasant manner, enjoying time to dawdle. We're working and loving what we're doing because we're occupying ourselves in our own way, on our own terms, in our chosen timing. Puttering takes the frustration out of tasks at home because we're actually doing things we profit from, experiencing pleasure rather than slogging through necessary chores in a methodical manner. When we're in charge of what we do, we cherish the experience and savor the moment. When I don't have a pen in my hand I tend to putter. This activity releases psychic energy and connects me to all the meaningful objects around the house, allowing me peace and quiet to savor whatever I'm doing. The only rules for puttering are simply to do whatever you wish to do at the moment. I adore my puttering time and indulge in this liberating activity with great regularity.

I do whatever I'm fond of doing when I putter and because I'm satisfying my own needs and wants, I feel a tremendous gratification. Puttering is not superficial; on the contrary, it is a way to soothe me, relax me, comfort me, and make me feel more at home. Whether I'm cleaning out the soot in the fireplace or looking through a box of family photographs, setting some aside to be framed and sorting others to go in scrapbooks, I'm using my vitality in the precise way I want to; the activity elevates my mood. Sometimes getting sweaty and dirty as I putter is enormously satisfying, although at other times I don't want to get dirty, preferring to sit and do something

Focus on what you love, what stirs your heart and soul, because you have little time and few resources.

The natural flights of the human mind are not from pleasure to pleasure, but from hope to hope.

SAMUEL JOHNSON

The most important thing about getting somewhere is starting right where we are.

BRUCE BARTON

at a desk or table. There are times when I'm in the mood to garden and other times I want to sew on a button, repair a hook and eye, or clean out a desk drawer.

Improving Our Spirit and the Spirit of Home

Puttering improves our mood and improves our house. Sometimes we'll want to preface our puttering with a vigorous walk in order to return home feeling more positive and less anxious. Being out in nature, in the light and exercising, improves our spirits, but so does puttering. Our home holds our emotional capital. Rather than leaving home, often we should stay at home and putter, especially on days when we're not feeling our best. When we walk around our house, we're soothed by all the meaningful things surrounding us. We're in awe at what good fortune we have, rather than worrying about problems that don't exist or that we can't do anything about. When we putter we lose our self-consciousness and do everything as though for the first time. Puttering is our way of adding little extra grace notes to whatever we do. We never think of expediency when we putter because we are not seeking a means of attaining an end; rather, we are finding imaginative ways to increase our enjoyment in the process. The result of how we spent our time is beneficial to our house, but we have also done something desirable to the way we feel about ourselves.

Puttering is one of our greatest tools of self-expression. We aren't working hard at working; we lighten up and brighten up as we improve our home and uplift our spirits. I was sewing a button onto one of Peter's blue-and-white-striped shirt-sleeves not long ago, and rather than use white thread, I used the exact shade of the blue in the shirt. I have the prettiest color thread that I buy on impulse because of my love of color, and I have fun finding ways to sneak a little color into my sewing. When you putter you make everything yours because you are not driven to anxiously produce efficiency

He is less desirous to make
progress than to know how
to live.

LIN YUTANG

and practicality, but you have the inclination to add your own touches to express something of yourself. Puttering's greatest benefit to us is the wide range of options we have in spending time helping our house. Because this is personal free time, when we're not in conversation with others, we're more in touch with ourselves. We're in charge of our timing and our style of working on our house as we're also figuring things out about ourselves. Puttering is a way for us to fuel the house with our loving energy and heal ourselves. Our home is the greatest nourishment to our soul, sustaining our passionate feelings, providing stimulation to our imagination. You can always go home to feel this sense of renewal and comfort.

Things are, and ought to be,
simple.

CLAUDE MONET

I putter when I feel on top of the world and also when I'm experiencing pain. Home is, or should be, a safe haven. I putter to have fun, get some exercise, and love up my home life. If I put on ballet slippers and dance to some favorite music I hear on the radio, no one can tell me to grow up and act my age because no one is there to criticize me. When I sing or whistle or dance I really don't care what other people think. I'm much more concerned with the fact that I'm having fun than with impressing others. Sometimes I skip when I putter, often I laugh at little ironies I experience.

The Fun Is in the Caring, the Doing

We experience a spiritual
opening up when we feel
at home.

I'm amused that I enjoy cleaning the house at this stage of my life. I could hire someone to do what I do if I wanted to, but I prefer the freedom and joy of puttering. The fun is always in the doing. One of the reasons everyone stops to watch someone else work is that they feel the fun is really in the doing. The healthier we are, the more active we tend to be, and the more active we are, the more we tend toward better health. There are a lot of people who walk around and sightsee in our village. You can spot them because they stop and look around.

They probably think we're poor suckers out there in the heat painting our fence, but I see it from a different perspective. I love to go on vacations where I am a sightseer. I become inspired by the natural beauty, the culture, and the customs of other countries and people, but I chiefly feel a yearning to bring all this novelty and newness home, to make our home a richer, more meaningful, more comfortable place.

A family vacation to Scandinavia inspired me to paint four-inch-wide blue-and-white stripes on the floor of the buttery in our cottage. Our favorite village in Provence in the South of France is reflected all over our home in the watercolor and oil paintings of scenes from this region by Roger Mühl. I still use black-lacquered rice bowls with gold trim that I brought back from India in 1960 when I went on a world trip. I wear clothes made by the Chinese in Chinese style. I always use Thai silk in my decorating because I fell in love with this material in Bangkok, Thailand, while on that trip. I still have a temple rubbing from Bangkok. We have tables purchased in Hong Kong, and red-lacquered chopsticks bought in Japan where I learned how to eat using them. I fell in love with black truffles in Sienna, Italy, over thirty years ago. We have touches of the style and flavor of every country where we've traveled, from cups from England to embroidery from Portugal. We brought back marbleized boxes from Florence and Venice as well as hand-blown glass from Italy. Where have you traveled and what are some of the things you've learned from these cultures? We always bring back a taste for the food or wines. All of these accumulated experiences come home and are interpreted in our own way.

Getting away gives us a chance to see our lives at home from a more enlightened perspective. We cook less, and travel more lightly, but whenever we're away from home, we miss our familiar things, our creature comforts, and our real life at home.

And thou wilt give thyself relief, if thou doest every act of thy life as if it were the last.

MARCUS AURELIUS

By a small sample we may judge of the whole process.

CERVANTES

Let our lives be our memorials.

SHAKER SAYING

Ninety-six Percent of Our Lives

To know when you have enough is to be rich.

LAO-TZU

When you are on vacation, is your mood generally better than when you are at home? A vacation for most of us is an escape from the day-to-day activities at home. The advantage of our vacations is that we return home with a fresh outlook. We are inspired to make improvements that will bring us more quality in our daily lives. But we don't escape often, and if we take a two-week vacation a year, as average Americans do, this means that out of the fifty-two weeks a year, we live at home fifty weeks. Ninety-six percent of our days and nights are spent at home; only 4 percent, on average, are spent away.

How's the Weather?

The best way to enhance the quality of each day at home is to pay attention to our mood. We can develop an internal barometer that makes us more self-aware. Of course, external circumstances affect us as well. We keep an antique barometer on a table in the living room. Peter likes to check the atmospheric pressure so he can forecast the weather. If the weather is turning bad, the indicator on the dial on the instrument goes down, and when the weather is improving, the indicator goes up. I think most of us are affected by the weather. When it's extremely humid, I don't have as much energy as usual, but I love rainy days when I can flop around the house reading have a cozy siesta. I blast classical music tapes to inspire and energize me as I putter around.

What Puts You in a Good Mood?

Write in your notebook when you are in the best possible mood, what you're doing, where you are, and what the circumstances are.

Take time to describe some scenes. Are you alone puttering at your workbench? Are you entertaining friends for dinner? Are you gardening with your spouse? Are you cooking? Studies prove that people's moods are usually better when they are with other people, yet we are alone at least one-third of our life. This is a most significant portion.

When is the last time you were grumpy? What caused you to be upset? What is the general climate of your mind and feelings? How would you describe your disposition? Do you tend toward mood swings? We're all mercurial with our ups and downs. Do you ever have fits of melancholy or have marked changes in your temperament? If someone around you is crotchety or gloomy, moping around the house, how does this make you feel? If someone you love is out of sorts, do you try to humor the person or do you go about your own business and let time heal? When you feel physically ill, are you emotionally happy?

For all human beings, wherever we may live, the quintessential place that cries out for our attention, nurture, and love is our home.

PETER MEGARGEE BROWN

Let us live and love.

GAIUS

Bicker, Bicker

When I was little and my parents quarreled, I thought I'd done something wrong. I kept trying to be a better child so my parents wouldn't fight. I heard my friends' parents argue, and I grew up thinking all people found fault with each other and bickered when they didn't have guests. It bothered me that couples seemed so frustrated with each other. It was in my early childhood, when I found solace in the garden or riding my horse at our farm in upper New York State, that I learned how content I was to be alone and to rely on my inner resources. To this day, I dread overhearing two people mean-spiritedly attacking each other.

Having those haunting memories of childhood, after Peter and I married, we seemed to get along so well living in an apartment that I wondered if we would continue to treat each other as graciously if we lived in a house. I remember confiding in Mrs. Brown about my

Wherever there is a human being, there is an opportunity for a kindness.

SENECA

What do we live for, if it is not to make life less difficult for each other?

GEORGE ELIOT

Death in any of its aspects is the fact which makes of the present hour something of absolute value.

ROLLO MAY

No matter how good the teacher, ultimately you have to do the inner work yourself.

JON KABAT-ZINN

fears. Peter gets paid to argue in a court of law and I didn't want our house to be a place where he tried out his skills on me. Mrs. Brown didn't encourage me to think about a house in the late seventies because she felt we had a wonderful life in our apartment home and we enjoyed traveling. "If everything is working out so beautifully, Sandie, why change things?" When we found the ugly house that was yearning to have us love it up, we sensed it had an innate sweetness to it, and we sat down one night and had a talk. We felt the house had a charm and an enchantment that would forbid misbehavior.

We made a pact. If we were to quarrel, we'd both go for a five-mile walk, come back, look at the house, and not enter until we'd made up. The whole idea of the pact made me feel secure. Young married couples who come to my lectures ask Peter and me for advice on how they can get along well over the course of their lifetime. Peter tells people who ask him, "Don't judge each other. Let things be. Don't pick, pick, pick." Living with other people every day exposes us to the reality of our own faults. We're not here to criticize others or to find fault. My advice is a little light-hearted. I tell the husband to put the toilet seat down. Chinese feng shui experts believe you should keep the lid of the toilet seat down so your fortune won't go down the drain. Whether or not this is purely superstitious doesn't matter. When a wife goes to the bathroom in the middle of the night and sits on a cold, possibly wet, toilet rim, she is usually not pleased. If the lid is down, the seat will be in place for a woman. This grace note, over a lifetime, will enhance the quality of each day.

A Happy Optimist

I have a wise older friend who is an inspiration to all of us fortunate to know her. She has more enthusiasm than any of our other friends. In the thirty-three years since our friendship began when I

helped to decorate her duplex apartment on Park Avenue, I have never heard this rare lady complain or say a mean word about someone. June simply refuses to lower herself to this mind-set. She is like a little girl, every day discovering new passions, laughing, and loving everything she does. June is dramatic, colorful, and vibrantly alive. She has a great gift of appreciation, feeling grateful for her good fortune.

June is determined to keep her energy positive no matter what is happening. Her home sings this joyful song in every place, in every way. There is nothing routine or lifeless about anything she does. She even pays her bills in a theatrical way, setting a huge arrangement of iris on her desk. She uses a fine fountain pen and has everything neat and pretty around her to inspire her. Then, before she begins, she sips some herbal tea and plays a tape of her favorite musical hits, singing along, smiling, having the best time. After an hour her bills are paid, there are favorite flowered stamps on the blue-and-white striped envelopes, and she's off to post them in the mailbox, smiling, whistling, and as happy as could be. This lady's flair has elevated daily life at home to an art.

Live to the Hilt

June has figured out how to live. She was an actress in her professional life and knows how to put on a good performance, not on stage, but at home, every day. Her heightened sense of her spiritual nature raises the day-to-day details of life, increases the depth of her soul, and strengthens her relationships with people, places, and things. Because she makes everything fun, whether we're making open-face tomato sandwiches together or zooming around Kmart with a cart full of bargains, she has a smile on her face and truly there is a song in her heart. She's never known the monotonous or dull because her romantic spirit doesn't have any room for the plain or the tired. She loves to be naughty. "I'm bad. I'm a bad girl," she'll say as she spreads the mayonnaise on the

Children have insights adults don't have.

PETER MEGARGEE BROWN

Without peace of mind, life is just a shadow of its possibilities.

JOAN BORYSENKO

Think naught a trifle . . .
Moments make the year.

EDWARD YOUNG

I was born modest; not all
over, but in spots.

MARK TWAIN

thin white bread over the butter hidden by the organic tomato. "I can't eat a tomato without bread, butter, and mayo," she confesses just before she laughs at herself.

We all know the quality of our day-to-day lives is largely up to us to invent and create. We all know we have this short time on earth to live our personal drama. Some of us live at ten (on a scale of one to ten) each day the way June does, and some of us live at one or two. Somehow, the whole concept of every day has been given a bad reputation, but every day is all we have. We can't fall into the bland, flat, humdrum routine and gradually find being at home alone uninteresting. We take our life day by day, finding ways to improve the way we feel, doing things that lift us up, maximizing what we have to work with. Certainly June's optimism and sunny disposition make her fun to be with, but when we're not with her, she still has the power to remind all of us who love her that we all can value ourselves more and live to the hilt.

When I lecture, I often say to the audience that today is a microcosm of our whole life. Right now is a miniature representation of who we are and how well we're living at home. There are seven days in a week, each one with rhythms of morning, noon, afternoon, and evening. Monday should be just as wonderful as Saturday. All days and all nights should be lived fully, as beautifully and as deeply as possible.

A Magical Day

One of my favorite illustrated lectures is entitled "How to Live a Magical Day." This is one of the happiest talks I give and it is poignant, because I show all the joy we can experience from the moment we wake up until the time when we rest our heads on a feather pillow under a cool, clean sheet and turn off the light. There is a great deal of fantasy; I'm off to Paris for a Claude Monet show and back at home in the cottage to have friends over for dinner and dancing under a full moon. All we have to do to tap into the magic is to be enchanted by everything we do, we see, we smell, we taste, and we hear. All day we are living a supernatural existence.

Write in your notebook what you would do to live a magical day. What time would you wake up? Who would be with you? What would your bedroom look like? What would you have for breakfast? Where would you sit? Would you read the newspaper? When would you leave the house? Where would you go? What would you do? Who would you see? Would you have lunch with a friend? Where? What would you want to be served? Would you go to a museum? Would you have tea with your mentor? Would you go shopping? Where? What would you shop for? Would you tinker around the house? What would you do? Would you be with your children or grandchildren? Would you have a dinner party? Who would you invite?

On my magical day, I did some writing in the early morning, took the girls to school, did some decorating, had lunch with Peter at one of our favorite New York restaurants, flew off to Paris to catch the exhibition of one of my favorite artists, had tea with Mrs. Brown at her apartment, did some power shopping on Madison Avenue, then packed up and went to the cottage with the girls and Peter where we had a dinner party for friends and family, dancing under lanterns, the stars, and the moon. After all the friends left and our family was asleep, Peter and I danced in the garden some more before going to sleep.

Other than going to Paris and Connecticut from New York in one day, most of this fantasy can be lived in one day. None of us stays at home all day, every day. We move about, but our home is our center, and it is where we can create the atmosphere and setting for a perfectly delightful, joy-filled day. With all the imperfections, the unfinished business, the lists of projects to be done, the unanswered letters, the unpaid bills, the dirty laundry, the weeds in the garden, and the refrigerator needing to be restocked, we can make a commitment to re-creating the quality of each precious day. The way we do this is to have fun no matter what we're doing.

Since we cannot change reality, let us change the eyes which see reality.

NIKOS KAZANTZAKIS

The greatest thing a human being ever does in this world is to see something . . . To see clearly is poetry, prophecy and religion, all in one.

JOHN RUSKIN

Transcending the Garbage

If in the past you found no satisfaction in emptying the garbage, transcend the garbage pail, rise above it. Look at the rubbish with a new attitude. This is our domestic waste; by collecting it and getting rid of it, we create a fresh beginning. We can pitch something out that we longer want or need. Trash keeps us from becoming messy, overwhelmed, or overtaken. Our house needs this regular cleansing as a catharsis, where we feel an emotional release. There is no reason to think negatively about your own trash. It is satisfying to know we can do the most menial task without feeling it is degrading or drudgery. People who practice transcendental meditation are detaching themselves from anxiety through meditation. What is transcendental is beyond our own experience and practical day-to-day observation. There is a higher level of vision and truth available to us, perhaps a sense of who we are and where we are. This form of meditation can have encouraging spiritual overtones and should be recognized and nourished. We transcend the low and the little and move to the big and the higher. This is the supreme transformation of enhancing the quality of each day. Empty the garbage; own the day.

For the next week, empty all the wastebaskets in the house and the garbage. When I do this task, I bring a plastic bag with me and some fresh white paper doilies for the bottom of each wastebasket. If you prefer, you can put six doilies in a waste basket at a time and peel off the top one when you empty the trash. Scrub the inside and outside of the garbage pail with Soft Scrub with bleach. Write in your notebook how it made you feel to do this task. What did you meditate about while you were emptying the rubbish? What music did you play? Did you whistle while you worked?

What Comes with the Territory

I'm fascinated by how uncomplaining dog owners are about using their pooper scoopers along the avenue. They love their dog and this comes with the territory, just as a parent changes a soiled diaper. We all understand that the more enjoyment we have from our children or a pet, the more maintenance there will be. We could hire a dog walker, but then we'd be depriving ourselves of the pleasure of our dog's companionship. We could hire a nanny for our baby, but this would mean we wouldn't be able to spend as much time with our infant.

Re-creating the Spirit of Home

When our children grow up and are no longer at home, our house is too neat, too quiet, and is never the same. There are fewer piles of dirty clothes on the floor, less wild music, less laundry, fewer dishes, and fewer of their friends hanging around. Yet, most of us wouldn't trade those years when our children were at home for anything. With Alexandra and Brooke grown up and on their own, I consider it an extreme compliment when they want to come home to be with us at the apartment and the cottage. Parents who maintain close ties with their grown children are richly blessed. The poetry, atmosphere, and magic of our collective lives at home reaches far beyond the limits of our private environment. There is an understanding that with love and care we will be able to re-create these emotions wherever we live, and parents, through their example, affirm and confirm that their children will be able to create this spirit in their own home. Each of us must have this living, breathing, welcoming home where they're free to come and go, to nest and to heal.

Five Percent

We all want to make a good impression, to have people come to our house and like what they see. But there is something far more profound that goes on at home. Ninety-five percent of our

We should surround ourselves with beautiful things throughout our day-to-day lives.

ELEANOR MCMILLEN
BROWN

Write it on your heart that every day is the best day in the year.

EMERSON

If I had enough ribbon, I could conquer the world.

NAPOLÉON

life is spent eating, sleeping and bathing. I wrote about these rituals in *Living a Beautiful Life.* Only 5 percent of our life is spent being engaged in special events—birthdays, anniversaries, weddings, religious holidays, and other celebrations. We can use our home, every day, as the center of our self-expression and celebration. We sometimes get stuck when we look outward and concern ourselves with the image of how we will appear to others. When people come to our home, will we be thought to have good taste? What will others think of our decorations, our colors, our personal treasures?

We naturally care what others think of us, but when we think well enough of who we really are at our core and focus on this person, how we feel as opposed to how we impress others, we'll be able to celebrate every day. Whenever we are true to ourselves, others accept us. It is the things we do to express our love of life that make us feel good at home. These loving gestures are sometimes seen in a sparkling white picket fence, but often they're felt in meditation or prayer or in quiet thoughts or intimate moments. Our home is not a status symbol indicating our rank or wealth or importance. It is a sacred environment that serves and uplifts us.

Redefining Who You Are

Repeat the exercise we discussed in Chapter 1—listing the qualities that define who you are. Redo your list without looking at the one you wrote earlier. Take some soul-searching time with this exercise, but try not to second-guess or edit yourself. If you've uncovered new items, that's fine. Look at your original list now and compare the two. Are they the same? Did the order change? How many of these important parts of who you are do you actually incorporate into your home each day?

This total vision will be your mantra for feeling at home.

You can watch this whole creative process unfold with joy and excitement, and thus enrich the quality of each day.

Flowers

If you have flowers on your list, look around your house. Do you see flowers in all your rooms? Do you have fresh flowers today? If flowers are central in your life, they are not a luxury to buy only when you have guests in your home. They are as important to you as food because they nourish you spiritually. Look around and think up ways to bring more flowers into your home. Have a flower budget and never live without flowers. Along with real flowers you can have flowers in the fabrics you select so your rooms will become gardens. You can have flowers on teacups, on dinner plates, on napkins, on tablecloths, on sheets, on lamp vases, or etched in glass; you can collect flower and gardening books to look at for inspiration. You can have a basket filled with gardening catalogues.

You might be inspired to hook a flowered rug. George Wells sells some beautiful rug-making kits with floral designs through The Ruggery in Glen Cove, Long Island, New York. The wool is vegetable-dyed in clear, flower-fresh colors. Hooking is fun to do and adds favorite flowers to a small rug you can place in your front hall or in the sanctuary of your bedroom. Maybe you'll be inspired to needlepoint some flowered dining room chair cushions or a living room pillow or even an eyeglass case. In your bathroom you might want to have a flower design on the floor tiles, or the tiles around the tub can include some hand-painted tiles of flowers.

Look in your closet. Do you see flowers on a necktie or scarf? I have flowered sundresses, summer suits, silk scarves, and blouses as well as flowered bands for my sun hats. Look at your umbrellas. They can have flower designs. I have a raincoat that is in bloom, as well as flowered paper cocktail

As we start something new—a new attitude, a new belief, a new way of life—something else ends. There should be a word that means beginning/end because nothing begins without something dying.

DR. RACHEL NAOMI
REMEN

It is when you are really living in the present—working, thinking, lost, absorbed in something you care about very much, that you are living spiritually.

BRENDA UELAND

napkins, wrapping paper, baby pillows, and watercolor botanicals. Most of our art depicts flowers, gardens, trees, and water. We are naturally drawn to the very things that define us.

Music and Dancing

If music is on your list, are you listening to something beautiful right now? One morning I was swept off my feet listening to a whole hour of march music on our classical station on the radio. Do you have a good music system and speakers? I have a client who calls her living room the music room. Ann has two pianos in this room, and she and her husband play duets for their own pleasure and for family and friends. When they are not playing, they are listening to symphonies; the speakers are placed throughout the downstairs of their large plantation-style house.

If you love to dance, do you have a sparsely furnished front hall or an area without a rug where you can dance? When's the last time you spontaneously invited your spouse to have a twirl with you? Behind our cottage is a Portuguese fisherman's society, and whenever they have a local band come to play, we dance on our patio under the stars.

Brooke's Love of Paris

Anyone who knows Brooke is aware of her passion for France, particularly Paris, where she went for the first time when she was five. She has found ways of returning ever since, whether literally or symbolically. Her New York City apartment is inspired by her love of this beautiful city. It is filled with photographs of Paris scenes and snapshots of her visits over the years, including one of her with her box camera taken by me on her first trip there. She collects prints and postcards of Paris, and French memorabilia is everywhere. Her dinner and dessert plates are French, bought in Paris when she had an apartment there; she writes with a French fountain pen on French paper she bought from a favorite stationery store, Marie Papier. She has a few French antiques and even her sheets are a French blue-and-white stripe, found in Paris. Looking around her apartment, you realize it could be in Paris. Her life at home in New York is intensified and infinitely more meaningful because her passion for Paris is expressed everywhere. Brooke keeps a Paris file for inspiration and to be more knowledgeable for her next trip. Even though she doesn't live there now, she still brings the essence of Paris to her apartment, right down to the graceful yellow French tulips she adores.

Remember, the delight of living is found as often on the byways as on the highways, that give us every day great joys of enlightenment.

PETER MEGARGEE BROWN

Blue, Blue, Blue, Blue, Blue

When Brooke was six, we went to Greece on a family odyssey and we all kept journals. Before we left, I was having a mother-daughter "groove" with Brooke. (A groove is when we take off on an adventure, look around and wonder at what we see, and end up having a cool drink or a snack and a talk.) I brought her blank book in my purse on this particular groove and asked her what she thought Greece would be like. She rolled her eyes around as though visualizing and told me, "The sky will be blue, blue, blue, blue, blue, and the water will be blue, blue, blue, blue, blue, blue, blue." Although she loves color passionately, blue has a spiritual quality for her. She has always studied the sky and water, and is passionate about the color blue, particularly French blue in clothing, and blue hydrangeas, which make her crazy with joy. This special affinity for the color blue began in early childhood from her love of nature's blues and has grown into a near obsession ever since.

Enlightenment is becoming conscious of the unconscious.

D. T. SUZUKI

Elephants

Brooke has remained true to herself and is faithful to her past and able to express her story visually. For example, when she was little she shunned playing with dolls in favor of Snoopy and Babar. How natural that one of Brooke's ten defining qualities is *elephant*. To my knowledge she's never been on an elephant, but she is faithful to her childhood companion and collects elephant pictures and elephant memorabilia and objects, from printed silk scarves to carved jade elephants—always with their trunks up for good luck.

Taste Is an Expression of our Exposure

The former president of Tiffany & Co., Walter Hoving, believed that taste is an expression of our exposure. Brooke's life experiences and extensive travels have helped her find and define, as well as refine, her personal style. She expresses something personal with every object in her home.

All too often we close off these connections and don't find places for them in our adult life, but they are all a part of our autobiography. If Walter Hoving was right, that we hone and mold our taste by what we've been exposed to, Brooke's upbringing was conducive to her expressing her creative outlets and passions. She was raised in a family that couldn't live without fresh flowers and has inherited her grandmother's and mother's love of flower arranging. The fact that she preferred Babar to dolls is her reality. Reviewing Brooke's list, as her mother and her greatest admirer, I see how her whole life is creatively integrated into her home, her work, and her passions.

And one perfect day can give clues for a more perfect life.

ANNE MORROW
LINDBERGH

If you were to ask what is most important in a home, I would say memories.

LILLIAN GISH

It is everything I long for.

AUDREY HEPBURN

Identifying Your Favorite Things

What are some of your indulgences, little things you take pleasure in that make a big difference to you? Maybe you love a certain kind of wineglass; you appreciate the shape, the thin lip, and the grace of the crystal's proportions. This refinement is not a waste of money because using this glass adds to your enjoyment of the wine and the occasion. You enjoy washing it by hand and wiping it dry so it sparkles in the light. You ritualize your glass of wine. The same enhancement could accompany your orange juice in the morning, as you use this favorite glass to start a new day. Think of your weaknesses for certain favorite things as your strengths, because in all the details of every day, you will have more and more things you love around you, helping you to stay open to your true nature.

—here, now, always—

T. S. ELIOT

A Passion for Ribbons

We should always look back in our life for the threads that tie everything together. When my sister, Barbara, and I were young, my mother sat at her French Provincial dressing table and put ribbons in our hair. She kept the colorful ribbons hanging down on either side of the mirror. As Mother brushed our hair, she would let us select a pretty ribbon. This special time with Mother was a real treat. She was always relaxed and seemed to enjoy this morning ritual. Mother loved ribbons and had a large ribbon drawer in a chest of drawers in the upstairs hall. I have happy memories of our wrapping presents together, and the ribbons always thrilled me. When I roamed our neighborhood picking daffodils in an abandoned field or wildflowers along the road, I'd tie them in a pretty ribbon and sell the bouquets door to door. I'd lay the bunches in a basket and gleefully skip around the neighborhood ringing doorbells, believing every household should enjoy fresh flowers tied with a pretty ribbon.

Ribbons are always festive, celebrating and happy.

I never outgrew my love of ribbons. When I was asked to decorate a table for Gorham in the late sixties using their silverware, china, and crystal, I knew I had to find a way to incorporate ribbons. I could have tied the napkins in a colorful bow, but it occurred to me that the entire tablecloth could be created of woven ribbons. I went to the ribbon market and had a look around. I ended up using a range of pinks, greens, yellows, and whites—solid colors, plaids, checks, and polka dots. I found some apple-green solid cotton for the background. I laid out ribbons in a pleasing design vertically, and then laid out the same patterns horizontally, but not in the same order, to add more variety. I wove the ribbons over and under each other, and where they intersected, I sewed a tiny white embroidered flower petal bought at a notions store. Much to my surprise the company loved the table setting. They thought the ribbon tablecloth showed off their products to great advantage and offered to pay me $500 for it. Although I wish now I hadn't sold this pretty cloth, I was thrilled at the time. They toured the country displaying their wares on the colorful tablecloth. A magazine photographed it and provided instructions on how to make it. I have a photograph in a scrapbook and a slide as a memory. I used some of the $500 to buy more ribbons, and I made another tablecloth in purples, greens, yellows, fuchsia pinks, and white, inspired by my love of pansies, and fortunately I still have it to enjoy.

One of my favorite fabric houses, Brunschwig & Fils, incorporated the woven ribbon design in its fabric line in five different color schemes. I had sundresses made for the girls and myself from the printed cotton, and I used the pattern as a quilted bed cover. I've had two of my books published with a pink-and-purple satin ribbon sewn into the spine. I'm usually outvoted by my publisher when I request this because it adds so much to the cost of the book. Not to be disappointed, I go to the ribbon market, buy a bunch of fifty-yard bolts, cut them up into bookmark length, and bring them with me on book tour to put into all the books I sign. Why do I love ribbons? They remind me of being three years old and awakening to life in my mother's garden with a sassy ribbon in my curly blond hair.

Caring is the greatest thing, caring matters most.

FRIEDRICH VON HÜGEL

One eats holiness and the table becomes an altar.

MARTIN BUBER

They remind me of all the gifts I've exchanged with my family and friends. We have a tradition in our family that we always use ribbons on our presents with lavish abandon so that the recipient may, in turn, wrap several gifts for loved ones using the ribbons. Of course, I find dozens of other ways to use them, too. I tie ribbons around storage boxes, hat boxes, and portfolios. I tie letters in ribbons and appreciate it when a box of stationery contains envelopes and paper tied in a ribbon. I use ribbons on the bottom edge of upholstered chairs and sofas and bind the edge of curtains and valances in ribbons. In our bathroom I used some French hand-scalloped hand towels as curtains, tied at the top with thin grosgrain ribbons. I use them as bookmarks and for my Filofax and day book.

Who loves the rain
And loves his home,
And looks on life with quiet
eyes.

FRANCES SHAW

I have a closet in the apartment I call the ribbon closet, with two shelves devoted to the storage of my extensive collection. When we bought the cottage, I was so thrilled to have a dining room with a fireplace and a narrow closet; I turned it into a space for all the tablecloths, napkins, and place mats. It looked so nice and neat; I tied some napkin sets in pretty ribbons. A lot of people would say this was a waste of time, and for most people it would be, but for me it was a meditation that brought me comfort and my eyes immense pleasure. Every time I open this shallow closet to select linens to set the table, I feel gratitude for the pleasure of having a dining room I love so much. These bundles of ironed napkins were gifts I gave myself and the ribbons made me happy.

It is wealth to be content.

LAO-TZU

We can indulge in these secret moments of beauty and luxury to enhance the quality of each day. They are really simple, inexpensive indulgences. Ribbons make me feel feminine, and I like seeing them in my home. They have color, texture, patterns, and beauty as well as nostalgia. For me, ribbons have the power to put me in touch with my feelings and express my attachment in positive ways at home. I don't tie ribbons around things because I'm a perfectionist or don't have anything better to do. I use ribbons in ways that will bring me joy and, in turn, bring joy to others. For me, ribbons are not frivolous or nonessential, but an important way for me to express myself.

I wrap ribbons around the neck of flower vases and I stake plants by wrapping ribbons around them. I buy ribbons wherever I travel and have some very old silk taffeta ribbons found in flea markets and country fairs. I can wash and iron them to be reused in different ways. For many years I used different ribbons as a strap on my watch. I have ribbon belts, and until a few years ago, I wore ribbons in my hair as bows in my headbands. I wear different ribbons in my straw sun hat and love selecting a different one each day. If I see something sad, ribbons come to mind. If you have an ugly old clothes rod, wrap it in a favorite blue ribbon with white dots and you'll think you're under the stars when you reach for a suit to wear. The chain holding up your chandelier could be wrapped in a colorful ribbon.

"I Travel Heavy"

Along with my fondness for ribbons, I adore boxes. Boxes are practical containers, and they can also be attractive. Often when we give or receive a present, it is in a box, tied with a ribbon. Boxes symbolize gifts to me. They can be as small as a pillbox or as big as suitcases, but whatever their size or shape, they are useful even if they're purely decorative, such as an antique tea caddy. The late interior designer, Mark Hampton, went to law school briefly before studying art. At his funeral last July, his roommate gave a eulogy remembering the first day of school when Mark arrived at the dormitory with trunks full of stuff. The roommate arrived first, unpacked his clothes and books, and left the room. Mark arrived with armloads of rhododendrons, three large marble obelisks (tapered pillars) and an army of boxes. Not one box had anything inside. When the roommate returned to the room that looked so different, he found Mark sitting on the floor arranging some boxes. "Hi, I'm Mark Hampton. I travel heavy."

I collect lots of pretty boxes. Many are empty, but sometimes I like to store seashells or sand from a favorite island escape, or smooth pebbles from a beach in Greece, or some colorful marbles. I love the element of surprise inherent in boxes; everyone's curious to know what's inside a pretty box. I use my weakness for boxes as an advantage, always on the hunt for a pretty color, a useful size, an interesting shape. I store newspaper clippings, magazine articles, letters, and postcards in boxes. I stack them under a table or against a wall. I couldn't feel at home without my box collection. They enhance and organize my life in so many ways, and because they're all colorful and attractive, I don't have to hide them. When I putter, tidying our rooms, I often put a bunch of old magazines and catalogues in boxes to be sorted and looked through at some future time.

Fun Drinking Glasses

What is beautiful to you? Build on what you have. There is a glass designer who created whimsical colored glasses with swirls and circles. They're clear with two colors—blue and yellow, or green and purple, or blue and pink. I adore these fun glasses and love to line them up on a kitchen counter where they catch the light and greet me each morning. They're childlike in their naivete and they charm me. I'm self-indulgent in my extravagance; I add to my collection, one at a time, as a gift I give the house and myself. Much to my satisfaction, everyone else enjoys these glasses also. We are really giving to others when we identify what we like ourselves. Whatever the drink, it's fun to choose and use one of these hand-blown glasses. They are works of art and elevate a glass of ice water into a sacrament. Wherever they are, they add color and pleasure to our eyes and our hearts.

A Fresh Eye

Last summer we spent most of our time at the cottage and, as a result, the apartment was not being loved up. Returning to it, I saw with a fresh eye how it really looked. Everywhere I looked I saw things I could improve, but before I got discouraged and felt overwhelmed, I called in some professionals to do the deep cleaning. Without our being aware of it, the apartment had gotten run down, one grade lower than lived in. To lighten up and brighten up I had the windows and mirrors cleaned, the cabinets scrubbed and the floors waxed. Everything sparkled and I felt lifted up. It was an invigorating experience that resulted in rewarding hours of reorganization and repairs. Some tiles needed to be replaced in the kitchen floor. We caulked around the bathroom sink. The lighting in the ribbon closet needed to be changed. One thing led to another. Closets were cleaned and styled. We packed up clothes to give to the thrift store. We felt we had neglected our apartment and in reality we had.

We Can Always Make Improvements

You'll always be able to improve how a room looks, feels, and functions. After this major transformation of our entire apartment, including reframing some pictures, I became acutely aware how much better we feel when we're surrounded by all the objects we love, polished and in good order. If we're in our own private world with our favorite colors and in a warm, comfortable, welcoming atmosphere, we're often shocked at the unnecessary coldness of a post office, a dentist's office, or a doctor's office. As an exercise, the next time you're in a space that is sad and barren and bleak, redecorate it in your mind. If you have to have your teeth drilled at the dentist, what would you like to see on the walls that would soothe you and make you feel more relaxed? When you're at the doctor's office waiting to take a stress test, what pictures would you like to see on the walls?

The energy to implement improvements in the quality of each day comes from our love of home. This opening up of our hearts to all the creative possibilities for enhancing our surroundings is key to our happiness at home. Light is so central to my soul that having dirty windows is a deviation from my truth. I know how important it is to have the sky and sunlight crisply invited into our rooms. We have a round magnifying mirror in our bathroom that didn't have a stand. Resting it on the counter reflected the ceiling. I found a brass plate rack to rest it on and placed it on the counter at an angle so it reflected the window. With light and a view, this small magnifying mirror became a luminous round window. All we have to do is be wide awake. Inspired by this newfound light and energy, I placed a small bouquet of miniature pink roses on the white tile ledge, complementing the delicate flowers hand-painted on the tiles; this way the pretty still life echoes in the round mirror.

Today is the first day of the rest of your life.

CHARLES DEDERICH

A Spa

My mantra for decorating is bringing light and nature's colors inside. I have a large box in the linen closet where I store soap. I'm fond of good soap and have a weakness for the scent of almond, jasmine, lemon, and freesia. I love the pretty packaging of bars of soap and keep them safe inside this box. The variety of scents mingles throughout the linen closet. Opening a new bar of soap is a private delight. I enjoyed a leisurely bath one lovely sunny morning using a freesia-scented bar of soap. I rested my head on the end of the tub and looked around. With the mirrors on the four walls sparkling and the window glass clean, I felt I was in a spa. I think of the beach when I'm alone in this bathroom because of the water, the seafoam-green paint under the sink, and the blue ceiling, and I often use seafoam or periwinkle-blue towels. When I use the lemon-colored towels, I feel yellow is the emotional color of the sun and I associate sunshine and beaches with it.

A day is a miniature eternity.

EMERSON

Women love their bathroom because it is the one place they can pamper themselves and often do so without disturbances. The bathroom is one of my favorite spots because we can indulge in some little luxuries that make a huge difference to our mood and energy. I believe in aromatherapy because it immediately vitalizes us and opens up not just our sense of smell but all our senses. We feel the comfort of the soft terry-cloth towel against our skin. We enjoy putting on some powder and skin cream. We all bathe regularly and we can enhance this practical necessity in hundreds of ways by paying attention to the smallest details. Write in your notebook your favorite soaps, herbs, essential oils, aftershave lotions, colognes, perfumes, and talcum powder. Write down your favorite size, color, and brand of towels.

Perfection

I use Caswell-Massey oval almond soap and often tuck a bar in each drawer that holds my underwear to make it fragrant. In *Living a Beautiful Life*, I wrote about my fondness for Crème 24 made in Grasse, France, by Mollinard. I received hundreds of letters inquiring where to purchase it—without having to fly to Nice and rent a car to go up the hill to Grasse, the perfume center of the world. Cambridge Chemists, at 21 East Sixty-fifth Street in New York City, carries this cream now. Mrs. Brown also used this snow-white wrinkle-preventing nutritive that is made of almonds, rose-hip water, and lemons. No one lives a perfect life, but there are perfect products that can give us pleasure and also be good for us in a wide variety of ways.

We might take a eucalyptus bath when the cold season comes or squirt some Vitabath moisturizing gelée in our tub. One day we might choose the original Spring Green and another time we might feel like the Fresh Floral Garden or the Vitabath Plus for dry skin. We can treat ourselves to a Crabtree & Evelyn's Persian Lilac foaming bath gel in the dark of winter to remind ourselves that spring is coming and the lilac tree will bloom again, faithfully promising us rebirth and rejuvenation. We can indulge in Crabtree & Evelyn's almond massage oil or their amazingly compelling citrus translucent soap. I have a white ginger body lotion that has as its ingredients ginger, oatmeal, milk, and honey. I use different perfumes, but find Allure by Chanel a favorite along with their classics, Chanel No. 5 and No. 19.

Having been the first female member of the board of directors of Fieldcrest Cannon before we sold the company, I have an immense loyalty to this company's products. I was raised with Fieldcrest Cannon towels and have always enjoyed them. I helped develop the colors of over a dozen towels while I was on the board and have a good supply I enjoy using to brighten up our bathrooms.

> *You will soon find that your joy in your home is growing, and that you have a source of happiness within yourself that you had not suspected.*
>
> ELSIE DE WOLFE

Hitting the Mark

By identifying exactly what we like, we can have exactly what we want without wasting time and money experimenting and being disappointed. What happens to me is that I have stuff around I don't enjoy and because I've made a mistake, I don't throw these duds away, so they hang around taking up precious space and blocking my energy. We can't give a used jar of body lotion to the thrift shop. We should have the courage to throw these things away that take up precious space. I have a hard time throwing things away. Usually Alexandra or Brooke helps me "de-thug." We should always have a strong connection to the objects we live with.

We can't expect others to buy us exactly what we have learned (by trial and error) that we enjoy. If we don't appreciate a vase or a set of napkins we have, we can always pass them on to someone who we know will like them. Often Alexandra or Brooke will give me a gift that has been given to them because it is more "me" than something they truly love. This is so sensible because they can enjoy seeing these items in our home even if they don't want them in theirs.

The products we use on ourselves for ourselves are not luxuries but necessities, and we deserve to treat ourselves as well as we can afford to. If we can have a perfect bath, perhaps we'll have more thoughtful, more profound meditations. The Buddha learned that he meditated better when he was comfortable and got off the rock and sat under a flowering tree. Anything we can do to make ourselves, our family, and

> *It has long been an axiom of mine that the little things are infinitely more important.*
>
> SHERLOCK HOLMES

our friends more comfortable at home should not be considered an extravagance because these seen and unseen details can make the difference between a house and a home. These little details are some of the thousands of ways we can turn something quite ordinary into an extraordinary moment and experience greater pleasure every moment at home.

Candles

I love to light candles because they have a spiritual dimension. Virtually all religious services light candles, even in daylight. I light candles for the illumination, the energy, the soft romantic and soulful light; they flicker and are alive but have only so many hours of burning time before they pass away. I light candles all the time—in the bathroom, a bedroom, at the kitchen table. I light a candle when I write and I put them all around when we have friends over in the evening. They help me to remember how precious, how fragile, and how temporary life is, and also, that each moment we're alive, we should celebrate and ritualize our time in order to create elevated, meaningful experiences.

They have changed eyes.

SHAKESPEARE

Because candles are important to me, I have a wide variety, ranging from bright-white jasmine-scented to fat, colored ones that are cylindrical, square, or round. Lighting a candle at the breakfast table or a pair when you're having a family lunch makes the occasion special. The way to live beautifully at home is to add beauty, comfort, and charm to whatever we do.

Touch-ups as Grace Notes

If something looks dull or sad, we can get out a pint can of paint and paint it. Whether you paint the bottom of a table, the underside of a bathroom countertop, the inside of a medicine cabinet, or the inside of a wastebasket, you can bring something unattractive into a new light. I didn't like the beige tone of the inside of a pink-and-white marbleized box, so I painted it a heavenly blue, the color of our kitchen trim. The next time you're at a paint store, buy some pint cans of latex paint in your favorite colors in order to be ready when inspiration strikes.

One of those heavenly days that cannot die.
WILLIAM WORDSWORTH

Old Friends

Take another look at your list of ten words that define you. Examine each one separately. Write in your notebook some ideas you may have that can improve the quality of each precious day at home. One of Peter's ten defining words is *old friends*. He makes new acquaintances all the time but he has old friends that go back sixty years or more. What can he do to preserve his memories and enrich these important relationships? As I tie ribbons around almost anything and light candles, Peter saves memorabilia from his friends—letters, photographs, invitations, programs, writings, news clippings, alumni news, and articles. He has all his friends' published books, and hangs framed pictures and interesting mementos in his writing room. Clients often ask me how many framed photographs they can hang in one space. If you ask Peter, he'd answer, "As many as will fit on the wall." His picture frames go from ceiling to baseboard. He likes living with his old friends, and this is one way he keeps his memories alive. Among all the photographs is a program from a Yale fortieth-reunion dinner. His friend Walter Curley noticed that most of the programs were left on the tables after the dinner. He scooped them up and wrote notes to his classmates on the page that had the words to the Yale song, "Bright College Years." Peter had the page with the song and Walter's message matted in a blue lacquer frame. "Old friends are the best! To Peter, From Walter. Fortieth Reunion, Class of '44." Peter loves this song that ends "For God, for Country, and for Yale!"

Difficulties are meant to rouse, not discourage. The human spirit is to grow strong by conflict.
WILLIAM ELLERY CHANNING

What I do must be done in the sunlight of awareness.
MARTHA GRAHAM

Because his college years were interrupted by World War II and many of his friends died, those who survived made a pact to remain good friends and make a contribution to the community. Peter sits at his desk in his writing room surrounded by photos of his friends, some who have died, others who are in failing health, and others who are thriving. This atmosphere encourages him to correspond regularly with these old friends because he believes they are the best.

I often think of Peter's defining personality traits:

Love	Dancing
Beach	Music
Old friends	Wine
Children	Lunch
Reading	Memories

Activity is contagious.

EMERSON

Waking up is a spiritual metaphor.

JIM WALLIS

The man is changed, no longer himself nor self-belonging; he is merged with the supreme, sunken into it, one with it: center coincides with center, for on this higher plane things that touch at all are one.

PLOTINUS

Recently he told me he is in a total enjoyment phase at home. Peter deeply appreciates being at home in the cottage and the apartment he also dearly loves. He's full of wonder and awe at his feelings of contentment and peace. None of us knows what the future holds, but we all have the present moments to live deeply.

There Will Be Lots of Surprises

When Peter asked me to marry him in 1974, he told me there would be lots of surprises. The biggest surprises are the transformation of the New York City apartment, over time, into a warm, comfortable atmosphere that welcomes us, uplifts us, and loves us. As we've loved up this personal environment, it speaks to us of our blessings. And then we took an ugly old dump of a house, and by doing a great deal of the work ourselves, transformed it into a charming sweet cottage where we also feel truly at home.

When we're at home we feel wholly ourselves, very much alive, enthusiastic, and extremely humble. We're so fortunate to be surrounded by all the objects that represent us and comfort us so completely. We're all born with the potential to bring our essence out. By being at home with ourselves and the atmosphere around us, we're able to appreciate these surprises. Because the divine mystery is not revealed to us in a big splash, but is rather hinted at in these surprises, we all have this powerful force within us. To realize the opportunity each of us has to express ourselves creatively at home each day is to be awake to life's deepest meaning.

When we're at home with ourselves, we increase this sense of wonder, of not knowing all the answers but being on a quest to know the truth. When we find out who we are and live the life we wish to live, we have found our true home. We don't retreat from the world. The universe is awesomely present because we connect to a larger view with a more sublime perspective. When we find our true home, we are free to go to the next level where we fuse with our divine nature. Here, at home, we lose our sense of separateness and feel connected. This is one of life's greatest mysteries. We need to feel at home at our core, as unique individuals, with our own gifts, talents, and idiosyncrasies. Once we do, we are free, at peace, united. This deeper place is where we live at home. We're able to live each moment with this ineffable joy because all our struggles and suffering teach us how fortunate we are to be alive right now, at home, and awake to this miracle. Peter and I had a wonderful conversation recently as we sat under an umbrella in our cozy walled garden looking up at the most incredibly intense blue sky. He told me we can all tell when our house or apartment becomes a sanctuary of harmony and peace—we yearn to be there; we feel the pleasure and contentment of being at home. Creating this atmosphere is worth all our struggles. In our lifetime there may not be anything else like it. At home is an epiphany. Feeling at home is a divine gift of grace. At home we see the world in a whole new light, a brighter, more luminous heaven on earth.

The most important and effective change, a change in our own attitude, hardly ever occurs to us, and the resolution to take such a step is very difficult for us.

LUDWIG WITTGENSTEIN

We have the power within us to create a perfect day.

A time filled with varied and interesting experiences seems short in passing.

WILLIAM JAMES

Conclusion

Feeling at Home Is Your Center for Happiness and Love

It is something to be able to paint a particular picture or to carve a statue, and so to make a few objects beautiful, but it is far more glorious to carve and paint the very atmosphere and medium through which we look . . . To affect the quality of the day—that is the highest of art.

—HENRY DAVID THOREAU

We are all spiritual beings temporarily in a physical body. The process of self-attunement and self-expression continues all the days of our lives. Our challenge is to love ourselves, and when we do, we can love our neighbors "as ourselves." When we love ourselves we can feel at home wherever we are. We take the positive energy and personal vision we live with at home with us everywhere.

Our home is the stage setting for every other experience we have. Our coming home is a wonderful map, a total summation of who we are. Feeling at home is a way of life, an inspiring journey of discovery as well as a bridge that leads us to greater appreciation, reverence, and beauty where we've transformed our spirit because we've learned how to follow our own heart.

All the love and sacrifices, the pains, the labor, the heartaches, the tenderness and caring that go into transforming a house or an apartment into a place where we feel wel-

Home is, or should be, a safe haven. Perhaps ideally a personal heaven for us here on earth.

PETER MEGARGEE BROWN

283

comed at home only deepens our appreciation for what we have. A house is a physical, man-made structure. A home is the spirit, the soul, our emotional and spiritual center. This everyday process of deepening our selves as we deepen our love of life at home infuses us with a powerful flow of loving energy that is sustaining and transcending.

We should try to make every day special. We can't risk saving up living for anniversaries and holidays in some unknown future we may or may not experience. We can awaken each day full of gratitude for the simple but powerful gift of life. Each day we can plant some seeds—in the garden, in the house, in our minds—that will bear fruit.

When we are open to this freedom and joy at home, we choose to be a resource to others, not a need. When we take care of our own needs at home and bring to our lives the love, caring, and beauty we all seek, we're then free to use all our gifts to express our unique creative talents in whatever ways we choose. When we affirm and confirm all that is positive, uplifting, light-filled, and loving in our own lives, our affirmation spills over into service to others.

Living well every day at home is the most liberating, exuberant way to celebrate our brief earthly journey. *Feeling at Home* is a personal love story, yours and mine. Whatever we do to add to our love of self and home will ultimately be our greatest gift to the world. Let your house or apartment be your teacher. We learn from our garden and intimate spaces at home how to be more caring and sensitive, more generous spirited, how to make every act a labor of love. Find colorful ways to love what you're doing and be glad to do what needs to be done. Once you start any task, you usually find it satisfying.

Have faith that being at home can be daily domestic bliss and live each moment in this belief. On days when you don't feel well, let your home comfort you, heal you, and love you. Everyday living is an expression of our creative energy. Work to improve the quality of each moment. Be awake to sudden flashes of profound depth. Contemplate the infinite possibilities open to us when we're courageous enough to be true to ourselves and live that truth every day at home. Express your interests and passions and boldly use your gifts and talents to love and serve others as you have learned to love and serve yourself.

In this way you will achieve your goal of serenity, freedom, and joy at home.

What lies behind us and what lies before us are tiny matters, compared to what lies within us.
—Emerson

Index

Index

G

H

I

imitation, 206
imperfections, 221–222, 233–236
impressing others, 263–264
India, 88, 255
instant gratification, 74
intuition, 17, 195–197, 199–200
ironing, 65–66, 74, 117, 152–153, 174,
  217–219
  of sheets, 171, 172, 247–248
Italy, 235, 242, 255

J

Japan, 191, 255
Jefferson, Thomas, 46, 164, 222, 226,
  232, 251, 253
Johns, Ruth Elizabeth, 88
Johnson, Samuel, 33, 141, 192, 194, 221,
  227, 252
journal writing, 209

K

Keller, Helen, 20, 202
kitchen, 15, 27–30, 46, 56, 68, 83,
  118–120, 130
  convenience of, 119–120
  table in, 46, 118–119
  wood floor in, 29–30, 47–48, 226
knives, sharp, 237, 247

L

lamps, see lighting
Larsson, Carl, xiii, 187–188
laundry, 151, 217–219, 247–248
  order in, 115
  outdoor clothesline for, 68, 240–241
  time management and, 65–66,
   152–153, 170–171, 173–174
laundry room, 40–41, 44, 68, 153, 201
  privacy and, 217–219

lawn mowing, 249–250
leisure, as term, 177
letter writing, 150–151, 208–209
Le Veau D'Or, 14
library, 14–16, 120–122
life passage, chapters of, 8, 213–215,
  250
light, 12, 27, 29, 32, 48, 61–62, 75–87,
  131, 197, 226, 274–275
  in dark rooms, 78–79
  deprivation of, 76–78, 80
  epiphany of, 82
  evaluation of, 83–84
  of fires, 86–87
  maximizing, 81
  mirrors and, 79, 82, 85–86
  mood and, 76–80, 85
  oversensitivity to, 84–85
  from shiny surfaces, 86
  solar, 82–83
light boxes, 84
lighting, 55, 61–62
  fluorescent, 80–81
  halogen, 61, 62, 77, 78, 79, 80, 226
  strip, 77, 83, 99
  see also candles
linen closet, 32–33, 130, 172, 195, 275
lithographs, 135
lived-in look, 231–232
living room, 29, 34–38, 48, 58–64, 165,
  215, 220–221, 237, 266
  changes in, 63–64, 138–139
  as drawing room, 240
  favorite things in, 60–61
  formal vs. informal, 49, 59, 138, 228
  as garden-reading room, 37–38, 41,
   48–49, 57
  livability of, 61–64
  outdoor furniture in, 58–59
  rarely-used, 34–35, 47, 228
loving up, 222, 225, 236–237, 258,
  273

M

About the Author

Alexandra Stoddard has designed the interiors of mansions and embassies as well as cottages and one-room studios for clients ranging from notable individuals to young people just starting out. Recipient of the first full scholarship ever awarded by the New York School of Interior Design, she brings more than thirty-six years of design experience to her work. For fourteen years she worked with Eleanor McMillen Brown, one of the doyennes of interior design, before starting her own design firm, Alexandra Stoddard Incorporated. She appears frequently on television and radio nationwide and has been featured in major magazines internationally. Author of twenty books, including her most recent book on decorating, *Open Your Eyes,* and her classic *The Decoration of Houses,* she is a sought-after speaker on the art of living. She lives with her husband, Peter Megargee Brown, in New York City and Stonington Village, Connecticut.